Scenario Visualization

Scenario Visualization

An Evolutionary Account of Creative Problem Solving

Robert Arp

A Bradford Book
The MIT Press
Cambridge, Massachusetts
London, England

MIT Press books may be purchased at special quantity discounts for business or sales promotional use. For information, please e-mail special_sales@mitpress.mit.edu or write to Special Sales Department, The MIT Press, 55 Hayward Street, Cambridge, MA 02142.

This book was set in Stone Serif and Stone Sans by SNP Best-set Typesetter Ltd., Hong Kong and was printed and bound in the United States.

Library of Congress Cataloging-in-Publication Data

Arp, Robert.
Scenario visualization : an evolutionary account of creative problem solving / Robert Arp.
    p. cm.
Includes bibliographical references and index.
ISBN 978-0-262-01244-7 (hardcover : alk. paper) 1. Visualization. 2. Problem solving—Methodology. 3. Creative thinking.
I. Title.
BF241.A77   2008
153.3'2—dc22

                                     2007032256

10 9 8 7 6 5 4 3 2 1

Contents

Acknowledgments   vii

Introduction: Routine Problem Solving versus Nonroutine Creative
Problem Solving   1

1 Organisms and Hierarchical Organization   11

2 Emergence and Function   29

3 The Visual System   57

4 The Evolution of the Visual System and Scenario Visualization   91

5 Scenario Visualization, Creative Problem Solving, and Evolutionary
Psychology   133

References   167
Index   207

Acknowledgments

Throughout the construction of this book, I learned firsthand that philoso-phy and the academic world, in general, are social enterprises. I could not have completed this book without so many helpful and rigorous people.

George Terzis, the director of my doctoral dissertation and philosophical mentor at Saint Louis University in St. Louis, Missouri, was most helpful and most rigorous. The amount of time, energy, care, wisdom, and concern he gave to me will never be forgotten. He is a true philosopher, a scholar, and a gentleman.

I spent as much time discussing this project with Brian Cameron. I have heard it said that, during one's graduate career, a person learns most about his or her particular discipline from a fellow graduate student. Other than Dr. Terzis, I owe the majority of my philosophical formation to Brian Cameron, who, besides having one of the keenest analytical minds, prob-ably was the most critical of my project every step of the way. I thank him for these criticisms and have tried responding to many of them in this book.

Another friend of knowing is Kevin Decker, who got me to thinking about issues in naturalism and evolution in the first place. What wisdom in me that was not gained from Dr. Terzis and Brian, I received from Kevin.

Given the interdisciplinary nature of my project, I have tried to make sure that all of the information in this book is accurate. Other top-notch philosophers, neuroscientists, biologists, and psychologists at Saint Louis University, Washington University in St. Louis, University of Missouri—St. Louis, and Southwest Minnesota State University took the time out of their busy schedules to look over earlier versions of this book and give me com-ments. They include Kent Staley, Richard Blackwell, Scott Berman, Michael Ariel, Jerry Morrissey, Charles Granger, Corey Butler, and Scott Peterson. In particular, I have learned a lot from Dr. Staley's comments and have tried to address many of his criticisms in this book. Also, Scott Berman was influential in getting me to think more deeply about the realism/antirealism debate.

I had fruitful conversations and correspondences with other thinkers and researchers about parts of my project as well, including Carl Craver, Charles Anderson, Jaakko Hintikka, James Maffie, Eric LaRock, Robert Wood, and Thomas Young.

I hand drew all of the illustrations in this book and, with the kind help of a computer graphic designer in St. Louis named Chuck Hart, was able to convert them into electronic format.

With his calming demeanor, Tom Stone, Philosophy Acquisitions Editor at MIT Press, was a relaxing influence for me during the book-writing process, and I thank him for believing in the project in the first place. I also want to acknowledge the dedication of referees, copy editors, proofreaders, copy setters, and other folks in the publication process who work for MIT.

I would like to thank Kim Sterelny, Anthony Freeman, Vincent Colapietro, Raymond Russ, and other editors of the following journals for the permissions to utilize sections of my previously published work in this book: *Biology & Philosophy, Journal of Consciousness Studies, Journal of Mind and Behavior, Journal for General Philosophy of Science, Journal of Speculative Philosophy, Journal of Critical Realism, American Catholic Philosophical Quarterly, History of Philosophy Quarterly, International Philosophical Quarterly,* and *Hobbes Studies.* Also, the reader can find the appropriate references to these journals under "Arp" in the References section of the book.

Finally, my wife, Susan Marie Arp, has looked over parts of my work and has given me comments to think about throughout this project (including my very first substantial criticism). I have the most profound respect for her, she continues to be my anchor, and I dedicate all of my projects to her.

Scenario Visualization

Introduction: Routine Problem Solving versus Nonroutine Creative Problem Solving

Imagine being a dentist in the early part of the nineteenth century. Now, imagine going to the dentist to have a tooth pulled in the early part of the nineteenth century. In those days, pulling teeth was a painful experience for the patient, as there were no known anesthetics in use at the time. The kinds of things a dentist used to help ease the patient's pain before a tooth extraction might have included having the patient suck on a medicinal herb that produces a numbing effect in the mouth, placing ice upon the gums, getting the patient to drink alcohol before the procedure, or any combination thereof. Such were the methods that Dr. Horace Wells likely used to solve the problem of pain associated with tooth extractions while working as a dentist in Hartford, Connecticut, circa 1844. These methods probably were nothing new, and we can imagine that dentists had been using these remedies for some time so as to alleviate or prevent the pain associated with tooth extraction.

One evening in 1844, Dr. Wells attended an amusing public demonstration of the effects of inhaling a gas called *nitrous oxide* with his friend, Samuel Cooley. Cooley volunteered to go up on stage to inhale the gas, and he proceeded to do things like sing, laugh, and fight with other volunteers who had inhaled the gas. As a result of the high jinks, Cooley received a deep cut in his leg before coming back to his seat next to Dr. Wells. Someone noticed a pool of blood under Cooley's seat, and it was discovered that Cooley had cut his leg; however, Cooley seemed to be unaffected by and was unaware of the wound. Upon witnessing this event, a light went on in Dr. Wells' head: "What if this laughing gas could be used during tooth extraction to ease a patient's pain?" The problem of pain associated with tooth extraction finally might be solved! In fact, over the next several years Dr. Wells proceeded to use nitrous oxide and was successful at painlessly extracting teeth from his patients, and the seeds of modern anesthesia were sown (Roberts, 1989).

Humans are resourceful animals. We can imagine Dr. Wells prescribing the various remedies with which he was familiar—the medicinal herb, the ice, the alcohol—in the attempt to ease a patient's pain during tooth extraction. In such a case, we would have an instance of what Mayer (1995) has called *routine problem solving*, whereby a person recognizes many possible solutions to a problem given that the problem was solved through one of those solutions in the past. People constantly perform routine problem solving activities that are concrete and basic to their survival, equipping them with a variety of ways to "skin" the proverbial cat, as well as enabling them to adapt to situations and reuse information in similar environments.

However, humans also can engage in activities that are more abstract and creative, such as invent tools based upon mental blueprints, synthesize concepts that, at first glance, seemed wholly disparate or unrelated, and devise novel solutions to problems. When Dr. Wells decided to use nitrous oxide with his patients, he pursued a *wholly new way* to solve the problem of pain. This was an instance of what Mayer (1995) has called *nonroutine creative problem solving*, which involves finding a solution to a problem that has not been solved previously. The introduction of nitrous oxide in order to extract teeth painlessly would be an example of nonroutine creative problem solving because Dr. Wells did not possess a way to solve the problem already, and he had not pursued such a route in the past.

Not only do people make insightful connections like that of Dr. Wells but they take advantage of serendipitous opportunities, invent products, manufacture space shuttles, successfully negotiate environments, hypothesize, thrive, flourish, and dominate the planet by coming up with wholly novel solutions to problems—primarily through the use of their visual systems. How is this possible? In this book, I give an evolutionary account of the human ability to solve nonroutine, vision-related problems creatively in their environments. I argue that, by the introduction of the Upper Paleolithic toolmaking industry near the close of the Pleistocene epoch, our hominin species evolved a conscious creative problem solving capacity I call *scenario visualization* that enabled individuals to fashion the tools and other products necessary to outlive other hominin species and populate the planet. Scenario visualization is a conscious activity whereby visual images are selected, integrated, and then transformed and projected into visual scenarios for the purposes of solving problems in the environments one inhabits. The evidence for scenario visualization is found in the kinds of complex tools our hominin ancestors invented in order to survive in the ever-changing environments of the Pleistocene world. In this book,

I also argue that this conscious capacity shares an analogous affinity with neurobiological processes of selectivity and integration in the visual system, namely, processes that enable animals to select relevant information from environmental stimuli and to organize this information in a coherent way for the animal. Further, I show that similar processes of selectivity and integration can be found in the activities of organisms in general. Because the brain is an evolved organ, a complete explanation of these processes and capacities must appeal to general biological and evolutionary principles. The evolution of these processes in our hominin past, I argue, helps account for the modern-day conscious ability of humans to utilize visual information so as to solve vision-related, nonroutine problems creatively in the environments they inhabit.

Principally, I am a philosopher of mind and biology, and, insofar as this is the case, I am concerned with two basic questions concerning human nature, namely, What are humans, in essence, that distinguishes them from the rest of reality? and How did we get this way? The hypothesis of scenario visualization—as one form of conscious activity—and its emergence in an evolutionary history are my small attempts to answer these fundamentally philosophical questions. Of course, I will not answer these questions *completely.* However, I will offer my hypothetical "piece to the puzzle" that only could have come about as a result of interdisciplinary dialogue and research. I believe that philosophy must work closely with other disciplines in figuring out the answers to the aforementioned questions, as well as any basic philosophical question (also see Arp, 2008d; Watson & Arp, 2008). When all is said and done, I support Churchland's (1993) claim that cognitive science should not be autonomous with respect to neuroscience, psychology, and the other empirical sciences. I endorse Fodor's (1998) observation that archeology and the biological sciences are good places to uncover the nature of the mind. I concur with Pinker (1994, p. 15), echoing Chomsky, that if research in artificial intelligence is to effectively study the mind, then it needs "constant integration across disciplinary lines." Further, I agree with Donald (1997, p. 356) that the "problem of cognitive evolution demands the widest possible range of information, (from) neurolinguistics, anthropology, paleontology, neuroanatomy, and especially cognitive psychology."

The ideas and arguments in this book are laid out in five chapters. The ultimate goal of my project is to explain how humans evolved a specific kind of conscious, vision-related, creative problem solving ability I call scenario visualization (also see Arp, 2005a, 2005b, 2006a, 2007a, 2008c). However, since conscious creative problem solving is a psycho-physiological phenomenon that is causally dependent upon the workings of the brain and nervous system in the human *organism*, in the first chapter I give a general philosophical account of organisms and use this account to explain facts regarding the functioning of the organism's subsystems and processes. I do this in order to offer a philosophy of biology that is comprehensive enough to account for the levels of biological phenomena that are relevant to my project, and the upshot is to lay the groundwork for showing that there is an analogous continuity of operation in the biological world, ranging from the activities of organelles in a cell to the complex workings of neural networks in a brain from which conscious abilities emerge (also Arp, 2005b).

I give further elucidation to Mayr's (1996, p. 103) description of organisms as "hierarchically organized systems that operate on the basis of historically acquired programs of information," as well as ratify Plotkin's (1997, p. 1) claim that biological phenomena "only make *complete sense* [italics mine] in light of evolutionary theory." I establish that an organism is a hierarchically organized living system made up of components that are engaged in processes constituting coordinated subsystems, with the product of these processes and subsystems being a *particularized* homeostasis relative to their operations that contributes to the overall *generalized* homeostasis of the organism. Besides being organized in such a way as to produce homeostasis in the organism, the processes in which the components of the organism are engaged possess certain properties. These properties include abilities to exchange data internally, selectively convert data to information, integrate that information, and process information from environments (also Arp, 2008a).

Having established these properties in the first chapter, in the second chapter I put forward what I call the *homeostatic organization view* (HOV) of organisms, whereby the components of organisms are organized to function so as to maintain the homeostasis of the organism at the various levels in the hierarchy (Arp, 2008a). Because of HOV, starting with the organelles that make up a cell and continuing up the hierarchy of systems and processes in an organism, we can maintain that there are clear instances of emergent biological phenomena. Using HOV, I endorse a form of what is known as *nomological emergence* in the metaphysical realm. Since the endorsement of a set of entities in the metaphysical realm requires an adequate description of those entities, I argue that it may be useful for a researcher to think like an *as-if realist* when describing the traits and processes of organisms (also see Arp, 2005c, 2005d). Whereas I use HOV to give credence to a version of nomological emergence in the metaphysical realm, I use as-if realism to give credence to a corresponding form of *representational emergence* in the epistemological realm. The end result is a better understanding of the epistemological views that underpin my metaphysical views in philosophy of science and philosophy of biology.

In the final section of the second chapter, having argued for HOV and as-if realism, I compare Cummins' (1975, 2002) organizational view of functions with the Griffiths (1992, 1993, 1996)/Godfrey-Smith (1993, 1994, 1996) modern history view of functions. In fact, it is essential to my project that I explain and defend a description of functions because my hypothesis concerning scenario visualization depends upon certain functional mechanisms of the mind having evolved to solve specific problems encountered in various Pleistocene environments (also Arp, 2006b). Whereas Cummins argues that a trait functions so as to contribute to the general organization of some organism's present structure, Griffiths and Godfrey-Smith argue that a trait functions because of its fitness with respect to the organism's recent evolutionary history. I show how these accounts can complement and be made compatible with one another. Given that structure, organization, operational flexibility, function, and evolutionary history are all factors to be considered in an organism's makeup, we should expect that the traits of an organism function the way they do because such traits presently contribute to the overall organization of the organism (Cummins) as well as having been selected for in the organism's species' recent ancestry (Griffiths/Godfrey-Smith).

Building upon the work of the first two chapters, in the third chapter I show how the subsystems and processes associated with vision in mammals comprise a hierarchically organized system exhibiting similar, analogous kinds of properties of information exchange, selectivity, and integration found in all organisms (also Arp, 2005b, 2008a). My analysis of the brain is restricted to the primary processes and mechanisms associated with the mammalian visual system for three reasons. First, there is a lot of empirical evidence supporting the mammalian visual system's structure and layout. Second, the visual system is present in many kinds of vertebrate species thought to be homologous to human beings. And third, the visual system plays a central role in the evolutionary account I give of the progression from noncognitive visual processing to conscious cognitive visual processing in terms of scenario visualization. As I go on to demonstrate, visual processing is an important factor—if not *the* most important factor—in the evolution of conscious creative problem solving capacities in humans.

In the third chapter, I also distinguish four levels of visual processing in animals. The first is a noncognitive visual processing that takes place at the lowest level of the visual processing hierarchy associated with the eye and its neural projections to the lateral geniculate nucleus and primary visual cortex. The second is a cognitive or psychological visual processing that occurs at a higher level in the visual hierarchy associated with the *what* and *where* unimodal areas of the brain. The third is a cognitive visual processing that occurs at an even higher level in the visual hierarchy whereby visual unimodal areas are integrated in the visual unimodal association area of the brain. The fourth is a conscious cognitive visual processing that occurs at the highest level of the visual hierarchy whereby the visual association areas are integrated with other sensory modalities, the limbic areas, and frontal areas of the brain (also Arp, 2005a, 2007b).

By the end of the third chapter, I show that the visual systems of mammals, in general, function so as to produce *visual cognition*. Visual cognition is the phenomenal representation of some object in the mammal's visual field that is the result of the integration of modular visual information received from that object in association with iconic memory, attention, and the synchronous firing of neurons in the areas of the brain relevant to the processing of the visual percept. Special attention is paid to visual modularity and visual integration. *Visual modularity* refers to the fact that the visual system is made up of distinctly functioning and interacting modules or areas having evolved to respond to certain features of an object in typical environments. *Visual integration* refers to a neurobiological set of processes that bind together the relevant information gleaned from visual modules/areas into a coherent cognitive representation of some object, enabling an animal to negotiate typical environments.

In the fourth chapter, after speaking about the general evolutionary principles of genetic variability and natural selection, I trace the evolution of the visual system from organisms that developed a light/dark sensitivity area to humans who are capable of the complex activities involved in conscious cognitive visual processing, including scenario visualization. I do this utilizing the anatomical evidence from fossils and living species thought to be homologous to ancient species. I also use archeological evidence from ancient toolmaking techniques, since I believe that the evolution of tool-types parallels the evolution from noncognitive visual processing, through cognitive visual processing, to conscious cognitive visual processing. The variety and complexity of tools discovered and dated by archeologists offer us compelling evidence that the brain and visual system have evolved with the passage of time (also Arp, 2006a, 2008c).

I suggest that advanced forms of toolmaking require *scenario visualization*, a conscious activity whereby visual images are selected, integrated, and then transformed and projected into visual scenarios for the purposes of solving problems in the environments one inhabits (also see Arp, 2005a, 2005b, 2006a, 2007a, 2008c). As a conscious process, scenario visualization is distinct from the cognitive processes of simply forming a visual image or recalling a visual image from memory; these activities can be performed by nonhuman primates, mammals, and certain other animals. Scenario visualization requires a mind that is more active in the utilization of visual images through the processes of selectivity, integration, and projection into future scenarios. It is not the having of visual images that is important; it is what the mind does in terms of actively selecting and integrating visual information for the purposes of solving some problem relative to some environment that really matters.

In this project, I am concerned mostly with the progression from cognitive visual processing to conscious cognitive visual processing, the relationship of these processes to one another, and, ultimately, how conscious cognitive visual processing—in terms of scenario visualization—evolved from cognitive visual processing. There is a huge amount of literature devoted to questions about the existence of psychological phenomena and whether psychological phenomena supervene upon or emerge from neurobiological phenomena (for starters, see Chalmers, 1996; Heil, 2004a, 2004b; Arp, 2007b, 2008d). Working out the problems associated with these issues constitutes solving several so-called *mind–body problems*. Now, no one has been able to give a satisfactory account of how it is that psychological states—particularly conscious psychological states—arise from, as well as interact with, the gray matter of the brain. Although I will not be able to completely solve the mind–body problem of how it is that conscious experience can emerge from and interact with the gray matter of the brain, my hypothesis concerning scenario visualization is an attempt to explain one aspect of our consciousness and the reason for its emergence in our species.

In order to fortify my hypothesis concerning scenario visualization and tell a concrete evolutionary story of the emergence of scenario visualization, I trace the evolution of the javelin from its meager beginnings as a stick through our *Homo habilis* → *Homo ergaster* → *Homo heidelbergensis* → *Homo sapiens* lineage. Given that modern humans evolved from early hominins, I further fortify the emergence of scenario visualization by presenting the psychological evidence that this kind of activity occurs in our species when trying to solve certain problems, as well as by presenting the neurobiological evidence showing that our brains are wired so that this kind of psychological activity can occur in the first place (also Arp, 2006a, 2008c).

We are the only kind of species that can scenario visualize, and what I suggest by the end of the fourth chapter is threefold. First, modern-day humans have the unique ability to actively select and integrate visual images from mental modules so as to transform and project those images in visual scenarios for the purposes of negotiating environments—this is scenario visualization.

Second, scenario visualization emerged as a natural consequence of our evolutionary history, which includes the development of a complex nervous system—through genetic variability and natural selection—in association with environmental pressures that occasioned the evolution of such a capacity. If an advanced form of toolmaking acts as a mark of conscious behavior, then what I suggest is that visual processing must be a significant way in which this consciousness emerged on the evolutionary scene. Considering that our early hominin ancestors not only had to select certain materials that were appropriate to solve some problem but also engaged in a number of mental steps that resulted in the construction of a variety of tool types, it becomes apparent that a fairly advanced form of cognitive activity had to occur. My suggestion is that such a process exhibits conscious mental activities associated with scenario visualization, since one must be able to segregate relevant visual information from irrelevant information, integrate those pieces of visual information into coherently organized mental pictures, and transform and project those pictures into various scenarios so as to construct tools that are adequate to solve problems in environments.

Third, our capacity to scenario visualize is a central feature of conscious behavior, an idea that comports well with Sternberg's (2001) notion of consciousness's entailing the setting up of future goals, Carruthers' (2002) idea that humans are the only kinds of beings able to generate, and then reason with, novel suppositions or imaginary scenarios, and Crick & Koch's (1999, p. 324) claim that "conscious seeing" requires the brain's ability to "form a conscious representation of the visual scene that it then can use for many different actions or thoughts."

In the fifth chapter, I further explicate the notions of routine problem solving and nonroutine creative problem solving, and I show how scenario visualization fits into the evolutionary psychologist's schematization of the mind to form a more complete picture of how it is that humans evolved the ability to solve vision-related, nonroutine problems creatively (also see

Arp, 2005a, 2006a, 2007a, 2008c). Routine problem solving entails a mental activity that is stereotyped and wholly lacking in innovation because there are simply perceptual associative connections being made by the mind of an animal. Images in perception or memory are associated with one another and/or with some environmental stimuli so as to learn some behavior or produce some desired result. If that result is not achieved, an alternate route is pursued in a routine trial-and-error fashion.

Unlike routine problem solving—which deals with associative connections within familiar perspectives—nonroutine creative problem solving entails an innovative ability to make connections between wholly unrelated perspectives or ideas. Koestler (1964) referred to this quality of the creative mind as a *bissociation of matrices*. In bissociation, humans put together ideas, memories, representations, stimuli, and the like in wholly new and unfamiliar ways. Thus, when we ask how it is that humans can be creative, part of what we are asking is how they bissociate, namely, take some idea found "way over here in the left field of the mind" and make some coherent connection with some other idea found "way over here in the right field of the mind," to put it crudely. Humans seem to be the only species that can engage in this kind of mental activity, principally with the usage of visual images.

I then build upon the ideas and arguments put forward by Mithen (1996, 1999, 2001) and other evolutionary psychologists that creative problem solving is possible because the mind is made up of a suite of encapsulated modules that evolved in our Pleistocene hominin past to deal with specific problems in erratic environments. According to Mithen, creative problem solving occurs because humans have evolved the mechanism of *cognitive fluidity*, a capacity for information to flow freely between and among mental modules. Mithen's idea of cognitive fluidity is supposed to explain our ability to bissociate because, on this view, the potential always is there to make innovative, previously unrelated connections between ideas or perceptions, given that the information within modules has the capacity to be mixed together, or fluidly intermingle.

While agreeing with the part of Mithen's hypothesis regarding the flexible flow of information between and among modules, I transform his account by arguing that human beings scenario visualize—they actively select, integrate, transform, and project visual information from mental modules into imagined scenarios—when they solve vision-related kinds of problems creatively. It is not enough that this modular visual information simply intermixes, as Mithen would have us believe, because then the information would be chaotic, directionless, and lacking in integrated coherency. The visual information must be selected and integrated relevant to a particular problem in an environment so that a solution becomes coherent for the problem solver, and a particular course of action can be pursued.

Finally, in the fifth chapter, I bring the entire discussion of the book around full circle, so to speak, by linking this conscious ability to select and integrate information to brain processes of the visual system, as well as other biological processes, that engage in similar selecting and integrating tasks. My claim is that just as biological processes, in general, exhibit selective and integrative functions, and just as visual integration performs the function of selecting and integrating visual module areas, so too, a certain form of consciousness emerged as a property of the brain to act as a kind of *meta*cognitive process that scenario visualizes, namely, selects and integrates relevant visual information from *psychological* modules for the purpose of solving vision-related, creative problems in environments (also see Arp, 2005b, 2008a). In this way, the mental and neurobiological processes of selectivity and integration are really analogous extensions of similar general biological processes. The upshot of my hypothesis is a biologically based account of vision-related, creative problem solving whereby the most complex psychological phenomena and processes are explained as emerging from neurobiological phenomena and processes, which, in turn, are explained as emerging from general biological phenomena and processes—all phenomena and processes being subject to evolutionary principles.

1 Organisms and Hierarchical Organization

1.1 Organisms as Hierarchically Organized Living Systems

The ultimate goal of my project is to explain how humans evolved a specific kind of vision-related, conscious, creative problem solving ability I call *scenario visualization*. However, since conscious creative problem solving is a psycho-physiological phenomenon that is dependent upon the workings of the brain and nervous system in the human organism, it is important for me to give a general philosophical account of organisms and use this account to explain facts regarding the functioning of the organism's systems and processes. I do this in order to offer a philosophy of biology that is comprehensive enough to account for the levels of biological phenomena that are relevant to my project. The further upshot is to lay the groundwork for showing that there is an analogous continuity of function in the biological world, ranging from the activities of organelles in a cell to the complex workings of neural networks in a brain from which conscious abilities emerge (also see Arp, 2005b, 2008a).

In general, biologists and other researchers who describe biological phenomena are aligned with Mayr (1996, p. 103) in his description of organisms as "hierarchically organized systems, operating on the basis of historically acquired programs of information" (Audesirk, Audesirk, & Beyers, 2002; Gould, 2002; Collier & Hooker, 1999; Eldredge, 1993, 1995; Bogdan, 1994; Lycan, 1995; Csányi, 1996; Zylstra, 1992; Terzis & Arp, 2008). What exactly is entailed in this description? There are numerous thinkers who describe organisms and their activities in various ways. In the next two chapters, I unify several of these conceptions while pointing to key characteristics of organisms that are relevant to my project as a whole. In this chapter, I further elucidate the idea that organisms are hierarchically organized living systems. In the next chapter, after using ideas and arguments from this chapter in support of certain forms of metaphysical and epistemological forms of emergence, I give further elucidation to Mayr's notion that organisms operate on the basis of historically acquired programs of information, as well as ratify Plotkin's claim that biological phenomena only make complete sense in light of evolutionary theory, by endorsing a hybrid view of functions based in both the Cummins organizational and the Griffiths/Godfrey-Smith modern history accounts.

According to Mayr (1996), an organism is a hierarchically organized living system. What exactly does this mean? We can define an *organism* as a hierarchically organized living system made up of components that are engaged in processes constituting coordinated subsystems, with the product of these processes and subsystems being homeostasis relative to their operations, producing the overall homeostasis of the organism. As a *system*, an organism is a unified entity that is explainable in terms of the properties of its components, the interactions of these components, and the overall coordination of these components. As a *living* system, an organism has to be made up of at least one cell, the basic unit of life. To understand what it means for an organism to be a *hierarchically organized* living system, we need to investigate the properties of the components of this kind of system. These properties include what I call (1) *internal–hierarchical data exchange,* (2) *data selectivity,* (3) *informational integration,* and (4) *environmental–organismic information exchange* (also Arp, 2005b, 2008a). When I describe each of these properties, the interactions of the components of this kind of living system, as well as the overall coordination of these components, will become evident.

However, before investigating the first of these properties in an organism, namely, internal–hierarchical data exchange, it is necessary to explicate the words *component* and *homeostasis* utilized in the above definition of an organism. The word *component* is a term that can be used analogously to refer to either a part of a process, a part of a subsystem, or a part of a system. In the most general of terms, an organism is a unified living system made up of subsystems. In turn, these subsystems are made up of processes, and these processes are the activities in which the components are engaged. The components of an organism range from the organelles performing processes in a cell, to cells performing processes in an organ, to organs performing processes in a subsystem, to subsystems performing processes in the whole system itself, that is, the organism. Thus, for example, the respiratory subsystem works with other subsystems in an organism like a dog to maintain its life: the respiratory subsystem would be considered as one component of the entire dog, envisioned as one whole system; the lung would be considered as one component of the respiratory subsystem of the dog; lung cellular tissue comprising one of the lobes of its lung would be considered as one component of the lung; and the particular kind of cell that comprises lung tissue is made up of organelles, the basic components of cells.

Homeostasis refers to the relatively constant or stable coordination of functioning among the components in the organismic hierarchy, given the interaction of these components with environmental pressures internal to and external to the organism. I will have more to say about internal versus external environmental pressures later in this chapter. For now, suffice it to say that there are environments exerting pressures upon the subsystems and processes internal to an organism, as well as environments exerting pressures upon the organism as a whole that are external to it. The components that make up an organism, as well as the organism itself, are able to respond effectively to the ever-changing environmental pressures by adjusting and readjusting their activities so as to continue their respective operations with a degree of stability. When a subsystem or process in an organism is operating with a degree of stability despite environmental pressures—for example, when the cell wall actually performs the activity of allowing nutrients into the cell, or when a heart actually performs the activity of pumping blood, or when the body of an animal actually cools itself through perspiration because its temperature has been raised above a certain degree—it is said to be functioning properly. I will have more to say about functions in the next chapter.

We can draw a distinction between what I will call *particularized homeostasis* and *generalized homeostasis*. Particularized homeostasis refers to the end product of the proper functioning of the *particular* processes and subsystems in an organism being the relatively constant coordination among the components that make up the processes and subsystems, given environmental pressures that are *internal* to the organism. Generalized homeostasis refers to the *overall maintenance of the life* of an organism being the result of the proper functioning of the processes and subsystems, given environmental pressures that are *external* to the organism. The overall homeostasis of the living system is maintained because homeostasis is maintained at the levels of the subsystems and processes.

If the various processes and subsystems of an organism are functioning properly in their internal environments—thereby producing particularized homeostasis—the organism is able to live its life effectively in some external environment. This proper functioning that yields internal homeostasis takes place at levels in the hierarchy of the organism ranging from the coordinated activities of organelles in the cell, to cells performing coordinated processes in an organ, to organs performing coordinated processes in a subsystem, to subsystems performing coordinated activities in an organism. Thus, in reference to our example of the dog: the dog is able to live its life in some external environment precisely because of the overall relatively constant coordination of the subsystems in its body; in turn, a particular subsystem, like the respiratory subsystem, functions properly because of the relatively constant coordination of cellular processes; and the cells themselves function properly because of the relatively constant coordination among the various organelles.

The subsystems and processes of an organism can be understood as functioning at various levels of operation, from lower levels to higher levels. The determination of a subsystem as existing at a certain level depends upon the way in which the processes of the subsystem operate and, in turn, the way in which the subsystems operate in the organism as a whole. Lower level processes operate in certain ways and form the basis for higher level processes and subsystems. In turn, higher level subsystems and processes are comprised of lower level processes and utilize the information from these lower levels to perform their own operations. In this sense, along with Audesirk et al. (2002), Lycan (1995), and Salthe & Matsuno (1995), we could say that higher level subsystems are the phenomena that literally *emerge* from lower level subsystems and processes. Later in this chapter and the next, I will have more to say about emergence as well as about higher levels exhibiting control over lower levels—in terms of higher levels selecting and integrating information from lower levels—in an organismic hierarchy.

The organism can be conceptualized as a hierarchical organization whereby levels of operation, in the forms of subsystems and processes, function interdependently with one another in this unified system. A schematization of this hierarchical system is shown in figure 1.1. The organism is represented by the large partitioned triangle that contains the smaller partitioned triangles within it; the biggest triangles within the one large triangle represent subsystems, the smaller triangles within those subsystems represent processes, the smallest triangles within those processes represent components of processes, and the partitions represent levels of operation. Some of the triangles overlap, signifying that the subsystems are interdependently related to one another. For example, in a hierarchically ordered system like the mammal, the nervous (sub)system is dependent upon the respiratory and circulatory (sub)systems, primarily for a process of oxygen transfer to the nerve cells and brain cells of the nervous (sub)system. At the same time, the processes of the respiratory and circula-

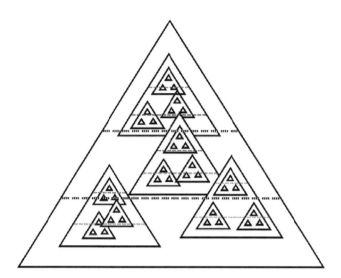

Figure 1.1
A hierarchically organized system

tory (sub)systems are dependent upon the processes of the nervous (sub)system—found, specifically, in the medulla of the brain—for their activities.

1.2 Internal–Hierarchical Data Exchange

Questions now arise as to how it is possible for the operations in this biological hierarchy to be carried out at a certain level, and also how the operations at lower levels are able to affect and be affected by higher levels, and vice versa? This is accomplished by what I call *internal–hierarchical data exchange*. By this, I refer to the fact that data must freely flow between and among the various levels of the organism. *Data* are the raw materials that are of the kind that have the potential to be useful for a process or operation. Data are exchanged between the components at one level of operation, among the various processes of a subsystem, and among the subsystems that make up the organism as a whole. In this sense, the operations and processes must exhibit a certain amount of malleability and flexibility so that data actually can be exchanged. The data can take the physical form of an electrical charge, an electron, a molecule, or a chemical transmitter, among other forms. Examples of this kind of data exchange abound in organisms, but we will take a look at one representative example.

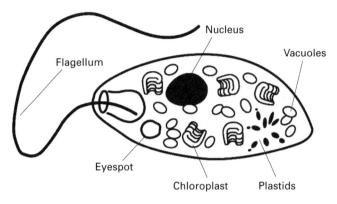

Nucleus

Vacuoles

Flagellum

Eyespot

Chloroplast   Plastids

Figure 1.2
A euglena

A euglena is a one-celled microorganism that is a member of the protist kingdom; in colloquial terms, it is known as a kind of algae (see figure 1.2). Euglenas are about 10 micrometers in length and look like a sperm cell with a more elongated body. They are equipped with a flagellum, eyespot, vacuoles, chloroplasts, plastids, and a cell nucleus. Each one of these components has a function in the euglena; the flagellum is a whip-like tail that enables the euglena to move around, the eyespot is light/dark sensitive so that the euglena can move toward sunlight (its food source), vacuoles allow for wastes to be disposed, chloroplasts transform sunlight to energy and food, plastids store the food, and the cell nucleus contains a nucleolus that synthesizes and encodes ribosomal ribonucleic acid (RNA), which is important for euglena structure and reproduction.

Referring again to our hierarchical model, an organism is an organized system composed of subsystems that are made up of components engaged in processes whose activities produce the particularized and generalized homeostasis of the system. For an organism like the euglena to function effectively in some external environment—basically, live its life in its microbial world—it is necessary that data be exchanged between and among the various subsystems of this system. Food storage in the euglena can be viewed as a subsystem activity, which itself is made up of processes concerning electron transport and oxygen exchange in photosynthesis. In this activity, the data consist of electrons and oxygen molecules. The data must be exchanged between the two processes; otherwise, there would be no storage of food. At the same time, this subsystem works with the subsystems concerning food acquisition and mobility. If data were not being exchanged between the eyespot and the flagellum, then there would be no movement toward sunlight; in turn, there would be no photosynthesis, and then no food storage.

1.3 Data Selectivity

Raw data are exchanged between and among the various subsystems and processes of the organism. However, not every piece of data is relevant or useful to a subsystem or process. There must be some property of the components of an organism that allows for discrimination or parsing between relevant and irrelevant data. Once a piece of data has been selected as useful for a process, it becomes informative for the process; the selected data ceases to be potentially useful and becomes actual information. Raw data have the potential to become information, and information can be understood as data of the kind that have been selected for as useful for a process or system in an organism. Thus, there are actually three categories of data, namely, (1) data that are *not* of the kind that are either useful or not useful for a subsystem or process, (2) data that *are* of the kind that are *not* useful for a subsystem or process, and (3) data that *are* of the kind that *are* useful for a subsystem or process, namely, information.

The term *information* can be defined in different ways, usually depending upon the intended goals of a particular intellectual discipline or methodology employed. Some molecular biologists use the term in the spirit of Shannon (1948) and Weaver & Shannon's (1949) information theory to describe any general communicative process that *selects* one or more objects from a set of objects (cf. Sacco, Copes, Sloyer, & Stark, 1988; Schneider, 1986; also the articles in Terzis & Arp, 2008). However, a few more conditions should be added to this definition in order to make it more appropriate for our discussion.

First, given the molecular biologist's definition, I think it is correct to say that information entails a selective process. As has been noted already, it is the selective capacity of the components of an organism that enables raw data to be considered as information. Consider that there are a multitude of activities being performed by organelles within the eukaryotic cell. The plasma membrane is the phospholipid bilayer that acts as the cell's shell. In the processes of endocytosis and exocytosis, materials are moved into and out of the cell through the plasma membrane. However, *not just any material* is allowed into or out of the cell. There must be some mechanism of discrimination employed in these processes so that the correct kinds of organic molecules come into the cell *as nutrients*, and the correct kinds of organic molecules get expelled *as wastes*. The data being exchanged in both cases are organic molecules. However, the cell processes can discriminate and select which molecules are useful and which molecules are harmful.

Second, these molecular biologists describe information as a communicative process. This seems correct, as information is a kind of medium between, on the one hand, something doing the communicating and, on the other hand, something doing the receiving in some environment. In other words, communication of information entails that there be some kind of afferent entity and some kind of efferent entity, as well as some kind of environment, in which this communication can occur. Insofar as this is the case, *information* can be considered as a communication on the part of some afferent entity (the communicator) that causes some kind of a change or modification in the efferent entity (the receiver) in an environment, influencing the subsequent activity of the efferent entity. Using our example of the eukaryotic cell, carbon, nitrogen, and oxygen molecules (the communicator) pass by the plasma membrane (the receiver) and can be understood as informative and incorporated into the body of the cell as energy (the influence). Conversely, organic molecules that are expelled as wastes by cell A (the communicator) can be understood as informative for nearby cell B (the receiver), to the extent that cell B does not intake cell A's waste (the influence).

Third, it would seem that some kind of storage or imprinting mechanism would need to exist in the receiver, even if this storage were to endure for only a short amount of time. Such a storage mechanism is necessary so that the information actually can be influential for the efferent entity. For example, when a cell divides in two during cellular mitosis, the offspring cell receives the genetic information from its parent cell. The genetic information from an initial parent cell (or parent cells) is housed in every one of the cells of a multicellular organism. This is why it is that biologists like Gould (2002) and Dawkins (1976) can refer to organisms as "genetic information houses." If that information from the parent cell was not stored somehow in the nucleolus of the offspring cell, then the offspring cell could not continue to pass on genetic information in its own process of mitosis.

Finally, afferent entities have the potential to become efferent entities, although not in exactly the same respect, and vice versa: cells are generated by mitosis but then generate their own mitosis, the plasma membrane takes in but then expels organic molecules, the medulla of the brain receives messages from and then sends messages to the heart and lungs, and drone bees perceive that food is present through the use of the visual system and then communicate this information to the rest of the hive by visual means. Organisms operate in such a way that information can be readily communicated and accepted by the same systems, processes, and traits. In this sense, there is a certain malleability or flexibility to be found in the subsystems and processes of an organism. Having both defined information and described the conditions concerning information exchange, we now can give a few more examples of this kind of activity in organisms.

Example 1   Successful gene transfer in reproduction entails that genetic information is passed along from parent organism to offspring organism. The parent organism acts as the communicator, and the offspring as receiver. The genetic code is the information that is communicated from parent to organism. The offspring is affected by this genetic information, since such information determines the offspring's structure and activity. The genetic information is stored in the deoxyribonucleic acid (DNA) located in the nucleus of the cell and, in conjunction with environmental factors, continually shapes the structure and activity of the organism throughout its life span (Audesirk et al., 2002; Mayr, 1997; Voet, Voet, & Pratt, 2002; Campbell & Reece, 1999).

Example 2   When a neuron produces an action potential—colloquially, when it *fires*—information associated with spiking signals is communicated between that neuron and at least one other neuron. The axon of one neuron, A, acts as a communicator, and the dendrites of another neuron, B—to which the axon of neuron A is connected—acts as a receiver. Protein synthesis in neurotransmitter release is the information that is communicated between neurons. Depending on the amount and intensity of the neurotransmitter emitted from the communicator neuron, the receiver neuron may become excitatory, making it more likely to produce its own action potential. Networks of neurons can fire more quickly when they are used more frequently, as if the information associated with the particular network's firing has been stored. The complex interworkings of trillions of these connections throughout an animal with a complex nervous system enable it to fight, flee, forage, feast, and so on (Kandel, Schwartz, & Jessell, 2000; Felleman & van Essen, 1991; Crick, 1994).

Example 3   Cells use energy, and one of the primary functions of the mitochondrion of an animal cell is to produce energy for the cell by converting sugars into a nucleic acid called adenosine triphosphate (ATP). However, this can happen only if there is a line of communication between other organelles of the cell and the mitochondria themselves. ATP acts as the material catalyst of information communicated between mitochondria and other organelles. When there are low levels of ATP, the mitochondria receive this information and convert more sugars; conversely, when sugars are converted, the other organelles receive this information and cellular homeostasis can be maintained (Audesirk et al., 2002; Voet et al., 2002; Campbell & Reece, 1999).

Example 4   A clear illustration of the communication of information in a systemic fashion is a mammal's muscle coordination in a *reflex arc*. In this activity, information is communicated to and from the spinal cord and a particular muscle group of the body (Kandel et al., 2000; Pelligrino, Fadiga, Fogassi, Gallese, & Rizzolatti, 1996). Consider a situation where a very curious cat decides to jump atop a very hot stove. The intense motion of the molecules from the stovetop is impressed upon the pads of the cat's paws. That motion affects the sensory neurons in the cat's skin, causing them to fire. The sensory neurons send a message to the interneurons and, in turn, a message is sent through motor neurons to the spinal cord. These *messages* consist of billions of action potentials and neurotransmitter releases, affecting cell after cell along the pathway of this particular reflex arc. In an instant, the spinal cord then sends a message back to the muscle groups associated with the cat's legs, diaphragm, and back. In a flash, the cat jumps off the stove and screams while arching its back. However, now the cat must coordinate its fall to the ground. This time, information is sent from the visual system to the brain and then back through the spinal cord to other muscles in the cat's body. All of this information must be integrated by the brain and motor responses must be orchestrated by the combined effort of brain–body communication of information. The cat narrowly avoids falling into the garbage can placed next to the stove.

We can now be more precise concerning the kind of activities in which organisms are engaged. This fourth example not only helps to demonstrate how information is communicated in organisms but also serves to bolster the claim that organisms are hierarchically organized systems of information exchange. This is so because information must flow between the subsystems of the organism, as well as within the particularized processes of the subsystems themselves, in order for an organized expression of the organism's activity to take place. Our curious cat utilized—at least—the endocrine, nervous, muscular, respiratory, skeletal, and visual subsystems in its body while jumping, screaming, and negotiating space. Similarly, for a euglena, there must be a flow of information between eyespot and flagellum in food acquisition, just as there must be a flow of information between chloroplasts and plastids in food storage.

1.4 Informational Integration

The mere fact *that* information is exchanged among the various processes and subsystems of an organism does not seem to capture fully or adequately the nature of an organism as a hierarchically organized system. The distinction between higher and lower levels in a hierarchy suggests that the higher levels exhibit significant *control* over the lower levels. This makes sense, since the more complex some process or system becomes, the more there is a need for mechanisms of control so that the process or system can operate efficiently. These mechanisms are like command centers where activity can be integrated and monitored, much like the central processing unit of a computer. In fact, Sperber (1994), Dennett (1991), Johnson-Laird (1988), and Dawkins (1986), each in their own way, envision computational systems equipped with central processing units as appropriate models of biological processes.

Now, there are at least two modes of control present in an organism conceived of as a hierarchically organized system, namely, *selectivity* and *integration*. Already, we have seen that selectivity is a mode of control, since this property of organisms acts as a kind of filtering mechanism that distinguishes raw data from information. Biologists and other researchers use the word *constraint* to describe mechanisms of selectivity associated with organisms, whether they are talking about cellular processes (Kulin, Kishore, Helmerson, & Locascio, 2003; Rosen, 1968), embryological development (Amundson, 1994), visual attentiveness (Hatfield, 1999), the fight-or-flee response (Nesse & Abelson, 1995), organismic homeostasis (Audesirk et al., 2002), or the adaptability of organisms to environments (Gould, 1980; Darwin, 1859).

In the four examples from the previous section, we can describe forms of selectivity that manifest a mode of control. In example 1, genetic information is passed along from parent to offspring, but the gene transfer in reproduction is *restricted* to a particular species. Genetic information cannot pass from euglena to cat, for example, or from human to euglena. With respect to example 2, proteins actually contribute in *regulating* the amount of neurotransmitters that can be released into a given synaptic cleft when a neuron fires. In example 3, mitochondria are said to *filter* any excess glucose to facilitate cellular homeostasis. Finally, in example 4, the brain ultimately can *control* the amount of force exerted in a jump (see Mayr, 1976; Hastings, 1998; Kitcher, 1992; Allman, 2000; Cziko, 1992, 1995; Pelligrino, Fadiga, Fogassi, Gallese, & Rizzolatti, 1996).

Once a useful piece of data has been selected for—thereby becoming information—it still has to be integrated into the overall workings of a process or subsystem. *Informational integration* is another mode of control in the organism viewed as a hierarchically organized system. It refers to the fact that the various processes and subsystems in an organism are equipped with a capacity to organize the information that has been selected for by the processes and subsystems so that, ultimately, generalized homeostasis can be achieved. Processes and subsystems achieve particularized homeostasis, the results of which contribute to generalized homeostasis in an organism. If there were not some mechanism by which the pieces of information were organized in processes and subsystems, then the hierarchy would not achieve generalized homeostasis, thereby ceasing to function or, at least, ceasing to function optimally in some environment. Selectivity and integration are like two sides of the same coin concerning control in an organism conceived of as a hierarchical organization—both are needed for proper functioning of the components and, consequently, for particularized and generalized homeostasis of the organism.

Consider an analogous thought experiment. If a painter selects all of the colors for a painting, but then splashes the colors on the canvas in a random fashion, there would be no organized piece of art produced (unless the goal is some modern art piece *intended* to be randomized). Or, consider that the very idea of a system entails a coordination of the components that make up the referent of such an idea. What would happen to a system if there were no integration of information to be found therein, that is, no coordination of components in the processes and subsystems that make up such a thing? The system would cease to be known as, and cease *to be*, a system, really. Instead it would be known as, as well as become, an aggregate of some sort. Although he cashes out an organism under the general rubric of a "mechanism," this is why Craver (2001, p. 59), echoing Wimsatt (1994, 1997) and Cummins (1975, 1983, 2002), can maintain that the "components of mechanisms, in contrast to those of mere aggregates, have an *active organization* [italics mine]."

Informational integration is achieved at many levels in an organism, from the coordinated operations of organelles in a cell, to the coordinated cellular processes in an organ, to the coordinated activities of organs in a subsystem, to the overall coordination of the subsystems of the organism.

Further, in a multicellular organism like an animal, all of these processes and subsystems function together in coordinated ways to produce the generalized homeostasis of the organism. In light of this property of organisms, the image of a triangle that I used in figure 1.1 is all the more appropriate as a schematization of an organismic hierarchy. The subsystems near the top part of the triangle control the entire system, just as the processes near the top of a subsystem control the subsystem, through the integration of information received from lower levels (see the papers in Terzis & Arp, 2008). Analogously, we can think of organizations like the Catholic Church or a corporation as manifesting this triangular model in their own actions and interactions. The pope and other bishops are at the top of the Church triangle and exhibit control over the rest of the Church as a whole. So too, the corporate members (CEO, chief financial officer, etc.) are at the top of the corporation triangle and exhibit control over the corporation as a whole.

1.5 Environmental–Organismic Information Exchange

Organisms interact with external environments. However, because organisms are hierarchically organized living systems composed of subsystems, processes, and components engaged in various operations, they have their own internal environments as well. Following Brandon (1984, 1992), an *environment* can be defined as any pressure or force that aids in the producing of some change in the organism's structure and functioning. We can draw a distinction between the information that is exchanged *within* the organism's environment and the information that is exchanged *between* the external environment and the organism. Thus, there are really two types of environments, namely, environments that are internal to an organism and environments that are external to an organism. In this section, I further elucidate these two types of environments and the relationship of these environments to the organism.

An environment is not limited to the external world surrounding an organism. There are environments internal to the organism. For example, the other organelles, nucleus, ATP, water, and various organic molecules act as the environment for a mitochondrion in the eukaryotic cell. Also, other eukaryotic cells, cancerous cells, water, and all kinds of organic molecules and chemical elements act as the environment for a typical eukaryotic cell. A myriad of molecules, including hydrogen, carbon, nitrogen, and oxygen, surround and exert influence upon organs in a multicellular organism's body. Further, a piece of food taken in from the environment external to the organism becomes part of the environment within the organism and, depending on the content, may be digested or expelled. These facts concerning internal environmental pressure add to the picture of an organism as a hierarchically organized system. Within this kind of living system, there are levels distinguishable from other levels. One way to describe the distinction is by comparing a certain level, say level(n), with other levels that act as environments exerting pressures, exchanging data, and communicating information with level(n).

At the same time, the organism itself is interacting with external environments that are exerting pressures, exchanging data, and communicating information with the organism. Concerning environments that are external to the organism, we see that organisms are members of species that live in populations. These populations usually coexist with other populations in communities. Many communities living with their nonliving surroundings comprise an ecosystem, and the sum of all ecosystems make up the biosphere of the earth. Other members of a species, different species, and the nonliving surroundings of an organism are all considered parts of the external environment for an organism. The organism constantly experiences environmental pressures, and these pressures can be described in terms of information that is exchanged between the environment and the organism.

External environmental information affects an organism in a one-way, environment-to-organism, external-to-internal causal fashion. This kind of information exchange can be witnessed as a result of research accrued and experiments performed by biologists and other thinkers.

It is common knowledge that an organism's survival is dependent upon both genetic and environmental factors (Gould, 2002; Berra, 1990; Mayr, 1969, 1976, 1982, 1991, 2001; Ayala, 1982). For example, if there is an alteration in a rodent's genetic makeup that causes it to have a malformed foot, then it is more likely to be eaten by a hawk out on the open range. However, if the same handicapped rodent lives in a forested area where it can hide under rocks and bushes, it is less likely to become a predator's victim. Also, if an environment happens to be made up of trees having fruit high up on its branches, and it just so happens that a fruit-eating animal's genes coded it to have a neck long enough to reach the fruit, then such an animal likely will survive. Conversely, if your animal genes coded you to have a short neck, it is unlikely you would survive in such an environment (i.e., if the fruit high up in the trees were your only food source). In the words of Berra

(1990, p. 8), "The environment is the selecting agent, and because the environment changes over time and from one region to another, different variants will be selected under different environmental conditions." These examples illustrate that there is a one-way, external-to-internal exchange of information between an environment and an organism existing in that environment.

Another famous example that illustrates the informational transfer between the environment and an organism in a one-way, external-to-internal fashion has to do with the finches that Darwin (1859) described on the Galapagos Islands during his voyage on *The Beagle*. These finches clearly exhibit *adaptive radiation*, that is, in the words of Berra (1990, p. 163), "the evolutionary divergence of members of a single phylogenetic lineage into a variety of ecological roles usually resulting, in a short period of time, in the appearance of several or many new species." Darwin noted several different beak shapes and sizes that apparently were modified in the finches, depending upon the ecological niche the particular bird inhabited. Some finches had massive beaks ideal for crushing their seed food source, others had thinner pointed beaks ideal for probing flowers, and still others had curved beaks ideal for picking food out of woody holes. In this set of circumstances, the environments the various finches inhabited were all different, and the finches with beaks most fit for a particular environment survived to reproduce.

Phenotypic traits are the physiological characteristics or behaviors of organisms that are under genetic control. The genetic information determines what a particular member of a species will look like, how fast it will run, what coloration it will have, how successful it will be at mating, and so on (Carroll, 2005; Mayr, 2001; Lewontin, 1992; Gould, 2002; Gordon, 1992). In the finch example, the different beaks represent the variety of phenotypic characteristics under genetic influence. If it just so happened that a certain beak style was effective in gathering food in an environment, then that finch would survive and pass its genes on to other finches. Soon, that particular niche would be dominated by the beak style that was most fit for that environment. I will have more to say about the general evolutionary principles of genetic variability and natural selection in the beginning of the fourth chapter.

Research has been conducted on animals to determine how the external environment affects the functioning of various systems of the body. One experiment has to do with occluding or removing the eyes of cats, rats, and birds at various stages of development to see if the neural connections of the brain necessary to the visual system either would develop abnormally or would cease to function altogether. These studies indicated that when occluding or removing the eyes, certain neural connections in the brains of these animals would not be made. This resulted in the cessation of certain visual processes, causing the overall subsystem to be underdeveloped in relation to other animals that had not had their eyes occluded or removed (Shatz, 1992; Shatz & Stryker, 1978; Clayton & Krebs, 1994; Black & Greenough, 1986; Cziko, 1995). This research illustrates what happens when information *is not* exchanged between environment and organism.

A further example that demonstrates environment-to-organism, external–internal information exchange has to do with research on the fruit fly, *Drosophila*. Experimenters are able to take out, move around, or add genetic sequences in the DNA of the fly, causing radical phenotypic alterations to result, such as the deletion of some organ, legs growing where antennae should be, and antennae growing where legs should be. The experimenter's adjustments to the genetic code of the fruit fly are analogous to the radioactive material and other kinds of natural external forces of mutation that alter the genetic codes of fruit fly populations. We find similar monstrosities in fruit flies when we study them in their natural habitats (Duncan, Burgess, & Duncan, 1998). Just as researchers tap into and alter the genetic codes of fruit flies in controlled experiments, so too, external forces "tap into" and alter the genetic makeup of fruit fly populations in nature. These fruit fly abnormalities are another example of the property of environmental–organismic information exchange found in organisms.

In this chapter, I have attempted to elucidate Mayr's idea that organisms are hierarchically organized living systems. So far, we have seen that an organism is a living entity, the components of which are hierarchically organized in subsystems and processes operating so as to achieve particularized and generalized homeostasis. These subsystems and processes possess certain properties including abilities to exchange data flexibly, convert data to information in a selection process, integrate information, and process information from environments. Among many other kinds of activities, organisms will engage in four basic operations— namely, some form of fighting, fleeing, eating, and reproducing—while constantly interacting with environments. Given the consequent pressures entailed in this kind of interaction, it makes sense that the subsystems and processes of an organism be coordinated and unified in a systemic fashion, so as optimally to engage in these activities while negotiating environments.

In the next chapter, after using ideas and arguments from this chapter in support of certain forms of metaphysical and epistemological forms of emergence, I give further elucidation to Mayr's idea that organisms operate on the basis of historically acquired programs of information, as well as ratify Plotkin's claim that biological phenomena only make complete sense in light of evolutionary theory, by endorsing a hybrid view of functions based in both the Cummins organizational and the Griffiths/Godfrey-Smith modern history accounts.

2 Emergence and Function

2.1 Metaphysical Emergence and Homeostatic Organization

In the previous chapter, the attempt was made to show that the processes in which the components of an organismic hierarchy are engaged produce homeostasis through abilities to exchange data internally, selectively convert data to information, integrate that information, and process information from environments. Now, it will be argued that the components and attending processes of an organism should be considered as emergent phenomena because of the way in which the components are organized to maintain the homeostasis of the organism at the various levels in the organismic hierarchy (also see Arp, 2008a).

Near the end of the first section of the previous chapter, the claim was made that higher level subsystems are the phenomena that literally emerge from lower level subsystems and processes of an organism conceived of as a hierarchically organized living entity. With respect to organisms and the descriptions of their components, processes, and properties, I endorse certain forms of metaphysical and epistemological emergence. As Silberstein (2002), Silberstein & McGreever (1999), and McLaughlin (1992, 1997) have clarified, there are metaphysical and epistemological forms of emergence. In Kim's (1995, p. 224) words, according to metaphysical emergentists, "a property of a complex system is said to be 'emergent' just in case, although it arises out of the properties and relations characterizing simpler constituents, it is neither predictable from, nor reducible to, these lower-level characteristics" (also see the discussions in Kim, 1999; Wimsatt, 1994, 1997; Emmeche, Køppe, & Stjernfelt, 2000; Craver, 2001; Lowe, 2000; O'Connor, 1994; Rueger, 2000; Zylstra, 1992). According to epistemological emergentists, the concepts, theories, models, or frameworks we utilize to describe phenomena at a certain level are nonreducible to the concepts, theories, and so forth at a lower level (see, e.g., the discussions in

Batterman, 2001; Cartwright, 1999; Primas, 1998; Sklar, 1999; Dupré, 1993; Crane, 2001; Van Gulick, 2001).

Further, as Silberstein (2002) and Silberstein & McGeever (1999) clarify, within the genus of metaphysical emergence, four kinds have been distinguished, namely, non-elimination, nonidentity, mereological emergence, and nomological emergence. Also, within the genus of epistemological emergence, at least two kinds of approaches have been distinguished, namely, predictive/explanatory emergence and representational/cognitive emergence. In light of the previous chapter, the metaphysical and epistemological forms of emergence that will be explored and defended in this chapter are the following: *nomological emergence*, understood by Silberstein (2002, p. 91) as "cases in which higher-level entities, properties, etc., are governed by higher-level laws that are not determined by or necessitated by the fundamental laws of physics governing the structure and behavior of their most basic physical parts," and *representational/cognitive emergence*, understood by Silberstein (2002, p. 92) as the thesis that "wholes (systems) exhibit features, patterns or regularities that cannot be fully represented (understood) using the theoretical and representational resources adequate for describing and understanding the features and regularities of their more basic parts and the relations between those more basic parts."

From the metaphysical perspective, nomological emergentists deny the general principle that the whole can be accounted for fully in terms of the physical parts, and so their view is contrasted with *nomological reductionism*. According to nomological reductionists, there are really no entities, properties, or substances that arise out of more fundamental physical ones, since, once the more fundamental ones have been described, that is all there is to the reality of an entity, property, or substance. Thus, for example, when people speak about water, they may take it to be a substance in its own right. However, according to the nomological reductionist, water *just is* hydrogen and oxygen—nothing new emerges when two hydrogen molecules combine with one oxygen molecule. Conversely, according to a nomological emergentist, there is something about water—for example, its liquidity or liquid property—that emerges from the hydrogen and oxygen molecules, making it such that this liquidity exists on a separate metaphysical plane from the molecules on which it depends. After all, reason nomological emergentists, liquidity appears to be something distinct from hydrogen and oxygen molecules, as well as their chemical bond.

From the epistemological perspective, representational emergentists are contrasted with representational/theoretical reductionists, who attempt to reduce concepts, theories, and so forth to their lowest common denominator, as it were, and this usually means a description in terms of physicochemical entities, properties, or substances and their attending laws or principles. Thus, if we took the cell as an example, according to a representational reductionist, the cell *can be described* completely within a physicochemical framework of concepts, theories, models, laws, and so forth associated with vectors and physical substructures and bonds (see the discussions in Churchland, 1995; Humphreys, 1997; Primas, 1998).

Some emergentists maintain that chemical bonds or basic physical structures—as well as our descriptions of them—are nonreducible to the molecules and atoms of which they are composed. Thus, there is an emergence–reduction divide even at the physicochemical level (see, e.g., the discussions in Hendry, 1999; Hellman, 1999; Belot & Earman, 1997). This physicochemical debate is avoided here, and instead I want to maintain that *starting with the organelles that constitute a cell*, and continuing up the hierarchy of components in processes and subsystems of an organism—including psychological phenomena—we have clear instances of emergent phenomena. The fundamental reason why these components and their attending processes must be considered as emergent phenomena has to do with the way in which the components are organized to function so as to maintain the homeostasis of the organism at the various levels in the hierarchy. I will refer to this position as the *homeostatic organization view* (HOV) of biological phenomena. Since homeostasis is ubiquitous as both a *concept* and as a *recognized reality* in biological, psychological, and philosophical communities (among many other disciplines), it makes for a natural point of discussion in the emergence/reduction debate.

In the first section of the previous chapter, a distinction was drawn between particularized homeostasis and generalized homeostasis. It was shown that because the various processes and subsystems of an organism are functioning properly in their internal environments (particularized homeostasis), the organism is able to live its life effectively in some environment external to it (generalized homeostasis). Here, the very existence of components and their activities at various levels in the organism's hierarchy is linked to the coordination of such components *so as ultimately to produce generalized homeostasis*. The components of an organism are organized in such a way that the resultant outcome of their processes becomes first particularized homeostasis and then generalized homeostasis. *That* components are organized to perform some function resulting in homeostasis is one feature that marks them out to be novel emergent entities distinguishable from the very physicochemical processes of which they are composed.

It was noted already that homeostasis first occurs at the basic level of the organized coordination of the activities of organelles in a cell. Researchers like Audesirk et al. (2002), Kandel et al. (2000), Voet et al. (2002), Campbell & Reece (1999), and Smolensky (1988) document cellular homeostasis. At this basic level of organelle interaction within the cell, we also would have the first instances of salient emergent biological properties that are distinct from the physicochemical properties upon which they depend. Consider all of the information being exchanged between and among the organelles of an animal cell. The nucleus is in constant communication with each mitochondrion, centriole, golgi apparatus, ribosome, and endoplasmic reticulum, each of which has its own function in maintaining the overall homeostasis of the cell (see figure 2.1): the nucleus contains the nucleolus and houses DNA, the mitochondrion supplies the cell with energy, centrioles are important for cell division, the Golgi apparatus stores

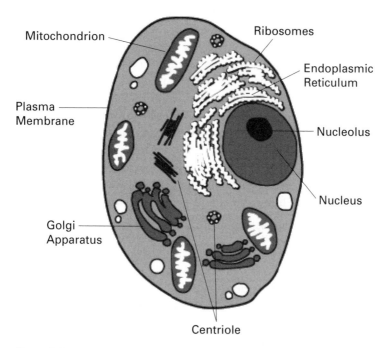

Figure 2.1
The major organelles of the animal cell

proteins, ribosomes are the sites for protein synthesis, the endoplasmic reticulum expedites the transport of cellular material, and the plasma membrane permits materials to move into and out of the cell.

In fact, *components* of organisms as they have been described—organelles, cells, organs, and subsystems, as well as the organism itself—all would be considered emergent entities. Referring to the schematization of an organism as one huge triangle containing smaller triangles that was used in figure 1.1 of the previous chapter, each one of those triangles—from biggest to smallest—represents a biologically emergent phenomenon. For example, although the organelles of a cell themselves are made up of physicochemical entities, they engage in coordinated kinds of activities that benefit the overall homeostasis of the cell; so too, although kidney cells are made up of organelles—which are made up of physicochemical entities—the kidney cells themselves engage in coordinated activities that benefit the homeostasis of the kidney; and so on, up the hierarchy of the mammal. This point was reiterated in my discussions with Jerry Morrissey at his lab at Washington University in St. Louis, where Morrissey conducts research on kidney cells (see the final section of Kaneto, Morrissey, McCracken, Reyes, & Klahr, 1998).

Now, in arguing for HOV, I am not advocating some "spooky stuff" principle (this terminology is borrowed from Churchland, 1993) of internal "vitalism" or external "design," the likes of which might be put forward by an organicist or a creationist (also see Arp, 1998, 1999, 2002). As was mentioned in the last chapter, the property of internal–hierarchical data exchange in an organism manifests upward causation, whereby the lower levels of the hierarchy exhibit causal influence over the higher levels. Likewise, the dual properties of data selectivity and informational integration manifest downward causation, whereby the higher levels of the hierarchy exhibit causal influence over the lower levels, in terms of control.

Consider that an organism like the human body is a complex multicellular entity made up of levels of independently organized entities that perform certain operations. These organized entities are hierarchically arranged from organ systems (e.g., the nervous system), composed of organs (brain, spinal cord, etc.), that are composed of tissues (nervous tissue), which are composed of cells (neurons, glial cells), each of which is composed of organelles (mitochondrion, nucleus, etc.), that are composed of organic molecules (carbon, nitrogen, oxygen, DNA, etc.). Each of these entities functions such that the operations at the lower levels contribute to the emergence of entities and their operations at the higher levels. Because of the activities of organic molecules, it is possible for organelles and their attending activities at a higher level to emerge, and because of the activities of organelles, it is possible for cells and their attending activities at a higher level to emerge, and so on.

Now, think of all of the complex upward and downward causal relations taking place when the human body simply gets up out of bed. Put crudely, the brain must exhibit downward causation, as a necessary condition, upon its own neurochemical constituents in order to cause the body to get up, while the neurochemical constituents must exhibit upward causation, as a necessary condition, for movement to occur in the first place. There is no "spooky" vitalism or design in any of this upward and downward causal interaction.

In fact, HOV provides an important addition to one standard interpretation of a hierarchical mechanism. In philosophy of science and philosophy of mind literature, it is now commonplace to find references to Craver's (2001) Cummins-influenced description of a mechanism hierarchy as some mechanism S, which is X-ing, composed of smaller entity Xs, which are Φ-ing. These Xs are little mechanisms themselves consisting of smaller entity Ps, which are σ-ing (also see Machamer, Darden, & Craver, 2000). This view has the benefit of describing some mechanism as a hierarchically organized system, in a nonspooky fashion, consisting of entities engaging in inter- and intraleveled causally efficacious activities. Also, this view is specifically supposed to account for *living* mechanisms, which classically have resisted a mechanistic description. In fact, Craver's view of a hierarchical mechanism maps onto my schematization of a hierarchically organized system schematized as nested triangles, and our two views have much in common.

However, as I pointed out to Carl Craver at a conference at Washington University in St. Louis, the problem with his view of mechanisms is that it neglects the more specified kinds of organized homeostatic activities in which the processes of organismic hierarchies are engaged. It is arguable that physicochemical entities—the so-called smaller entity Ps, which are σ-ing, that make up the organelles, which are Φ-ing—themselves are not coordinated in such a way so as to produce homeostatic results; they are not *organized to do something*, or achieve some result *in this homeostatic manner*. Further, it is arguable that physicochemical entities are not organized in hierarchical ways such that we could say they are engaged in particularized homeostatic processes contributing to a generalized homeostasis.

Organisms are responsive to their environments in such a way that they can adapt to changes. A callous on your foot is a simple example of the integumentary subsystem of your body adapting to a change in its external environment. Organisms, as well as the subsystems and processes of which they are composed, exhibit a certain amount of flexibility and malleability in relation to their internal and external environments. In fact, as we have already seen, the subsystems and processes of organisms produce particularized and generalized homeostasis, namely, a relatively constant coordination among the components of an organism, given the interaction of these components with environments internal to and external to the organism. Homeostasis and adaptability are two sides of the same coin. As was intimated already, this property of adaptability in relation to environments is yet another essential feature that distinguishes living entities, properties, or substances from nonliving ones. Another way to say this is that the adaptability of processes and subsystems in organisms can be pointed to as a clear way in which to distinguish the biological from the physicochemical realms.

Consider a rock. A rock would be classified as a nonliving, physicochemical entity because it does not have this ability to adapt to environments and situations the way that living, biological entities do. If a rock is hit by a hammer with a certain amount of force, it breaks up into pieces, the pieces fall where they may according to physicochemical laws, and that is the end of the story—this is its "response" to the environment. Alternatively, if one's forearm is hit by a hammer such that a bone breaks, the various systems of the body go to work to repair the damage so that some form of homeostasis can be reachieved. The body *adaptively* responds to this environmental pressure, and the hierarchy goes to work on fixing the problem. Further, if the bone does not heal correctly or the muscles surrounding it have atrophied because of the blow, the subsystems and processes of the body can compensate for the injury. If the hierarchy cannot fix the problem, it adjusts or readjusts if necessary. Homeostasis in an organism entails adaptability as a necessary condition, for it is the organism's response to its ever-changing environment that will occasion the need for either particularized or generalized homeostasis. Of course, biological entities are constructed of physicochemical components and are subject to the same physicochemical laws as any other piece of matter in the world; again, there is upward physicochemical causation that acts as a necessary condition for biological functioning. However, biological entities, as hierarchically organized living systems, have this distinguishing property whereby the subsystems and processes adaptively respond to their environments in ways that other physicochemical entities do not.

2.2 Represenational Emergence and as-if Realism

So far I have argued for a nomological form of metaphysical emergence—in terms of HOV—whereby parts of a biological system are envisioned as genuine emergent entities, starting at the level of the organelles of the cell. According to HOV, the components of an organismic hierarchy are organized to function so as to maintain the homeostasis of the organism at the various levels in the hierarchy. A question may arise as to how it is that a corresponding epistemological form of emergence may be possible so as to describe the metaphysically emergent biological phenomena. Could there be a representational/cognitive form of epistemological emergence that complements this nomological form of metaphysical emergence? This question of the relationship between metaphysical and epistemological forms of emergence is central to any discussion of emergence/reduction, as it would seem difficult to justify ontological claims without appealing to epistemological claims, and vice versa. Given this intimate relationship between metaphysics and epistemology, it may be that once a particular ontic level has been identified as emergent, then a whole new set of concepts, hypotheses, theories, and so forth will have to be introduced to account for the emergent phenomena.

Issues surrounding epistemological emergence and reduction are particularly poignant when describing organisms. This is so because it would appear that biology has its own set of laws and organisms have their own sets of properties that, despite being dependent upon physicochemical laws and properties, are nonreducible to them (see Mayr, 1969, 1996; Ruse, 1971, 2003; Gould, 2002; Lennox, 1993). In biological matters, an antireductionist's use of epistemological emergence accepts or implies that biological descriptions may emerge that are not reducible, even in principle, to physicochemical descriptions. Thus, the issue thinkers confront when trying to give a description of organisms and the functioning of their components can be put in the form of a question: Has the biologist given us a description of organisms and the functioning of their parts that is so basic as to be *un*achievable by a physicochemical description? In other words, in describing organisms and the functions of their systems and processes, does the biologist give us something that the physicist or chemist leaves out?

The HOV I endorse with respect to the functioning of organisms can be described within a biological framework that utilizes the language of teleology or functionality. In the rest of this section, as well as in the following section, I will be arguing that it is legitimate and appropriate to use this kind of language for describing the traits and processes of organisms in the biological sciences. Thankfully, the language of teleology already is being used by biologists, psychologists, philosophers, and other researchers to describe biological phenomena (for starters, see the essays in Ariew, Cummins, & Perlman, 2002; Perlman, 2004). As Ruse (2003) has pointed out, researchers thinking about biological matters since Aristotle cannot get around using the concepts and language of purpose, function, and organization to describe biological phenomena, even if to describe phenomena *as if* they were organized in a teleological manner (see Arp, 1998, 1999, 2002, 2005c, 2005d). Our descriptions of these kinds of entities seem to resist a reductive explanation to the levels of chemistry or physics. *That* researchers cannot get around describing biological phenomena as if they were organized with goals toward homeostasis may already be an indicator of an epistemological form of emergence. If one adopts a realist strategy for describing the biological realm—or an as-if realist strategy (cf. Rescher, 1997, 2005)—then it is easy to see how one could connect an epistemological form of emergence with a metaphysical form. Here, the descriptions of biological phenomena resist reduction and must be *described* with a set of emergent terms, precisely because that is the way in which we believe biological phenomena are homeostatically organized out there in the world. This may be why we cannot seem to jettison the language of teleology/functionality from our vocabulary.

It seems something is left out of the description of an organism if we say that, for example, a dog *just is* a mass made up of chemical properties having certain kinds of bonds, subject to laws of electromagnetism, gravity, and so forth. This kind of description might work well for, say, a rock because we do not see the properties of a rock as engaged in coordinated kinds of activities contributing to hierarchies and producing homeostasis. We do not ask what the components of a rock are *doing* for the rock as whole, or how they function, other than to say that the chemical bonds comprising its matter are of the kind that keep it solidified in some patch of space and time. However, an organism like a dog would seem to require a different kind of description as an entity having components whose emergence is related to the coordination of those components and their homeostatic outcomes in a hierarchically organized system; otherwise, one is in danger of *under*describing a dog's subsystems and processes *just as* a mass made up of chemical properties having certain kinds of bonds, subject to laws of electromagnetism, gravity, and so forth. There is more to a description of a dog's kidney, for example, than can be captured by the language of physical laws and chemical bonds. As a biologically emergent entity, the dog's kidney has a specific function it performs in the dog's digestive subsystem, and it is related to other organs in the system as a whole in such a way so as to aid in the maintenance of the dog's life.

Above, I hinted that it is possible for one to adopt either a realist or an as-if realist strategy when describing organisms. This may sound somewhat counterintuitive, given the existence of pragmatic, neo-pragmatic, and other forms of coherentist, intuitionist, or constructivist antirealisms that are prevalent in philosophy of science. In what follows, I will argue that it may be useful for a researcher to think like an *as-if realist* when describing the traits and processes of organisms. I want to give further specificity to the representational form of epistemological emergence I endorse, as well as show that an as-if form of realism in the epistemological realm can be combined with HOV, which is a form of nomological emergentism. The end result will be a better understanding of the epistemological views that underpin my metaphysical views in philosophy of science and philosophy of biology (also see Arp, 2005c, 2005d).

Godfrey-Smith (1996, p. 7) is correct in noting that realism and a "Dewey-style pragmatism" are two of the prominent competing metaphysical worldviews in the contemporary philosophical scene. Realists admit the existence of mind-independent realities (e.g., Fumerton, 2002; Plantinga, 2000; Devitt, 1997; Kitcher, 1993; Wright, 1993; cf. Dummett, 1982), and a host of pragmatists consider themselves antirealists unwilling to admit the existence of mind-independent realities (e.g., Rorty, 1998; Putnam, 1981, 1987, 1995; Brandom, 1994; Habermas, 1984; cf. Dickstein, 1998; Will, 1996). It seems to me that the antirealist has scored a victory in noting that there is a veil of perceptions and ideas that mediates between the world (if it exists) and the mind. In fact, one could consider this veil of perceptions and ideas—and its attendant skepticism—to be the fundamental insight that drives any antirealist project. Given the existence of our perceptions, there is, in principle, no way to know the nature of reality with *absolute certainty* or to know whether a reality beyond our perceptions really exists. When all is said and done, a philosopher, scientist, or any other kind of serious thinker ultimately has to confront the question as to whether there are mind-independent realities or not, and such thinkers will have to choose a side in the debate.

When Wittgenstein (1953) argued that a word's meaning is contextualized by and dependent upon the language-games of a particular group, this went a long way in convincing contemporary thinkers that propositions, sets, numbers, and truth itself need not be abstract objects. Carruthers (1993, p. 240) takes this idea one step further in his criticism of realism:

One can thus believe in a class of objective analytical truths: believing that all internal relations between senses were determined, independently of us, as soon as the senses of our expressions were determined; believing, indeed, that these are genuine objects of discovery. And one can believe that an analytic truth is an eternal truth: constraining our talk about remote items, and about counter-factual situations, just as much as it constrains our talk about the present. And yet one can, consistently with both beliefs, believe that sense depends for its existence upon our existence: only coming to exist when we first begin to use a language in which that sense may be expressed.

Rorty takes *one more step further* and disposes of the transcendent altogether. According to Rorty, we cannot get beyond our own language setting because *there is nothing beyond* our own language setting. Rorty (1991, pp. 22–23) calls his view pragmatic and, accordingly, pragmatists

see the gap between truth and justification not as something to be bridged by isolating a natural and trans-cultural sort of rationality which can be used to criticise certain cultures and praise others, but simply as the gap between the actual good and the possible better. From a pragmatist point of view, to say that what is rational for us now to believe may not be *true*, is simply to say that somebody may come up with a better idea. . . . For pragmatists, the desire for objectivity is not the desire to escape limitations of one's community, but simply the desire for as much intersubjective agreement as possible, the desire to extend the reference of "us" as far as we can.

In Rorty's pragmatic setting, the so-called "objective" would extend only so far as the accepted ideas of a particular scientific or philosophic community. Also, this objective would be the result of a common consensus.

Such views presented by Carruthers and Rorty wed pragmatism to constructivism and antirealism (cf. Fumerton, 2002; Kulp, 1996; Young, 1995; Rosen, 1994; Collins & Pinch, 1993). This is so because, from this perspective, ideas are constructed by minds (constructivism), and, insofar as they are constructed, these ideas have no independent existence without minds doing the constructing (antirealism). Peirce (1966, p. 96) summarized the intersection of these positions effectively when he stated that we

may fancy that this (pragmatic settlement of opinion) is not enough for us, and that we seek, not merely an opinion, but a true opinion. But put this fancy to the test and it proves groundless; for as soon as a firm belief is reached we are entirely satisfied, whether the belief be true or false. And it is clear that nothing out of the sphere of our knowledge can be our object, for nothing which does not affect the mind can be a motive for mental effort. The most that can be maintained is, that we seek for a belief that we *think* to be true.

From the Rortyan pragmatic perspective, positing a realm of abstract objects whose existence, by definition, exceeds the common pool of constructed ideas seems to be a form of philosophical elitism or esotericism that can only lead to, in the words of Tiles (1988, p. 26), "ways of insulating faulty doctrines from proper criticism, ways of begging questions in favor of certain conceptions of thought and its activity, the mind and its relation to objects." From their epistemological and metaphysical high horses—divorced from experience—such intellectualistic, rationalistic, and logicistic philosophers, scientists, and mathematicians could then arbitrarily claim "what is" and "what is not" precisely by *pre-determining* a priori notions and apodictic realities. This comprises one of the dangers associated with realism (cf. Dewey, 1982).

Some pragmatists do think that there can be a positive role for truth understood not as an apodictic and dogmatically determined eternal certainty discovered by the scientific community but as an ongoing process of formulation and reformulation in which no beliefs or propositions— even those associated with logical laws (Dewey, 1982; Erdmann, 1892)— are immune to open-ended discernment and the possibility of falsification (Dewey, 1941, 1982; Rorty, 1991, 1993, 1998). In this sense, classical pragmatism like that of James (1975) and Dewey (1982) began the process of replacing a realist, foundationalist notion of truth with an antirealist coherentism and helped pave the way for neo-pragmatism as well as deflationist theories that deny any reality to truth whatsoever. Alston (1996, pp. 189–190) has expressed the move away from realism toward pragmatism in this manner: "The truth of a truth bearer consists not in its relation to some 'transcendent' state of affairs, but in the epistemic virtues the former displays within our thought, experience, and discourse. Truth value is a matter of whether, or the extent to which, a belief is *justified, warranted, rational, well grounded,* or the like."

The end result of pragmatism is a probabilism—the quest for truth and certainty becomes nothing more than a quest for inquiry and security (Dewey, 1929a; Peirce, 1960; Putnam, 1995; Rorty, 1982, 1987, 1993). The pragmatic attempt to "fix belief" may leave some thinkers—for example, realists—wanting for a more robust epistemological justification and metaphysical resting place in *the* truth. In this sense, analogous to Moore's open question regarding the good, namely, "It may bring us pleasure, but is it good?" a realist may ask of our epistemologies, "It may be a rationally justified belief in terms of intellectual and technological fecundity, BUT IS IT TRUE!" Recalling Peirce's (1966) idea that an open-ended science will fix belief, one wonders how such an account serves to quell the agitation of doubt. It seems that, from the pragmatic perspective, metaphysics as such is replaced by an epistemological process and, further, this process must rest content with a kind of contingent truth. One may ask, "Whence is derived the *ultimate* justificatory force?" Consider the words of Mack (1968, pp. 72–73) in the final pages of his work concerning pragmatism: "The notion of the necessary specificity of any appeal to immediate experience points to a conclusion about the quest for a 'resting-place' for thought: thought never does find a final resting-place in Reality, but is always carried on to new problems—there is no complete rest for thought except in the sense in which consummatory experience is final."

However, we never can reach this consummatory experience. How can the resting content with a contingent truth be made consistent with the quelling of doubt entailed in the fixation of belief? Belief would seem to be fixed momentarily on what is taken to be the truth of the times. This may satisfy a lot of thinkers, but there will always be those who remain unsatisfied. Peregrin (1996, p. 4) puts this dissatisfaction with pragmatism another way: "The trouble with pragmatic theories of truth is that they seem to give us too much freedom with respect to truth. . . . Truth becomes far too circumstances-dependent, which is contrary to the intutition that some of our statements, if they are true, are true forever."

Enter the as-if realist. It is possible to show the value of thinking like a realist, even for the pragmatist. The commitment to the pursuit of abstract objects could become instrumental in guiding the life of philosophy and science in a limited, *as-if* manner. Kant (1929) spoke of the value of the regulative ideas as not only aiding in the rounding off of our systematic picture of reality but also prompting us to do further research and investigation. Thinkers are to act as if there is god, cosmos, and soul in order to further benefit our intellectual and moral lives. According to Kant, such a concession—albeit at root agnostic—has pragmatic benefit in keeping both our scientific endeavors and the philosophical dialectic alive (also see Arp, 2007c). So too, working as if there are truth conditions to be satisfied "out there" has a similar function and appeal. If we behave as if we hold certain beliefs about the truth conditions surrounding propositions, even if we are not completely clear about the metaphysical reality—the *ding-an-sich*, as it were—of those conditions, then such beliefs can be beneficial to us in our intellectual pursuits. Something valuable for the pragmatist can be gleaned from a realist metaphysics and methodology when such realism is tempered in this as-if manner. This tempered version of realism can be referred to as *as-if realism*.

I want to put forward an epistemological and metaphysical project that acknowledges the strengths of both antirealism and realism. The antirealist is correct about ultimately not being able to know, *for certain*, whether there are things that exist outside of the mind. The realist is correct that, despite this ignorance, we can and should act as if there are realities outside of the mind to be known. For, as I will show, such as-if realist thinking has pragmatic value, and it would be miraculous if our descriptions did not match up with some reality.

A few questions now emerge. What does this as-if realism offer to us that cannot be had by a pragmatist community of belief holders? After all, as McTaggart (1921) and Sellars (1963) have shown, it is possible to hold both that truth consists in a correspondence with facts *and* that these facts are mind-*dependent* realities. Does this as-if realism regarding truth do any real work for a scientific or philosophic community? What does this realism offer us over and above a Rortyan-style pragmatism such that this pragmatism alone is epistemologically and/or metaphysically insufficient?

I will attempt one line of response to these questions by utilizing, and modifying, an argument that has its roots in the realism of Aristotle and Plato called the *argument from the sciences*. In the *Metaphysics*—for example, at 1025b20, 1032b5, 1037a5–1038b—Aristotle notes that in order to do science, we cannot have a science of particulars, since such particulars are constantly in flux as well as indefinable; hence, there must be some general essence or form that comprises the object of a science. For example, anthropology cannot deal with the particular instances of humankind like Plato, Napoleon, or Elvis Presley per se (principally because these particular instances are constantly changing and cannot really be defined) but must instead deal with the general essence of "humanity" in which Plato et al. share per se (in this sense, anthropology can deal with Plato, Napoleon, or any other individual human, at best, in a *per accidens* fashion). According to Aristotle, when we do anthropology, we take as the object of our science a really existing humanity or human nature. Aristotle's naive form of realism can be traced back to Plato. In the *Republic* at 511c, Plato puts forward a realist position, arguing that "pure ideas" or universals/essences/forms make things in the visible world both *be* what they are and *be known as* what they are (see Vlastos, 1981; Annas, 1981).

This realist argument from the sciences continues throughout medieval philosophy with Thomas Aquinas (e.g., *Prooemium, Com. Meta.*; see Wippel, 1984) and Duns Scotus (1995). We can also find this realist argument present in Descartes' rationalism, Husserl's phenomenology, and Frege's attack of psychologism. Clarke (1992, pp. 272–273) notes that Descartes' "common sense" ideas regarding the sciences are "very close to scholastic philosophy." Also, Husserl (1995, p. 154) takes "world, Nature, space, time, psychological being, man, psyche, animateorganism, social community, and culture" to be realities that make "genuine sciences" possible. For Frege (1964, 1966, 1977, 1979), senses (or meanings) and thoughts (or propositions) are abstract objects that form the very basis for our ability to communicate beliefs and claims to one another in the sciences, and the True and the False are unique kinds of abstract objects that justify our beliefs and claims.

The case can be made that such notions as "the nature of AIDS," "the function of the heart," and "what is best for my child," as well as the propositions communicated about these notions, not only are nonreducible to the beliefs of a particular thinking community but also actually are abstract objects having a truth value that is discoverable. This is to say that there are genuine truth conditions pertaining to propositions and the objects they name that cannot be reducible to assertibility conditions—the circumstances under which thinkers would be justified in asserting such propositions—in a Dummett-style (1978) antirealist fashion.

When scientists, researchers, and other thinkers get together to figure out what a disease like AIDS actually is so they can cure it, they are wondering about the *very nature* of AIDS itself, not about *Sue's belief* regarding the nature of AIDS or the *scientific community's beliefs* regarding the nature of AIDS. So too, when people are trying to discern the function of the heart, they really are concerned with *the actual* functioning of the heart, irrespective of the myriad thought experiments and counterexamples that present themselves through the intersubjective community of minds in the dialectic of journal pages and conferences. Further, when Johnny's parents are considering what is best for him, they want what *is* truly best for him, not what Johnny *believes* is best for him or what the pediatrician *thinks* is best for him, or even what they as parents *take to be* best for him. Johnny's parents want simply what is best for Johnny and will adjust their beliefs as well as assent to those propositions that align themselves with what is truly best for him.

We can grant that a parent, scientist, or any other thinker has to make decisions, conduct experiments, or construct theories based upon the best available information at the time. Further, we can grant that the circumstances under which persons are justified in asserting propositions become significant in terms of the outcome of our belief systems. However, there seems to be an implicit recognition that the beliefs of the particular thinking community *ultimately* are not going to be enough to justify our beliefs—we may have to settle for Lockean probabilism, but we really want Cartesian clarity and distinction. Research continues to be done concerning AIDS, philosophers of science and biology continue to discuss the heart's function, and moral theorists continue to debate what is best for some Johnny knowing that the current theory or set of beliefs is not going to be the "end of the story." In this sense, it could be said that "*the* nature of AIDS," "*the* functioning of the heart," and "*what is* best for Johnny" are taken to be something real, "out there" so to speak, having properties and aspects that hold true irrespective of our beliefs regarding them.

It may be that realism is reproachable and dispensable because it suffers on at least two fronts: it calls us to engage in a Sisyphean epistemological task promising some kind of knowledge that cannot be had, and it calls us to accept a notion of truth and other metaphysical entities that are really delusional "wretched makeshifts" to use a Freudian (Freud, 1964) term. However, we seem to think and work like *as-if realists*. At present, problems concerning vagueness, other minds, logical paradoxes, truth gaps, and the like plague epistemologists, mathematicians, logicians, and metaphysicians. It would seem that no one—realist and antirealist alike— seriously doubts that these problems *cannot* be solved. The work being done in these areas betrays antirealist or intuitionist sentiments. Mathematicians right now are trying to solve the Goldbach's conjecture problem (Vaughan, 1997), or the problem associated with mapping artificial languages onto natural languages (Hodges, 2001). Epistemologists are mounting responses to the preface paradox (Rosenberg, 2002), the liar paradox (Gupta, 2001), and the indexical identification problem (Corazza, 2002). Logicians are devising "supertruths" to deal with vague predicates (Lambert, 2001), and metaphysicians are debating the existence of consciousness and the nature of the heart's functioning (Chalmers, 1996; Perlman, 2004; Arp, 2006b).

Contrary to those who align themselves with intuitionism or constructivism, thinkers, in fact, must believe that the principle of bivalence holds with respect to past events, or other minds, or certain mathematical and logical issues; otherwise they would not (in some cases) spend their entire lives devoted to solving these problems. All of these thinkers—intuitionists, constructivists, realists, and pragmatists alike—do their problem solving work as if the answer is out there to be had. Pragmatists may claim, along with Dewey (1951), that a lot of the work done by epistemologists and metaphysicians aims at some "unapproachable" or "irrelevant" truth. However, why then do we aim at the truth (and falsity) concerning these issues? Why should such work matter to us if we *didn't* think that there was something real to be gained by doing the work? It would seem that the *spirit* of realism and its methodology is of value to thinking communities whether they choose to admit this or not.

Now, if this is an accurate description of how the scientific, philosophic, or any other research community works (*and* if it is the case that I am *not* setting up some kind of false dilemma), then we can draw one of two conclusions: either (1) there are these realities out there, or (2) we act *as if* there are these realities out there waiting to be discovered, even though we know we could never discover them because we can't have a god's eye view, or we are always "trapped" behind a veil of our own ideas, or they are just not there. If we deny the conclusion that there are realities out there, we still seem to act as if there are realities out there; we still want to get at what we take to be the *nature* of AIDS, the *actual function* of the heart, and *what is* best for Johnny, despite our epistemological limitations or nihilism. The truth of this conclusion is demonstrated by the way our thought processes work concerning the problems we are trying to solve.

So far I have hinted at a *descriptive* account of *how it is* that scientific and philosophic communities work like as-if realists. However, someone may wonder *why we should* act like as-if realists. My response is utilitarian in tone, and it is simply that acting in such a way has pragmatic benefits. Strange and equivocal as it may sound, *I am advocating that pragmatists should be nonpragmatic, by showing that realism is of pragmatic value!*

Thinkers like Trout (1998), Kitcher (1993), Boyd (1991), and Miller (1987) already have shown the many benefits that result from holding to scientific realism. My argument can be looked at as an addendum to what has been known in philosophy of science circles as the *argument from miracles*, popularized by Smart (1963) and Putnam (1975). The proponents of this argument conclude that unless there were actually existing entities as part of the furniture of the world, and the theories put forward by thinkers approximated these entities, then the success of science certainly would be a miracle. In other words, it would be miraculous if there were not a real world out there to which our perceptions and ideas correspond given the fecundity of our scientific, philosophic, and other research endeavors. This realist attitude, and its attendant inference to the best explanation, should filter into other philosophical and logical areas precisely because of the evidentiary success of thinking in this fashion.

Stated simply: thinking like a realist works best for scientist, as well as for mathematician, logician, and epistemologist alike. It is of no theoretical or practical use to think *solely* like a Pyhrronian skeptic, or a nihilist, or a Rortyan antirealist. Where would our thinking be if Aristotle, or Galileo, or Hawking had *not* challenged the intersubjective communities in which they found themselves by thinking there must be something more that is *really* "out there" to be grasped, understood, or assimilated?

It would seem, then, that we should not have *mere* "coherence of beliefs" regarding Johnny's benefit, or "agreement" regarding the nature of AIDS, or "consensus" regarding the function of the heart transitorily understood by the intersubjective community. We should have coherence of beliefs *and* we should know that what we are doing *is actually best* for Johnny; we should have agreement regarding the nature of AIDS *and* that agreement should be the result of our understanding of what AIDS *actually is*; we should have consensus regarding the heart's function *and* that consensus should be based in the *actual functioning* of the heart. It is good to have realists in the scientific or philosophic community reminding these communities not to rest on the laurels of coherentist pragmatism; the question will always remain as to whether coherence is enough.

To put the point another way, Dummett-style assertibility conditions are fine to articulate, and we should seek to express them as accurately as possible, but what we ultimately must confront are the *truth conditions* surrounding propositions. Notice that we still do not fully know the nature of AIDS, or the heart's functions, or cancer, or consciousness, or concepts, just as we may never know if what we have done for Johnny is in fact *the* best thing for him. At the same time, we continue to seek the nature of these things and ponder whether we could have made better choices for Johnny as if there was something to be gained in the search—we would be remiss to do otherwise.

When all is said and done, it may be useful for pragmatic communities of thinkers to act as if there was truth "out there" so as to guide its inquiry in the same way that, say, Kant asks the scientific community to act as if reality was governed by the regulative ideas. Kitcher (1989) has made this kind of claim, and Rescher (1997) has argued for a version of realism on pragmatic grounds. Such a view, paradoxically enough, tries to wed a foundationalist epistemological program having realist leanings with a coherentist epistemological program having antirealist leanings. But, such foundationalism and realism should not rattle the coherentist. As Audi (1993, p. 13) maintains in *The structure of justification*, after a lengthy discussion of the possible integration of foundationalism and coherentism: "Foundationalism, then, is not the rigid, incorrigibilist, atomistic view some have thought it to be. It can be moderate, fallibilist, commonsensical, and psychologically realistic. It can also provide a role for coherence in understanding justification and, in some contexts, in generating it."

2.3 Organisms and Function

In the last two sections of this chapter, I have argued for a nomological form of metaphysical emergence, in terms of HOV, and I began to argue for a representational form of epistemological emergence, in terms of an as-if realism. In the final section of this chapter, I will continue to argue for both forms of emergence by an investigation of *function* (also see Arp, 2006b). That organisms have functions and that we must describe—or, at least, *as-if* describe—the actual functioning of those organisms are central to my metaphysical and epistemological versions of emergence. Further, it is essential to my project that I explain and defend a description of functions because my hypothesis concerning scenario visualization depends upon certain functional mechanisms of the mind having evolved to solve specific problems encountered in various Pleistocene environments. As a *biologist* (of sorts), the realist in me says that organisms really do have functions. As a *philosopher* of biology, the antirealist in me realizes that no one can know, for sure, if organisms really do have functions, principally because of the veil of perceptions that mediates between the mind and world (if there is a world). However, we still must proceed to describe organisms as if they have functions because (1) such a description is useful and (2) it would be miraculous if our descriptions did not match up with what we take to be the real functions of organisms as we perceive them.

Organisms, and the subsystems and processes that comprise them, tend to operate in certain ways on a regular basis. This operational regularity not only aids biologists in identifying certain traits but enables biology to be considered an autonomous science with its own domain of laws (also see the sections on function in Arp & Ayala, 2008; Arp & Rosenberg, 2008; Terzis & Arp, 2008). Genetic information is communicated from parent organism to offspring, mitochondria convert sugar to ATP, the heart pumps blood, the medulla controls breathing, the complex interactions of the subsystems and processes of multicellular organisms tend toward the maintenance of a dynamic equilibrium (homeostasis)—all of this happens in fairly predictable and reliable ways. Another way of describing the tendency for processes and subsystems of organisms to operate in predictable and reliable ways is in terms of the organism's *functions*.

In the biological realm, a complete explanation of a trait seems to include an explanation in terms of function. It is natural to ask of some trait, What is its function? or What purpose in the organism does the particular trait serve? or What is the goal of its activity? Thus, for example, to explain the existence of the human heart as *merely* a red mass of tissue located in the chest cavity of the torso that pulsates and reverberates according to the natural laws of physics and chemistry strikes us as an incomplete explanation. However, as has been argued quite convincingly by Mayr (1996), Walters (1998), Lennox (1993), Sober (1993), Gould (1977), Sterelny (2001), Dawkins (1986), and others, biology has its own legitimate scientific principles and terminology (cf. Machamer, Darden, & Craver, 2000; Tabery, 2004; Glennan, 1996). In line with a biological explanation, it seems we can talk about the heart's function or purpose in the human body as an organ that pumps blood. An important part of explaining the heart is to say that it exists *so as to* pump blood, or that pumping blood is the heart's *operation* or *function*.

Beginning in the 1960s with Nagel (1961) and Hempel (1965), philosophers of science and biology have not only proposed a variety of definitions for the term *function* but have attempted to specify the conditions where it may be appropriate to predicate functions of natural and artificial things, and to appeal to these functions in explanations (see Cummins, 1975, 2002; Wright, 1973, 1976; Mayr, 1982, 1988; Millikan, 1984, 1989, 2002; Buller, 1999; Ayala, 1998; Mahner & Bunge, 2001; Neander, 1991, 1999; Hardcastle, 1999; Perlman, 2004). Some thinkers, like Dennett (1987, 1995) and the Churchlands (1986, 1989), offer a promissory note that talk of functions in biology will be eliminated altogether once a more accurate, value-free system of terms is invented to describe the operational traits of organisms. Searle (1990b, p. 414) seems to hold the similar view that functions are solely the product of intentional and intensional minds, and that functions are "never intrinsic but are always observer relative." And Ruse has affirmed (1971, 1973) and reaffirmed (2003) a position similar to that of Dennett, the Churchlands, and Searle, namely, there is nothing like an intrinsic or extrinsic *ontological* purpose or design to be found in nature. Talk of functions is just that—*talk* of functions.

Yet Ruse and other thinkers admit something about the biological sciences that Kant (1987) had admitted in his third *Critique*; with respect to organisms, it is useful to think *as if* these entities have traits and processes that function in goal-directed ways. Thinkers cannot seem to get around Trivers' (1985, p. 5) claim that "even the humblest creature, say, a virus, appears organized to *do* something; it acts *as if* [italics mine] it is trying to achieve some purpose" or Arnhart's (1998, p. 245) observation that "although the evolutionary process does not serve goals, the organisms emerging from that process do. Darwin's biology does not deny—rather, it reaffirms—the immanent teleology displayed in the striving of each living being to fulfill its specific ends. . . . Reproduction, growth, feeding, healing, courtship, parental care for the young—these and many other activities of organisms are goal-directed" (also see Bogdan, 1994; Stout, 1996; FitzPatrick, 2000; Sterelny & Griffiths, 1999; Arp, 1998, 1999, 2002, 2006b).

In the last section, I argued for an as-if realism. This approach acknowledges that we could never know the nature of anything outside of our own perceptions *for certain*. At the same time, as-if realism affirms that we must act as if there is a reality out there to be understood and described; it would be miraculous if there were not a real world out there to which our perceptions and ideas correspond, given the fecundity of our scientific, philosophic, and other research endeavors. With this as-if realism in mind, we can still attempt to describe the functions of the traits and processes of organisms. Thus, I am in agreement with Ruse and other thinkers who do not attempt to explain away descriptions of the functions of traits. The as-if realism I endorse works together nicely with this as-if description of the functioning of biological traits—the as-if realist in me acknowledges that organisms act as if they are organized so as to function in specific ways. In fact, as noted already, it is essential to my project that I lay out and defend a description of functions because, as will be shown in later chapters, my hypothesis concerning scenario visualization depends upon certain functional mechanisms of the mind having evolved to solve specific problems encountered in various Pleistocene environments.

There are several views concerning the appropriate definition of function for biological matters, and Perlman (2004) has done a fine job of laying out all of these views as envisioned in the history of Western philosophy. The two views of function with respect to living things that, in my estimation, have the most credibility are Cummins' (1975, 2002) organizational account and the Griffiths/Godfrey-Smith modern history account (Griffiths, 1992, 1993, 1996; Godfrey-Smith, 1993, 1994, 1996), and I am not alone in this assessment (cf. Boorse, 2002; Millikan, 2002; Schwartz, 2002; Collier, 2000; see also Arp, 2006b). Ultimately, I want to maintain that these two accounts need not be in competition and, actually, can complement one another. Further, as will be shown later, my hypothesis concerning the emergence of scenario visualization will rely upon parts of both of these accounts.

Cummins explains the function of some trait in terms of the role it plays in maintaining the overall organization and survival of the organism in its present state. Traits only have functions in relation to other traits within the organization of the system as a whole. The function of the heart is a standard case utilized in discussions. Thus, the heart's function is to pump blood because this fulfills its causal role in relation to the organization of the animal as a whole. There are two things to notice about this account.

First, a trait can have—or could have had, or could have—any variety of functions in relation to the organizational whole. In other words, a single part could have a variety of functions, depending upon the organization of the system. The heart could have filtered urine if the overall organization of the animal were different in the past, or it could be co-opted to perform some other function if the overall organization of the animal changed in the future. Thus, there is a certain flexibility or malleability in some trait's functionality. I find this to be a virtue of Cummins' position, as it is now common knowledge that certain traits may actually be exaptations or preaptations, rather than adaptations. Although, as we will see, the flexibility in a trait's functionality makes it difficult to define exactly what a trait's *present* function in the overall organization of an organism actually is.

Second, Cummins purposely develops his account independent of any evolutionary factors that would contribute to the historical origin of a trait's functionality. According to Cummins, for a trait to perform some function, the basic structural components of the trait must already be present so that it can perform that specific function in relation to the organization of the organism as a whole. In other words, because the function of some trait cannot precede the presence of that trait, and only comes to have a function in relation to the contribution it makes to the organization of the organism as a whole in its present state, it makes no sense to speak about an evolutionary history with respect to that trait. Thus, hearts pump blood because of their contribution to the overall maintenance of the animal's life, *not* because they conferred a survival-enhancing capacity in the animal's evolutionary ancestry. Whereas the flexibility and/or malleability exhibited in a trait's functionality acts as a virtue of Cummins' position, I find the neglect of a trait's history to be a vice of Cummins' position, as I will demonstrate in a moment.

Conversely, according to the Griffiths/Godfrey-Smith modern history account, the function of some trait or process X in an organism is defined by what the trait was naturally selected for doing in the organism's species' recent past. This is to say that *past* advantages to the organism are what define functions. Griffiths and Godfrey-Smith add the qualification that the past advantage must be a *recent* addition in the species' history, stemming from the fact that the original selection for any trait may have favored an entirely different effect than the one that counts as the trait's current function. Thus, for example, the heart pumps blood or the kidney filters urine in a cat because these traits enabled the cat's most recent ancestors to survive. The hearts that pumped blood and the kidneys that filtered urine most adequately were naturally selected for as a trait in the feline species, and cats today have hearts and kidneys that function so as to pump blood and filter urine *precisely because* of this fitness. Ayala (1998, p. 45) favors a historical account of functions and notes that some trait is functional "if it contributes to the reproductive efficiency of the organism itself, and if such contribution accounts for the existence of the structure or process." Ayala (1998, p. 40) further notes that these traits in organisms are "biological adaptations. They have arisen as a result of the process of natural selection. The adaptations of organisms—whether organs, homoeo-static mechanisms, or patterns of behavior—are explained [functionally] in that their existence is accounted for in terms of their contribution to the reproductive fitness of the population."

According to Cummins, the function of some trait X has to do with the trait's contribution to some greater capacity or propensity of the organism to survive rather than its evolutionary history. From Cummins' perspective, to say that the heart's function is simply its adaptive ability to pump blood—as proponents of the Griffiths/Godfrey-Smith modern history account want to do—is to miss other relevant effects of the heart that contribute to the overall survival value of the organism. The heart produces sound, weighs a certain amount, and has a certain structure, and these are all factors *besides* its pumping of blood that supposedly contribute to the overall maintenance, survival, and propensity for survival in the organism (cf. Bigelow & Pargetter, 1998; Bechtel, 1989; Allen, Bekoff, & Lauder, 1998; Staddon, 1987; Horan, 1989).

Unfortunately, the problem with this description of functions is that it is too broad. Cummins fails to distinguish effects it is the function of a trait or organ to produce from those it is not its function to produce. Almost *any effect* can be understood as contributing to the survival value of an organism on this interpretation of function. In other words, describing functions *purely* in terms of organizational capacities and propensities for survival puts us in the awkward position of not being able to distinguish between the salient and nonsalient purposive features of traits. Concerning the example of the heart, Cummins wants to say that weighing a certain amount, producing sound, having a certain structure, *and* pumping blood are all potential functions of the heart. However, there does not seem to be any significant evidence or theoretical precedent to show that the heart's producing of sounds or weighing a certain amount per se confers any propensity for survival in an organism.

There is a further problem with Cummins' account. Recall that a trait can have—or could have had, or could have—any variety of functions in relation to the organizational whole. A single part *could have* a variety of functions, depending upon the organization of the system. However, it does not seem right to speak about the function of some trait by reference to a propensity that will confer future advantage, because the future has not occurred for us to know *if in fact* the advantage will be conferred. As Cummins himself acknowledges, it is possible that a trait adapted to function in an environment *now* may be co-opted for a different use in that same environment later. The ability to fly in birds may have come about in this way. Feathers probably were selected for in archaic birds to protect them from the cold but eventually became co-opted for flight (Feduccia, 1996; Ostrom, 1979; Gould & Vrba, 1982).

Also consistent with Cummins' account is the fact that the environment may change, possibly making it such that a trait that functioned in the previous environment will become nonfunctional in the present environment. It is likely that the existence of vestigial organs testifies to this kind of change (Berra, 1990). Further, it may be possible that an environment changes, and a trait adapted to function in the previous environment gets altered and co-opted for a different use in the present environment. This may be the way in which conscious decision making arose in humans when the hominin line was forced to move from jungle to savanna in Africa during the Pleistocene epoch (see Tattersall, 2001, 2002; Arp, 2005a, 2006a). Thus, we never really can say that a trait will have some future functioning advantage. At best, we look at its *present* functioning in relation to some environment and surmise about its *past* functioning—again, *recent* past, as per the qualification of Griffiths and Godfrey-Smith—in some similar or dissimilar environment.

So, Cummins seems to do at least two things that are misguided. First, he inappropriately neglects the role that recent evolutionary history plays in a trait's functional development. Second, in the tongue-in-cheek words of Achinstein (1977, p. 344), he "saddles us with a bevy of unwanted functions." Most biologists would agree with the Griffiths/Godfrey-Smith account and want to say that the proper function of the heart—given its recent selection in evolutionary history—is to pump blood, and only *in an ancillary way* is the heart's function to produce sounds, weigh a certain amount, or have a certain structure (see Neander, 1999; Ayala, 1972; Sober, 1993; Millikan, 1984, 2002; Mayr, 1993; Dawkins, 1986; Ruse, 1973).

Nonetheless, it seems to me that the accounts of Cummins and Griffiths/ Godfrey-Smith can complement and be made compatible with one another. The part of Cummins' account of functions that seems correct has to do with the function of a trait understood as both (1) contributing to the overall organizational structure of the organic system and (2) being flexible or malleable enough to be co-opted for some other function. These qualities can complement the idea that the functioning of a trait must arise within the context of an evolutionary history. There is nothing incompatible or contradictory in maintaining that some trait functions so as to contribute to the general organization of some organism's structure while at the same time describing the emergence of that trait's functional contribution to the organizational structure of the organism by reference to a recent evolutionary history. So too, there is nothing incompatible or contradictory in maintaining that some trait is malleable enough to be utilized for several potential functions while at the same time describing the present status of that trait in reference to a recent evolutionary history. Given that structure, organization, operational flexibility, function, and evolutionary history are all factors to be considered in an organism's makeup, we should expect that the traits of an organism function the way they do because such traits presently contribute to the overall organization of the organism (Cummins) as well as were selected for in the organism's species' recent ancestry (Griffiths/Godfrey-Smith).

In attacking historical accounts of function, including the modern history account, Bigelow & Pargetter (1998) entertain the thought experiment that the tenets of evolutionary biology may turn out to be false. For example, your grandparents could have been put together randomly out of swamp material, and hence, you would have no evolutionary history to speak of. If that happened to be the case, then the backward-looking, historical explanation of function would lose its very *backward* support! I will risk sounding ad hominem and point out—as Churchland (1993, p. 746) has done—that this kind of thought experiment suffers from the flaw of most armchair philosophical thought experiments, namely, "too much thought and not enough experiment!" One of the marks of good scientific theorizing has to do with being open to the possibility that a well-established theory may one day be debunked by evidence that disconfirms the theory. In other words, good science entails the falsification of theory. The swamp grandparents thought experiment hints at this falsification with respect to evolutionary theory. However, as Millikan (1989, 2002) and Neander (1991) affirm, there is enough evidence to suggest that we should not abandon evolutionary theory just yet, despite such a thought experiment. I will point to a lot of this evidence when I build my case for the evolution of the brain, visual system, and scenario visualization later in this book. The work of biologists, neuroscientists, geologists, archeologists, psychologists, philosophers, anthropologists, and zoologists, among legions of other thinkers and researchers, establishes evolutionary theory on a firm footing.

Despite the divergent views concerning the definition of a biological function, both proponents of Cummins-style functions and proponents of Griffiths/Godfrey-Smith-style functions agree that evolution has taken place and continues to take place. Given that evolution is understood as the result of the complex workings of such factors as differential reproduction, artificial selection, sexual selection, mutation, genetic drift, and genetic recombination in a *historical context*, this historicity lends further support to approaching the functions of traits from the perspective of the modern history account.

The modern history account gives elucidation to Mayr's (1996, p. 103) description of organisms as "operating on the basis of historically acquired programs of information." Crudely and simply put, the information that organisms acquire is to be found in the particular genetic code received from their parent(s). However, as Plotkin (1997, p. 1) has observed, "nothing in biology makes *complete sense* [italics mine] except in light of evolution." Therefore, any description of biological phenomena must include an evolutionary perspective to be considered as a fully explanatory description of the biological phenomena under investigation.

The account of functions I endorse is an evolutionary adaptationist explanation. It is well-known that the primary mechanism of evolution is natural selection. Through natural selection, environmental influences affect populations of organisms, and the chance that beneficial traits will dominate in successor generations is increased by the adaptive ability and reproductive success of individuals possessing optimal genetic variants. When a trait contributes to the fitness of the organism in its current environment, it is said to be *functionally adaptive*. For example, as was mentioned in the previous chapter, the various kinds of finches that Darwin described on the Galapagos Islands have different beak structures as a functionally adaptive response to their particular food source. Dawkins (1986, p. 178) is correct in maintaining that adaptations "affect every part of the body, its shape and colour, its internal organs, its behaviour, and the chemistry of its cells."

A Cummins-style explanation is a necessary ingredient in the description of a biological function, given the dual emphasis placed upon a trait's role in the overall organization of the organism and the flexibility associated with a trait's function. However, a complete account of the function of some trait requires an explanation of *how* the trait came to be useful for the organism. Thinkers who utilize the evolutionary adaptationist methodology view traits as adaptations that have evolved due to past contributions to the fitness of the organism in some environment. Sober (1993, p. 83) is representative of this kind of thinking, and he links adaptation to a historical account in a clear fashion: "To say that a trait is an 'adaptation' is to comment not on its current utility but on its history. To say that the mammalian heart is (now) an adaptation for pumping blood is to say that mammals now have hearts because ancestrally, having a heart conferred a fitness advantage; the trait evolved because there was selection for having a heart, and hearts were selected because they pump blood."

The biologist in me takes it as a real given that evolution has occurred and that accounts of the functioning of traits and processes require an evolutionary explanation. The philosopher of biology in me is not sure if there is anything real out there to speak of as having a function; however, my as-if realism tells me that it makes sense to proceed as if there were realities out there with functions based in an evolutionary history. Thus, in the end, given my endorsement of the modern history account as necessary to explain how it is that organisms have become hierarchically organized functioning systems, I take Plotkin's claim that a biological phenomenon only makes complete sense in light of evolutionary theory seriously.

In the first chapter, I described an organism as a living entity, the components of which are hierarchically organized in subsystems and processes operating so as to achieve particularized and generalized homeostasis. The subsystems and processes possess certain properties, including abilities to flexibly exchange data, convert data to information in a selection process, integrate information, and process information from environments. In this chapter, I endorsed a form of metaphysical emergence whereby entities, properties, or substances arise out of more fundamental entities, properties, or substances and yet are not wholly reducible to them. I argued for this form of emergence based upon HOV, namely, the fact that the subsystems and processes of organisms coordinate their functions so as to produce particularized and generalized homeostasis. I also argued for an epistemological form of emergence that is rooted in the language of teleology and as-if realism.

In completing my account of organisms understood as hierarchically organized systems, I argued that the components of organisms function the way they do as a result of recent past adaptive advantages. The evolutionary explanation I endorsed is a type of causal explanation of how it is that the recent history of a trait has had certain adaptive effects, which have facilitated the selection of that trait. We will see in subsequent chapters that the brain and visual system, as well as the psychological phenomena emerging from brain processes that enable humans to solve problems creatively, exhibit similar biological properties and abide by the same evolutionary principles laid out and explained in these last two chapters.

3 The Visual System

3.1 The Hierarchical Organization of the Mammalian Visual System

In the first chapter, I established that an organism is a living entity, the components of which are hierarchically organized in subsystems and processes operating so as to achieve particularized and generalized homeostasis (HOV). The subsystems and processes possess certain properties, including abilities to exchange data flexibly, convert data to information in a selection process, integrate information, and process information from environments. In the second chapter, after using HOV and as-if realism to give credence to nomological and representational emergence, respectively, I argued that the Cummins organizational view and the Griffiths/Godfrey-Smith view can be made compatible with one another in providing a complete definition of biological function. We should expect that the traits of an organism function the way they do because such traits presently contribute to the overall organization of the organism (Cummins) as well as were selected for in the organism's species' recent ancestry (Griffiths/Godfrey-Smith). The work of the first two chapters was accomplished for the twofold purpose of giving further elucidation to Mayr's description of organisms as hierarchically organized systems that operate on the basis of historically acquired programs of information, as well as ratifying Plotkin's claim that biological phenomena only make complete sense in light of evolutionary theory.

In the next chapter, I deal with the evolution of the mammalian visual system. In this chapter, building upon the work of the previous two chapters, I show how the processes associated with vision in mammals comprise a hierarchically organized system exhibiting the same kinds of properties of information exchange, selectivity, and integration found in organisms in general (also see Arp, 2005b). I restrict my analysis of the brain to the primary processes and mechanisms associated with the mammalian visual system and visual cognition. I do this for three reasons. First, there is much empirical evidence supporting our understanding of the mammalian visual system's structure and layout (van Essen, 1985, 1997; van Essen & Maunsell, 1983; van Essen & Gallant, 1994; van Essen, Anderson, & Felleman, 1992; van Essen, Anderson, & Olshausen, 1994; van Essen et al., 1998; Allman & Kaas, 1971; Desimone & Ungerleider, 1989; Mishkin, Ungerleider, & Macko, 1983; Rueckl, Cave, & Kosslyn, 1989; Casagrande & Kaas, 1994; Kosslyn & Koenig, 1995). Second, the visual system is present in many kinds of vertebrate species thought to be homologous (i.e., having evolved from a common ancestor) to human beings (Kaas, 1993, 1995, 1996; Northcutt & Kaas, 1995; Preuss, Qi, & Kaas, 1999; Harvey & Pagel, 1991; Desimone, 1992; Desimone, Albright, Gross, & Bruce, 1984; Karten & Shimazu, 1989; Butler & Hodos, 1996; Tyler et al., 1998). Finally, I restrict my scope to the visual system because it plays a central role in the evolutionary account I give of the progression from noncognitive visual processing to conscious cognitive visual processing in terms of scenario visualization. I fortify what thinkers like Barton (1998), Crick (1994), Carruthers (2002), and Allman (1977, 1982, 2000) have maintained, namely, that visual processing is an important factor in the evolution of conscious behavior, including creative problem solving.

The mammalian visual system is situated within the vertebrate nervous system, while at the same time it is composed of neurons that are specialized in their own processes. Recalling the schematization of triangles in figure 1.1 in the first chapter, the visual system is like a medium-sized triangle made up of smaller triangles (the neuronal processes), existing in a larger triangle (the nervous system) along with other systems like the auditory, olfactory, and so forth. All of these triangles exist within the largest triangle (the organism) as is schematized in figure 3.1. There is an elegant consistency in the hierarchical organization exhibited from the microlevel of the neuron to the macrolevel of the vertebrate nervous system. This consistency is echoed in Bear, Connors, & Pardiso's (2001, p. 161) claim that the "signaling network within a single neuron resembles in some ways the neural networks of the brain itself." Hierarchies exist within hierarchies, and, as we will see, the visual system is one of those hierarchies that functions so as to aid in producing the architectonic organization of the nervous system of an animal.

In the first chapter, I proposed that these hierarchies are able to interact with one another because of internal–hierarchical data exchange, whereby data—the raw material that are of the kind that have the potential to become useful for a process or operation—are exchanged between and

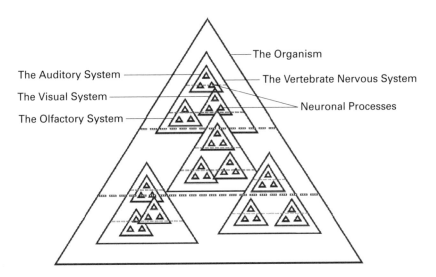

The Organism

The Auditory System

The Vertebrate Nervous System

The Visual System

Neuronal Processes

The Olfactory System

Figure 3.1
The visual system hierarchy in relation to the organism

among the processes and subsystems at various levels of operation in an organism. In their textbook devoted to the principles of neuroscience, Kandel et al. (2000, p. 353) describe the processes associated with perception in the cerebral cortex using a hierarchical model: "Sensory information is first received and interpreted by the primary sensory areas, then sent to unimodal association areas, and finally to the multimodal sensory areas. At each successive stage of this stream more complex analysis is achieved, culminating eventually, as with vision, for example, in object and pattern recognition in the inferotemporal cortex."

Kandel et al.'s text is a standard work in neuroscience, and I use it as my primary reference throughout this book. Kandel et al. actually divvy up the hierarchy of sensory systems into four parts, namely, (1) the primary sensory areas, (2) the unimodal areas, (3) the unimodal association areas, and (4) the multimodal association areas.

The primary sensory areas act as base levels, and they refer to the parts and processes associated with information that is initially communicated to the spinal cord and/or brain through one of the five sensory modalities, namely, touch, hearing, taste, smell, and vision. For example, in the visual system the primary sensory area comprises the eye, the lateral geniculate nucleus (LGN), and the primary visual cortex located in the occipital lobe of the brain. The unimodal areas build upon the data received from some prior particular primary sensory area and refer to the parts and processes associated with a higher level integration of the data received from one of the primary sensory areas. In the visual system, there are two primary unimodal areas that process information concerning *where* an object is and *what* an object is, located along trajectories between the occipital lobe and parietal and temporal regions, respectively. The unimodal association areas, in turn, refer to parts and processes associated with an even higher level integration of the data received from two or more unimodal areas. In the visual system, the unimodal association area integrates data about the color, motion, and form of objects and is located in the occiptotemporal (also called *occipitotemporal*) area of the brain. Finally, the multimodal association areas refer to parts and processes associated with integrating the data received from the unimodal association areas and, depending upon the sensory modality, process this information in either the parietotemporal, parietal, temporal, and/or frontal areas of the brain.

Having given this general overview of the hierarchy concerning perception in the cerebral cortex and related areas, we now can give a more specified description of the visual hierarchy, along with its components and processes. The components of the visual hierarchy are comprised of groups of specialized neurons that "fire" according to certain external and internal stimulus cues, and the various processes of the visual hierarchy are active when an object "comes into view," as it were, namely, when an object is recognized as present in a mammal's visual field. In essence, what follows is a description of the neural wiring and functioning associated with mammalian object recognition in the visual system.

The primary sensory area of the visual system comprises the pathway that starts with the retina of the eye and projects through the LGN of the thalamus to the primary visual cortex of the occipital lobe (V1 or Brodmann area 17). Photons of light are transduced into electrical signals by the photoreceptor neurons that lie on the innermost layer of the retina known as rods and cones. Rods are sensitive to dim light, while cones are sensitive to brighter light. The photoreceptors make synapses with other kinds of neurons known as horizontal and bipolar cells. The horizontal cells primarily are responsible for the center-surround organization of the receptive field of the bipolar cell. The bipolar cells receive synapses from photoreceptors, horizontal cells, and other neurons known as amacrine cells and relay data from the photoreceptors to the ganglion cells, which send their axons to the brain via the optic nerve. The ganglion cells project to a number of sites, including several cortical areas through the thalamus, the hypothalamus, and midbrain. The major cortical projection is via the LGN of the thalamus to the primary visual cortex in the occipital lobe (Kandel et al., 2000; Zigmond, Bloom, Landis, Roberts, Squire, & Wooley, 1999; Bear et al., 2001).

The LGN consists of six layers in primates. The inner two layers, with their large neurons, form the magnocellular laminae (literally, *big-celled layers*); while the remaining four layers, with their smaller neurons, constitute the parvocellular laminae (*small-celled layers*). Intercalated between these principal laminae are the koniocellular neurons (K cells). In their firing responses, the magnocellular neurons (M cells) are sensitive to motion especially, while the parvocellular neurons (P cells) are responsive to color.

Like the LGN, the primary visual cortex in the occipital lobe (again, known as V1 or Brodmann area 17) is made up of six primary layers in primates. The LGN mainly projects to layer IV of V1, and to a lesser extent to layer VI, with the M and P channels having different synaptic targets within these laminae. There is also a projection from cells in the intralaminar part of the LGN directly to layers II and III of V1. The layer IV neurons project on to adjacent neurons in such a way as to form what are known as orientation-specific columns, ocular-dominance columns, and blobs. Orientation-specific columns are responsible for the decomposition of objects of the visual field into short line segments of varying orientation form. Ocular-dominance columns are responsible for the combination of input from the two eyes so as to perceive the depth associated with an object and its background. Blobs are responsible for processing wavelength information, which ultimately contributes to the recognition of various colors of objects.

The occipital lobe is split into many visual-related areas, each processing an aspect of an object in the visual field. V1 is responsible for initial visual processing and can be subdivided into different subregions, each containing a full representation of the visual field for the contralateral world. However, after the initial processing in V1, the processing that takes place in other regions of the occipital lobe is more specialized: V2 is responsible for stereo vision, V3 for distance, V4 for color, V5 for motion, and V6 for object position. Van Essen et al. (1992) have recorded more than thirty primary visual areas in the macaque monkey. Through positron-emission tomography (PET) and functional magnetic resonance imaging (fMRI) scans, Zeki, Watson, Weck, Friston, Kennard, & Frackowiak (1991) and Sereno et al. (1995) have demonstrated that there are multiple visual areas in humans devoted to specific analysis of the properties of an object in the visual field.

So far, I have described what Kandel et al. would call the visual *primary sensory area* of the visual hierarchy. From this area, another level is added to the hierarchy as cortical projections are laid out along two visual *unimodal areas*, namely, the M cell and P cell pathways. The M cell pathway is also known as the parietal or dorsal pathway, and it consists of visual areas laid out along a trajectory from the occipital region, through V1, V2, V3, V5, and V6, to the parietal region of the brain. Research suggests that the M cell pathway is responsible for guiding our actions in our visual environment, since depth, motion, and object position—that is, *where* an object is, independent of what the object is—appear to be processed along its stream. Conversely, the P cell pathway is also known as the temporal, or ventral, pathway, and it consists of visual areas laid out along a trajectory from the occipital region, through V1, V2, and V4, to the temporal region of the brain. Research suggests that the P cell pathway is responsible for the color and form recognition of an object—that is, *what* an object is, independent of where the object is (see Desimone & Ungerleider, 1989; Ungerleider & Mishkin, 1982; Ungerleider & Haxby, 1994; Goodale et al., 1994).

Yet another level is added to the visual hierarchy as neurons from the parietal and temporal visual unimodal areas project to the visual *unimodal association area* in the occiptotemporal cortex of the brain. This area is considered more complex than the unimodal areas because neurons there are involved in integrating the processed data received from the parietal and temporal unimodal areas concerning color, motion, depth, form, distance, and the like. Research has shown that there is a division of labor concerning an animal's abilities to distinguish what an object is from where an object is. However, there are times when an animal must perform both of these tasks, and given the neuronal projections from the parietal and temporal areas to this common site in the occiptotemporal cortex, it makes sense that an animal be able to integrate visual information about what and where an object is in its visual field at the same time.

At the highest level of the visual hierarchy, the visual unimodal association area projects to the *multimodal association areas* of the prefrontal, parietotemporal, and limbic cortices. This is the level at which visual information is integrated with other sensory information, as well as where motor planning, attention, emotion, language production, and judgment take place.

There are a number of other parts of the central nervous system (CNS) that exchange data with the visual system, including the posterior parietal cortex, the subcortical structures of the hypothalamus, and upper brainstem. The neurons in the posterior parietal cortex respond to stimuli of interest and are probably involved in visual fixation and tracking. The superior colliculus in the midbrain is a multilayered structure wherein the outer layers are involved in mapping the visual field, the intermediate areas are involved in saccadic eye movements, and the deeper layers are involved with more complex sensory integration involving visual, auditory, and somatosensory stimuli. There is a projection from the optic tract to the pretectal nuclei of the midbrain that, in turn, projects to the Edinger–Westphal nucleus. This projection provides the parasympathetic (i.e., autonomic) input to the pupil of the eye, allowing it to constrict. Also, there is a direct retinal input to the suprachiasmatic nucleus of the hypothalamus that is important in the generation and control of circadian rhythms.

Other extrastriate cortical areas receive projections from the LGN, as well as the pulvinar region of the thalamus. An area in the inferotemporal (IT) cortex has been found to respond selectively to faces. This area has been described as *face-selective* without implying that when one recognizes a face, only cells in this area participate in this recognition (Tovee & Cohen-Tovee, 1993; Tovee, 1998). IT cortex also has been shown to be involved in storing visual memories, as well as encoding the properties of objects (Kosslyn & Koenig, 1995). Finally, the visual unimodal *and* multimodal association areas are linked up with other areas in the frontal, temporal, and parietal lobes and the hippocampus so that visual images can be made, stored, recalled, inspected, and possibly utilized in planning, judging, feeling, and other complex voluntary activity.

As has been said, the systematic distributions of parts and processes in the visual system, and related systems, are hierarchically organized. The multimodal areas build upon information received from the unimodal areas, and the unimodal areas build upon information received from the primary sensory area, as is schematized in figure 3.2. It should be clear from the aforementioned description of the neural wiring and functioning associated with the mammalian visual system that there must be a massive coordination and organization of processes in the CNS for a seemingly simple activity—like recognizing an object—to occur. When I visited him in his lab, Michael Ariel, a neuroscientist at Saint Louis University in St. Louis who specializes in the visual systems of turtles, affirmed this point (see, e.g., Martin, Kogo, Fan, & Ariel, 2003). The realization that the

The Primary Visual Area and Pathways

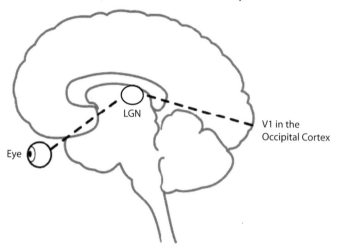

The Unimodal Visual Area and Pathways

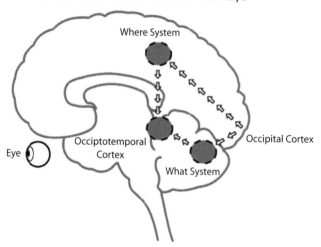

Figure 3.2
The primary sensory, unimodal, and multimodal areas and pathways of the visual system

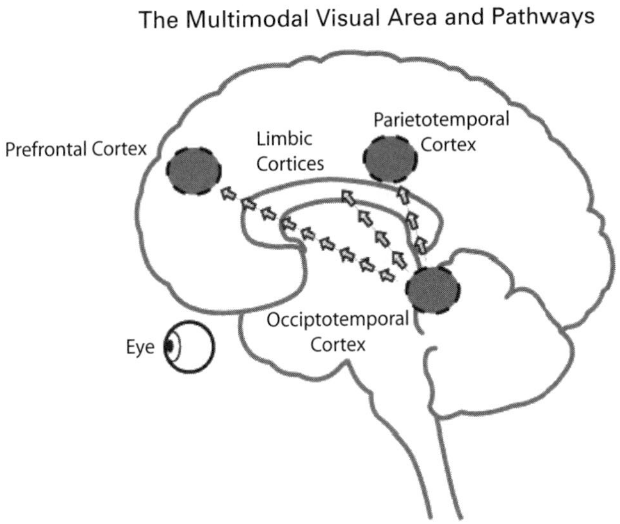

The Multimodal Visual Area and Pathways

Figure 3.2 (continued)

nervous system is such a grandiose architectonic has caused Gray (1999, p. 31) to maintain, "The inescapable conclusion is that sensory, cognitive, and motor processes result from parallel interactions among large populations of neurons distributed among multiple cortical and subcortical structures."

Data are exchanged at the various levels of the visual system and CNS and, because of these exchanges, an animal is able to form a coherent picture of an object in its visual field. However, a final qualification must be made about the hierarchical processes of the visual system. We must draw a distinction between a *serial* hierarchy and a *dynamic*, or *interactive*, hierarchy. In a serial hierarchy, information flows in a one-way direction from the lowest level to the highest level of the hierarchy. Conversely, in an interactive hierarchy, information flows bidirectionally among and between the lower and higher levels of the hierarchy.

Consider a small, fictitious corporation consisting of a worker, a manager, and a CEO. The worker is the lowest member of the hierarchy, the manager is one step above the worker, and the CEO is at the top level of the hierarchy. The worker communicates two ideas to the manager who, in turn, communicates these two ideas plus two more of his own ideas to the CEO. Once the first two ideas are communicated from worker to manager, there is no further contact between the two people; likewise, once the four ideas are communicated from manager to CEO, there is no further contact between those two people. This worker → manager → CEO setup would be an example of one-way information flow in a serial hierarchy.

There is only one sense in which the visual system can be considered as a serial hierarchy; otherwise it is most appropriately envisioned as an interactive hierarchy. The information flow from retina through LGN to V1 occurs in a one-way direction, like the flow of information from worker to manager to CEO in the small corporation. There is no information feedback from V1 to the retina, just as there is no information feedback from CEO to worker in our fictitious corporation. This makes sense, since the inputs of primary sensory areas themselves are passive and automatic in-takers of information (see Sekuler & Blake, 2002).

Unlike the one-way flow of information between retina and V1, there is the possibility for a dynamic, interactive, two-way flow of information between and among the primary visual, unimodal, and multimodal areas of the visual hierarchy. For example, Kosslyn & Koenig (1995) present evidence that emotions (present at a higher level in the hierarchy) can affect the visual system's performance in terms of visual priming and coded anticipation of certain visual scenes (present at a lower level in the visual hierarchy).

Also, in their experiments with monkeys and humans, Sigala & Logothetis (2002) show that visual categorization determines, in many ways, what specific features of a face will be focused upon. In effect, the experiments show that if a face is categorized *generally* in a certain way as expressive of some particular emotion, then this categorization will influence what *particular* features of a face—for example, basic lines, symmetries, and the like—the animal subsequently will focus upon. The neural correlates of visual categorization are found higher up in the visual hierarchy associated with the occiptotemporal and parietotemporal cortices, while the neural correlates concerning the processing of particular features of the face, in terms of lines and symmetries, are found at a more basic spot in the visual hierarchy associated with the trajectory between the temporal and occipital cortices of the *what* system.

Here, we have an instance of a dynamic, interactive flow of information in the visual hierarchy because, in addition to information regarding a face's particular features flowing from the *what* system to the occiptotemporal and parietotemporal cortices in facial categorization, there is flow of information *back* from these cortices to the *what* system in terms of this categorization's determination of the particular features of a face that are focused upon by an animal. Referring to the fictitious corporation, this kind of information flow would be analogous to the CEO's being in some form of dialogue with the manager about his or her ideas, such that the CEO has influence upon the manager's ideas, and vice versa.

3.2   Selectivity in the Visual System

As I showed in the first chapter, not every piece of data is relevant or useful to a system or process in an organism. Thus, I posited data selectivity as the property of a subsystem or process that allows for discrimination between relevant and irrelevant data. Data selectivity is necessary so that the raw data actually can become informative for a subsystem or process. Data that have been selected cease to be of the kind that are potentially useful and become actual information. It should be clear that data selectivity is integral to the processing of information in the subsystems and processes of a hierarchically organized system. However, as I went on to note, the processing of information also requires flexible communication between afferent and efferent entities, in an environment, so that a change can be evoked in the activity of the efferent entity. Finally, some kind of storage or imprinting mechanism would have to exist so that the information can be influential for the efferent entity.

Now, in the very simplest of terms, the complex processing of information in the nervous system seems to require the fourfold steps of (1) detecting data in some environment, (2) discriminating between relevant and irrelevant data, (3) integrating information, and (4) initiating some kind of response, as Audesirk et al. (2002), Sekuler & Blake (2002), and Kandel et al. (2000) each have noted in their own ways. The goal of this section is to focus upon the second step of this process, namely, discriminating between relevant and irrelevant data. I will demonstrate that there is data selectivity occurring at virtually every level of visual processing, from the activities of photoreceptors in the retina, to the columnar and blob-cell firings, all the way up through the *what* and *where* unimodal systems, to the unimodal and multimodal association processes occurring in the occipitotemporal, parietotemporal, prefrontal, and limbic cortices. This data selectivity makes it possible for the components of the visual system to process data and make use of this data as information.

Visual processing is already occurring in the retina, and this entails that the various kinds of neurons therein actively are selecting data that are relevant to their specific function. The retinal cells are specialized to detect differences in the intensity of light falling upon them, since the rods selectively attend to dim light, while the cones selectively attend to intense light. Sekuler & Blake (2002, p. 91) underscore this selective capacity in the retina by noting that "events in the retina shape vision by emphasizing some information and by de-emphasizing other information." This information from the retina then is sent through the ganglion cells to the brain. Data selectivity continues in the occipital lobe where orientation-specific and ocular-dominance columns respond to lines and depth, respectively, while the blobs process wavelength information, which ultimately contributes to the recognition of various colors of objects. The specification of functions in the M and P cell pathways further attests to this data selective property of the visual system, since the M cells respond to depth, motion, and object position, while the P cells respond to form and color.

The most complex level of the visual system makes connections in the multimodal association areas of the prefrontal, parietotemporal, and limbic cortices. Research shows that the prefrontal areas primarily are responsible for motor planning, judgment, some memory, and language production, while the limbic cortices are responsible for olfaction, emotion, and some memory formation as well. Research also shows that the parietotemporal lobe aids in sensory integration of visual space and language but, most importantly, *spatial attention* (Lux, Marshall, Ritzl, Zilles, & Fink, 2003; Milner & Goodale, 1995; Wurtz, Goldberg, & Robinson, 1982).

Treisman (1977, 1988), Julesz (1983, 1984), and Desimone & Duncan (1995) have proposed a mechanism of attention whereby the brain selectively associates the disparate features of the visual scene for a short time. The associated data are considered as *spotlighted* and comprise the coherent visual scene of which an animal is aware (cf. Wurtz, Goldberg, & Robinson, 1982; Posner & Peterson, 1990; Posner & Dahaene, 1994). Treisman (1988) has performed psychological tests on humans demonstrating this association, while tests on macaque monkeys—as well as PET and fMRI tests on humans—reveal areas of the occipotemporal cortex to be active while subjects try to make a visual scene coherent (Brefczynski & DeYoe, 1999; DeYoe, Felleman, van Essen, & McClendon, 1994; DeYoe, Trusk, & Wong-Riley, 1995; Beason-Held et al., 1998; Buckner et al., 1995; Honda, Wise, Weeks, Deibel, & Hallett, 1998; Rushworth, Daus, & Sipila, 2001).

The spotlight metaphor is helpful, since the data from experiments suggest that neuronal processes *ignore* or *discard* nonuseful data while *selectively attending to* or *spotlighting* relevant data. This is why Kandel et al. (2000, p. 504) can maintain that "selective attention acts to limit the amount of information that reaches the highest centers of processing in the brain," and Bear et al. (2001, p. 569) claim that attention "has to do with *preferential* [italics mine] processing of sensory information" (also see Sekuler & Blake, 2002; Fink et al., 1996).

Animals are bombarded with sensory data in droves. There would be no way for the sensory systems of the animal to take in all of this data; if they did, the animal probably would cease to function altogether, much like an overloaded computer that shuts down (cf. Johnson-Laird, 1988). Thus, there are selectivity mechanisms—kinds of filtering devices—that exist at the various levels in the visual hierarchy, segregating relevant from irrelevant data. The relevant data become processed as information, while the irrelevant data are simply ignored. As was communicated to me by Charles Anderson at a neuroscience conference at Washington University in St. Louis, the visual system exhibits its own checkpoints of selectivity, from the interactions among organelles in the neuron, to the retina's ability to detect differences in the intensity of light, to the spotlighting of visual information at the higher levels of the visual hierarchy. This is why, while researching the visual system, Anderson and his colleagues (van Essen et al., 1994, p. 271) call our attention to mechanisms "for dynamically *regulating* [italics mine] the flow of information within and between cortical areas." Also, as Zigmond et al. (1999, p. 822) note, in the visual system "high-level neurons classify visual stimuli by integrating information that is present in the earlier stages of processing, but also by ignoring information that is independent of that classification."

3.3 Informational Integration in the Visual System

In the first chapter, I argued that the mere fact information is exchanged between and among the various processes and systems of an organism does not fully capture the nature of an organism as a hierarchically organized system. The hierarchical nature of an organism suggests that the more complex levels exhibit an amount of information control over less complex levels. There seem to be advisory mechanisms that emerge from these complex operations, and this would make sense, since the more complex a process or system becomes, the more there is a need for mechanisms of control so that these processes or systems can operate efficiently (cf. Poggio & Hurlbert, 1994; Johnson-Laird, 1988; Cziko, 1992, 1995). However, I posited that this control is more than merely a selection of data for its usefulness, or a segregating of useful data (information) from nonuseful data. The more complex processes and systems in these hierarchies not only select relevant data for their usefulness as information but also coherently *integrate* information in manifesting a control of that information so as to respond efficiently in some environment.

In the last section, I noted that the complex processing of information in the nervous system seems to require the fourfold steps of (1) detecting data in some environment, (2) discriminating between relevant and irrelevant data, (3) integrating information, and (4) initiating some kind of response. The third step in this process, namely, integrating information, will be the focus of this section, as I show that integration is a key feature of the visual system, especially when considering the relationship the animal has to its external environment. True, the visual system detects and then selects or segregates information; however, since selection alone cannot account for how this information is organized for some purpose, neural networks possess an ability to integrate the information so as to aid the animal in optimally negotiating some environment. Once the information has been selected, it must be organized in a coherent manner so that an animal can go about the business of feeding, fighting, fleeing, reproducing, and the like in the most optimal and efficient manner possible.

For example, through the visual unimodal association area, such integration is made evident in the visual system's ability to align shape and color in the *what* system with distance and position in the *where* system so as to visually process an approaching predator (Goodale et al., 1994; Goodale & Murphy, 2000; Kosslyn & Koenig, 1995). Another example of this integration is the ability of the higher areas of the visual system to extract a coherent three-dimensional picture of a visual scene from two-dimensional images on the retina (Zigmond et al., 1999). Other examples include the integration of information specifying relations of depth among objects, as well as the integration of information specifying the distance between a perceiver and an object (Bruno & Cutting, 1988).

It would seem that any organized hierarchical system—including the visual system—must come together part by part, with the separate parts, at first, functioning so as to solve a certain distinct problem. This is how computer networks are built up from the fundamental *ifs* and *thens* or the *1*s and *0*s to the more complexly functioning Big Blues or World Wide Webs (see Sperber, 1994; Johnson-Laird, 1988; Barto, 1985; Chellapilla & Fogel, 2001; Copeland, 1993; Arp, 2007a, 2007b). This is also the way natural/historical processes appear to work in evolutionary advances (see Deacon, 1997; Berra, 1990; Gould, 1977; Dawkins, 1996). Thus, it is understood by neurologists, philosophers, psychologists, and other thinkers that the mammalian visual system is made up of parts, or *brain-process modules*, that have been selected for in an evolutionary history to process color, shape, depth, motion, the edges of objects, and the like (Goodale & Murphy, 2000; Casagrande & Kaas, 1994; Edelman & Tononi, 2000; Shallice, 1997; Marr, 1983; Sereno et al., 1995). At the same time, such an organized hierarchical system seems to have evolved advisory mechanisms that can both segregate or select certain parts as relevant, *as well as* integrate or bind relevant parts together, so as to adapt to an environment. Thus, van Essen et al. (1994, p. 271) maintain that the "need for highly flexible linkages between a large number of physically separate modules" requires a mechanism that *controls* and *integrates* the information gathered from such modules.

It is important for an animal's survival that it be able to select relevant visual information about color, shape, distance, and the like from the environment and then integrate that information so as to know whether to fight, flee, eat, mate, and so forth. In other words, the recognition and discrimination of objects is key to an animal's survival. A question now arises: How is it that the disparate pieces of selected data that have been carried by separate pathways at the various levels of the visual hierarchy are organized into a coherent visual perception, enabling object recognition and/or discrimination? This is actually a kind of *binding problem* question, of which there are probably many at the various neurobiological and psychological levels of the visual system (Roskies, 1999; Gray, 1999). Another way to frame the question is this: How is it that the parallel processing of lines, shapes, forms, colors, motion, distance, depth, and the like are combined in such a way as to yield the image of a particular object in one's visual field, not of something else entirely? How is this information coherently integrated or *bound together* so as to become informative for the perceiver?

I suggest that this is possible through the phenomenon of *visual modularity* and the mechanism of *visual integration*. When relevant visual areas are bound together so as to make coherent sense out of some external stimuli in terms of object recognition or discrimination, this *bundle* comprises the integration of visual modules.

Visual modularity refers to the fact that the visual system is made up of distinctly functioning and interacting modules, parts, or areas, having evolved to respond to certain features of an object in typical environments. A *module*, in this sense, is simply a brain process or brain system devoted to some specified task concerning object recognition and/or discrimination. The concept of the module is nothing new and has been utilized by neuroscientists, biologists, evolutionary psychologists, and other thinkers for years (see Fodor, 1983, 1985; Bruno & Cutting, 1988; van Essen et al.,

1994; Mithen, 1996; Gardner, 1993; Bear et al., 2001; Kandel et al., 2000; Zigmond et al., 1999; Kosslyn & Koenig, 1995).

For example, we have noted already that the visual cortex and related pathways are split up into many areas, each processing a different aspect of the visual field; V1 is responsible for initial visual processing, V2 for stereo vision, V3 for distance, V4 for color, V5 for motion, and V6 for object position. Each of these processes can be viewed as a module as Marr (1983) makes clear in his famous work on vision. DeYoe et al. (1994, p. 151) have shown that the blobs and interblobs of V1 and V2 in macaque monkeys contain neurons with distinctive visual response properties suggesting, as they call it, "modularity" and "multistream processing." Also, Broca's area and Wernicke's area would be considered as other examples of brain-process modules, since grammar–usage and language comprehension appear to be localized in these areas, respectively (see Lueders et al., 1991; Patterson & Wilson, 1987; cf. the new research of Petrides, Cadoret, & Mackey, 2005). Further, the face-recognition area in IT cortex already mentioned is another example of a brain-process module (Tovee & Cohen-Tovee, 1993; Tovee, 1998; cf. the new research in Sinha, Balas, Ostrovsky, & Russell, 2006).

The parallel processing associated with the visual system would be considered as a suite of coordinated physiological or brain-process modules— the information processed about color is one brain-process module, the information about distance is another module, the information about form still another module, and so forth. In fact, the very idea of parallel processing *entails* modularity, since the processes are made up of components that operate independently in completing tasks. The brain can be represented as a host of modules, some of which are located in a single spot (like Broca's area for grammar–usage) and others of which are dispersed over the entire cortex. Finally, these brain-process modules are viewed as nested within hierarchies, and one can envision larger modules coordinating input from smaller modules, which themselves collate neural processes from still smaller neural bundles, and so forth.

The phenomenon of visual modularity works with the mechanism of visual integration to produce a coherent visual perception. *Visual integration* refers to a neurobiological process or set of processes that bind together the relevant information gleaned from visual modules into a coherent, cognitive representation of some object, enabling an organism to function in typical environments. As Zigmond et al. (1999, p. 822) note, in the visual system "high-level neurons classify visual stimuli by integrating information that is present in the earlier stages of processing."

What areas of the brain would be likely candidates for visual integration? We know that the *what* and *where* visual unimodal systems are laid out along trajectories from V1 in the occipital lobe to the temporal and parietal regions, respectively. And we know that different aspects of an object— color, form, distance, and the like—are processed along each one of these trajectories. There appears to be some kind of integrating mechanism that allows the primate to determine either what an object is or where an object is that is present in each of these systems. Information about an object from V1, V2, and V4 must be integrated somehow along the trajectory that forms the *what* system; likewise, information about an object from V1, V2, V3, V5, and V6 must be integrated somehow along the trajectory that forms the *where* system. We can infer that integration of information is taking place from the fact that if the *what* system is nonfunctioning, a primate still may be able to distinguish where an object is; conversely, if the *where* system is nonfunctioning, a primate still may be able to distinguish what an object is (Goodale et al., 1994; Goodale & Murphy, 2000; Desimone & Ungerleider, 1989; Ungerleider & Haxby, 1994). How would an animal be able to determine, coherently, the what or the where of an object *independent of one another* if the information from these areas was not somehow integrated along the individual trajectories?

Further, the very concept of an *association area* implies an integrating mechanism. Thus, it is likely that the visual unimodal association area of the occiptotemporal cortex acts as the integrative mechanism for the information processed from the *what* and *where* visual unimodal systems. This area is involved in processing the information received from the parietal and temporal unimodal areas concerning color, motion, depth, form, distance, and the like. We know that there is a division of labor concerning a primate's abilities to distinguish what an object is from where an object is. However, there are times when a primate must perform both of these tasks and, given the neuronal projections from the parietal and temporal areas to this common site in the occiptotemporal cortex, it makes sense that a primate be able to integrate visual information about what and where an object is in its visual field at the same time. Kandel et al. (2000) claim that these areas integrate information about form, color, and motion, noting that their evidence comes directly from studies of humans who have suffered brain injuries, experimental studies on monkeys, and radiological imaging techniques of humans. Beason-Held et al. (1998) have shown through PET scans that the occiptotemporal lobes are active in elementary form perception in humans. Also, Honda et al. (1998) noted the activation of these areas in PET scans when humans performed visuomotor tasks in a matching-to-sample test where both the *what* and the *where* systems were utilized.

Further, it is plausible to posit that the multimodal areas act as the neuronal integrating mechanism for the information that is processed through the highest level of sensory systems and those systems associated with memory, attention, planning, judging, emotions, and motor control. Kandel et al. (2000) name the prefrontal, parietotemporal, and limbic cortices as the most likely neural candidates. Roberts, Robbins, & Weiskrantz (1998), Uylings & van Eden (1990), and Rees & Lavine (2001) point to these areas as primary integrating mechanisms for higher level functions, including conscious awareness. Through PET scans, Macaluso, Frith, & Driver (2000) have shown that the unimodal and multimodal areas are active in tasks involving the utilization of both the visual and somatosensory systems (also see Eimer & van Velzen, 2002; Calvert, 2001).

Consider a possible exchange between two chimps: chimp A has food, and chimp B wants chimp A's food. If chimp A is being approached by chimp B, it must be able to visually judge space and shape (*What* is this thing coming at me?), along with distance and size (*Where* is this thing in relation to me?), as well as interpret the facial expressions of its approacher. As we have seen already, the *what* and the *where* systems follow trajectories from the visual cortex to the temporal/ventral and parietal/dorsal areas respectively, and facial recognition has neural correlates found in the IT cortex. All of this modular processing occurs in a parallel fashion, by separate modular processes, as neuroscientists indicate (e.g., Felleman & van Essen, 1991; Desimone et al., 1984; Crick, 1994).

When facial recognition, body position, and proximity are brought to cognition—as when chimp A communicates to chimp B something like "this is my food; don't touch it or I'll bite you"—there must be an integration of this modular information so that the chimp can form a coherent perception. Further, there are various sorts of stimuli coming in through the other sensory modalities that must be integrated with the visual system so that chimp A ultimately can initiate a response in terms of either fighting, fleeing, making friends, or making some other response. The brains of our chimps bind together the various modules of the visual system, as well as binding together the visual system with other systems, while negotiating this exchange. The phenomenon of visual modularity and the mechanism of visual integration work together to explain how this exchange between these two chimps is possible.

3.4   Levels of Visual Processing

In the previous section, I noted that visual recognition and discrimination of objects are key to an animal's survival, and I went on to suggest that these activities are possible because of the phenomenon of visual modularity and the mechanism of visual integration. There is more to the story concerning an animal's visual cognition of an object than simply visual modularity and visual integration. Numerous studies indicate that (1) iconic memory, namely, a form of short-term memory that lasts no more than a second or so, as well as (2) attention and (3) the synchronous firing of the neurons in the areas relevant to the visual percept, seem to be necessary for visual cognition. These parts and processes may not comprise the sufficient condition for an overall coherently unified visual percept; this is to say, there may be some element or elements missing. However, the empirical evidence seems to indicate that such parts and processes are necessary for a coherent visual scene.

Before discussing these additional conditions necessary for visual cognition, I want to distinguish the various levels of visual processing, of which visual cognition is a part. We can distinguish four levels of visual processing in the visual system. The first level is a *noncognitive* visual processing that occurs at the lowest level of the visual hierarchy associated with the eye, LGN, and primary visual cortex. At this level, the animal is wholly unaware of the processing, as the brain receives the disparate pieces of basic information in the visual field concerned with lines, shapes, distance, depth, color, and so forth, of an object in the visual field (Gray, 1999; Julesz, 1984; Merikle & Daneman, 1998; Rees, Kreiman, & Koch, 2002).

Evidence for this level of processing comes from data gathered from *backward masking experiments* as well as from patients who suffer from *visual form agnosia, prosopagnosia, visual neglect, blindsight,* and *color anomia* (Farah, 1984, 1990, 1997; Cowey & Stoerig, 1995; Crick & Koch, 1998; Marcel, 1983). The patients in these experiments are able to process visual information, seemingly without being aware or cognizant of that information. In his blindsight experiments, Weiskrantz (1986, 1988, 1997) has shown that limited stimulus detection and movement toward objects is possible in patients who claim they "cannot see," that is, have no awareness of the stimulus. Graves & Jones (1992) also draw a distinction between nonconscious visual processing and visual awareness as a result of their experiments with blindsight patients. Humphrey (1992) notes a case of color anomia where a woman was able to process colors without being aware that she was making mistakes in her conscious reporting of those colors (also see Oxbury, Oxbury, & Humphrey, 1969).

In his backward masking experiments, Eagle (1959) documented interesting cases where people were shown a quick image of a man wielding a knife—approximately one-tenth of a second—followed by a longer lasting image of the same man standing and smiling. They then were asked to describe the character of the man in the second longer lasting picture. Interestingly enough, many subjects were unaware that the first picture occurred and yet still would judge the character of the man in the second picture according to what was processed by their visual system in the first picture. These studies seem to indicate that there is noncognitive visual processing occurring, despite the absence of awareness and/or conscious visual experience.

The second level of visual processing is a *cognitive* visual processing that occurs at a higher level of visual awareness associated with the *what* and the *where* visual unimodal areas. When it is said that an animal visually perceives what an object looks like or where an object is located, this means that the animal is *cognitively aware of* or *cognitively attends to* that object in the visual field. We can infer that cognitive visual processing is taking place from the fact that if the *what* system is nonfunctioning, a primate still may be able to distinguish where an object is; conversely, if the *where* system is nonfunctioning, a primate still may be able to distinguish what an object is (Goodale et al., 1994; Goodale & Murphy, 2000; Ungerleider & Haxby, 1994).

The move from noncognitive visual processing to cognitive visual processing is a move from the purely neurobiological to the *psychological* dimension associated with the brain's activities. I am using words like *cognition, awareness,* and *perception* to refer to similar psychological discriminatory abilities of an animal. Cognition enables an animal with a complex nervous system to negotiate environments as optimally as possible. In the previous chapter, I argued that the components of an organism are emergent entities nonreducible to the physicochemical parts of which they are composed, based upon the way in which the components are organized to do something directly related to the generalized homeostasis of this hierarchically organized living system (also see Arp, 2008a). The psychological dimension associated with the brain's activities can be considered as another level of emergent phenomena—psychologically emergent phenomena—added to the neurobiological hierarchy. Cognition is an emergent phenomenon because the parts and processes associated with it appear to be organized in such a way so as to aid an animal in discriminating information in environments. However, the kind of end result or end product of cognition—although similar to other activities in the animal's hierarchy in having generalized homeostasis as the goal—is different in that such a product is a *psychological* phenomenon that aids in generalized homeostasis.

There is a huge amount of literature devoted to questions about the existence of psychological phenomena and whether psychological phenomena supervene upon or emerge from neurobiological phenomena (for starters, see Heil, 2004a, 2004b; Stich & Warfield, 2003; Chalmers, 1996; McGinn, 1982; Hasker, 1999; Hatfield, 1999; Mesalum, 1998; Kim, 2000; Lycan, 1995; Searle, 1992; Arp, 2005b, 2007b, 2008d). Working out the problems associated with these issues constitutes solving several so-called *mind–body problems.* Now, no one has been able to give a satisfactory account of how it is that psychological states—particularly conscious psychological states—arise from, as well as interact with, the gray matter of the brain. However, my intuition concerning the emergence of psychological states is that just as the components at various levels of neurobiological and biological hierarchies—such as organelles, cells, tissues, and organs—cannot be reduced to the physicochemical parts of which they are composed, so too visual cognition, although dependent upon neurobiological processes, is not reducible to such processes. Again, the main reason why psychological phenomena are nonreducible to neurobiological phenomena is the same reason why neurobiological and biological components are nonreducible to the physicochemical parts of which they are composed, namely, such components and phenomena emerge as a result of the way in which they are organized to do something directly related to generalized homeostasis of the organism. I will have more to say about this in the next two chapters when I speak more directly about the evolution of scenario visualization in our species' psychology.

The third level of visual processing is a cognitive visual processing that occurs at an even higher level of visual awareness concerned with the *integration* of the disparate pieces of visual unimodal information in the visual unimodal association area. There are times when an animal must determine *both* what an object is and where it is located, and this level of visual processing makes such a determination possible.

The fourth level of visual processing is a *conscious cognitive* visual processing that occurs at the highest level of the visual hierarchy associated with the multimodal areas, frontal areas, and, most probably, the summated areas of the cerebral cortex. This is the kind of visual processing related to human visual awareness and visual experience, and evidence for this level comes from reports made by individuals, as well as from observing human behavior (Roth, 2000; James, 1890; Chalmers, 1996). As I will make clear in the next two chapters, one form of conscious cognitive visual processing is scenario visualization, namely, the selection and integration of visual images from mental modules, as well as the projection of visual images into future scenarios for the purposes of negotiating environments.

In this project, I am concerned mostly with the progression from cognitive visual processing to conscious cognitive visual processing, the relationship of these processes to one another, and, ultimately, how conscious cognitive visual processing evolved from cognitive visual processing. This is so because, as I show, conscious cognitive visual processing—in terms of what I call scenario visualization—is necessary for vision-related, nonroutine creative problem solving. Although I will not be able to solve *completely* the mind–body problem of how it is that conscious experience can emerge from and interact with the gray matter of the brain, my hypothesis concerning scenario visualization is an attempt to explain a *part* of our conscious abilities and the reason for its emergence in our species.

We can think of the four levels of processing in relation to the various species in the animal kingdom. All vertebrate species in the phylum Chordata with a rudimentary visual system—mammals, birds, reptiles, amphibians, and fish—exhibit noncognitive visual processing of some kind. These same vertebrate species also exhibit cognitive visual processing to some degree or another. Besides the numerous studies on apes, monkeys, dolphins, cats, dogs, birds, and turtles that seem to indicate that they have cognitive abilities such as awareness and associative learning (for starters, see Marten & Psarakos, 1994; Byrne, 1995; Pearce, 1997; Stamp Dawkins, 1993; Parker, 1996; Tomasello et al., 1993; Weir, Chappell, & Kacelnik, 2002; Eimer & van Velzen, 2002), I have witnessed my own cat's abilities to perceive and recall where her treat is located in the cabinet, as well as her abilities to expect the treat and go for the treat when I have left the room. (Sometimes, she actually would open the cabinet where the can of treats was kept and knock the can to the counter below!) Given the data, I agree with Roth (2000, p. 95) that "it is fair to assume that all vertebrates with larger cortexlike structures, particularly those with cortices showing cross-modality information transfer, have awareness about what is going on around them." However, within the order primates, human beings alone seem to exhibit *conscious* cognitive visual processing to a full degree, while the other primates may do so to a lesser degree (cf. Parker, 1996; Whiten et al., 1999; Mitchell, 1993).

3.5 Iconic Memory

Having laid out these four levels of visual processing, we can now discuss visual cognition as being dependent upon iconic memory, attention, and the synchronous firing of the neurons in the areas relevant to the visual percept. Iconic memory is implicated in visual cognition because the visual representation has to be held in mind, so to speak—if even for a very short time—so that unification of the various parallel processes that contribute to cognition can occur. The idea is that if the disparate pieces of information were too fleeting, then there would not be enough salience in the visual field to be able to encode the incoming information. In studies where individuals are shown quick flashes of objects on a screen and then asked to identify them, if the object does not remain on the screen for at least 250 milliseconds (a quarter of a second), then the individual does not "see" the object or thinks that the test had not begun. This is so because the object is flashed on the screen at such an incredibly fast rate that the visual system is not even aware of the occurrence (Barrett, Dunbar, & Lycett, 2001; Julesz, 1983). Through PET scans, activity in the left prefrontal cortex has been shown to be active in individuals who attempt to encode visual information (Kosslyn et al., 1999a, 1999b, 2001).

Further, the existence of iconic memory acts as a bridge between non-cognitive visual processing and cognitive visual processing. We are wholly unaware of the processes in the lowest level of the visual hierarchy comprising the trajectory from retina, through LGN, to V1. Iconic memory is kind of like the paused scene on a movie you rent or a snapshot photograph in your mind that enables you to be aware of or cognitive of a visual scene—although such a scene or photo can be held in mind for only an incredibly short amount of time.

When we think of memory, what comes to mind are recollections of mental maps, events, sights, sounds, smells, and the like. Further, these recollections are not a jumbled mass of confusion but are organized into coherent picture-like scenes. With respect to visual memory, these scenes are, in effect, visual images that we have stored somehow in our brains and deliberately can recollect if necessary. So how does this storage take place?

Following leads from Hebb (1949, 1966), Bliss & Lømo (1973) demonstrated that the hippocampus of the mammalian brain exhibited alterations in synaptic strength of neurons, depending upon the amount of stimuli applied. They termed this alteration in synaptic strength *long-term potentiation* (LTP). LTP could last for hours in brain slices, while in the intact animal it could last for days. Malenka & Siegelbaum (2001, p. 419) note that LTP is a "ubiquitous property," since it has been observed in the excitatory synapses of a variety of areas of the brain, including the hippocampus, all layers and areas of the cortex (including the visual cortex), the amygdala, the thalamus, and the cerebellum.

In addition, Kandel's (1976) groundbreaking work associated with the gill-withdraw reflex of the marine snail, *Aplysia*, showed that simple forms of learning—habituation, sensitization, and classical conditioning—could produce changes in the synaptic strength of neurons resulting in memory storage. It seems clear that there exists some kind of storage mechanism at the cellular level. This is something important to keep in mind, as the organs and processes of the brain are comprised of these collections of neurons (cf. Maviel, Durkin, Menzaghi, & Bontempi, 2004; Fink, 2003; Hoffman & McNaughton, 2002).

However, this is not the full story concerning memory storage. Studies of patients whose association areas are damaged have shown that different representations of an object are stored differently. For example, a person suffering from *associative visual agnosia* whose posterior parietal cortex has been damaged can identify objects by drawing them but cannot name them. Conversely, a person suffering from *apperceptive visual agnosia* whose occipital lobes are damaged can name objects but cannot identify them to draw them (Farah, 1990). Another example is *prosopagnosia*, the inability to recognize familiar faces or learn new faces that results from damage to the IT cortex. People who suffer from prosopagnosia, although unable to process or recall faces, still can process and recall other objects, such as animals and tools (Geschwind, 1979). These studies indicate that the visual image is a product of multiple representations in the brain, each having their own neural correlates and each concerned with a different aspect of the visual image. This implies that there is no *one* deposit memory storage area. Rather, there are multiple storage areas, and recollection is itself a process of building up disparate pieces of information.

In this section, I discussed a storage mechanism in the visual system for at least two reasons. First, such a mechanism is necessary in information exchange so that a receiving afferent entity actually can be influenced by the information communicated by an efferent entity. Think of an action potential and neurotransmitter release in the synaptic cleft of a neuron A and how that affects a neighboring neuron B, possibly causing another action potential in neuron B. Or, think of the DNA transfer when neurons differentiate. In both of these processes, the effects in some way must be *imprinted* within the efferent entity so that the communicated information evokes some kind of change in the efferent entity. These processes are representative of the myriad exchanges of information taking place throughout the entire nervous system.

Second, a memory mechanism is integral for visual imaging. When I want to deliberately recall my spouse's face, a process begins whereby the IT cortex, hippocampus, and other temporal cortical areas are activated. That I can recall my spouse's face means I had to imprint her face, and this process *also* involved the IT cortex, hippocampus, and other temporal cortical areas (see Kosslyn, 1987; Kosslyn et al., 2001). Alternatively, say I wanted to hold an object in my hand—like a shirt off the rack at a department store—and analyze an aspect of it to check and see if it has any imperfections. In order to accomplish this task, some kind of temporary memory would be necessary to sustain its image long enough in my visual field.

3.6 Attention

Besides iconic memory, visual cognition seems to depend upon an attention to the visual scene in terms of an *alert* or *arousal state*. In fact, damage to the pathways that make up the arousal systems within the thalamus and hypothalamus has been shown to impair cognition and consciousness (see the papers in Parasuraman, 1998). As I have noted already, selection mechanisms are necessary for visual processing. Animals attend to certain areas of their visual field that they find interesting, and attention enhances detection (Wurtz, Goldberg, & Robinson, 1982; Moran & Desimone, 1985; Posner & Peterson, 1990; Desimone, Chelazzi, & Duncan, 1994).

Singer (2000) and Kandel et al. (2000) liken attention to a filtering mechanism that both limits the amount of information reaching the cortex and enhances the responses of neurons in many brain areas relevant to the processing, storing, and recalling of the visual percept. This makes sense, since the thalamus, one of the parts of the brain implicated in attention, is *the* only mechanism by which information from the CNS is relayed to the cerebral cortex. Research on monkeys has shown that when they selectively attend to visual stimuli, the posterior parietal cortex, S-II neurons at the gateway to the temporal lobe, and V4 neurons in their brains are active (Steinmetz, Roy, Fitzgerald, Hsiao, Johnson, & Niebur, 2000).

3.7 Neuronal Synchrony

Along with iconic memory and attention, the synchronous firing of neurons in areas relevant to the processing of information gathered from a visual scene has been posited as a kind of neuronal binding mechanism. One version of the hypothesis, put forward most forcibly by Crick & Koch (1990, 1998, 1999, 2003), is that sets of cortical areas related to the parallel processing of visual information are coordinated in the thalamus at a firing rate of around the 40-Hertz range. Von der Malsburg (1981), Gray (1999), Singer (1999, 2000), and Singer & Gray (1995) have put forward similar positions that a coherent visual scene results from the synchronous firing of cooperative interactions of neurons in the cortical network. The idea is that the synchronous firing would bind the cells responding to different features of the same object together for a short amount of time, so as to produce a coherent visual perception. Neuronal synchrony has been accepted by many as a plausible binding mechanism, since experimental evidence has shown that relevant neuronal areas associated with the awareness of a visual scene, even areas that are quite a distance from one another, fire at about the same rate (Kosslyn & Koenig, 1995; Castalo-Branco et al., 1998; Engel, Kreiter, König, & Singer, 1991; Fries, Roelfsema, Engel, König, & Singer, 1997; Gray, Knig, Engel, & Singer, 1989; Rodriguez, George, Lachaux, Martinerie, Renault, & Varela, 1999; Roelfsema, Engel, König, & Singer, 1996; Usher & Donnelly, 1998; Vaadia, Aertsen, & Nelken, 1995; Lumer, Edelman, & Tononi, 1997; Ritz & Sejnowski, 1997). Such synchrony could be the "holy grail" the scientist is seeking as a plausible neurological correlate for the unified phenomenal visual perception.

In one of their final papers together, Crick & Koch (2003) added to the neuronal synchrony hypothesis by putting forward the idea that cognitive visual processing is sustained by shifting coalitions of neurons. The neurons in a particular coalition support one another directly or indirectly and increase the activity of their fellow members, much like what is known as a *synfire chain*. A synfire chain, originally put forward by Abeles (1991), refers to a significant pool of neurons whose simultaneous firing raises the potential of adjacent pools of neurons to allow them to fire. Coalitions of neurons are in a kind of competition, and attention may help in giving one coalition a dominant position over another. When an animal attends to a visual scene, that is, when such an animal is cognitively aware of that scene, the neural correlation of this coherent visual scene is simply the *winning* coalition. This is yet another attempt on the part of Crick & Koch to address the binding problem, since the coalition of neurons acts as the correlate to the bound, integrated, and coherent features of a single object in a visual perception.

Crick & Koch's latest idea has initial intuitive appeal because not only do they pull together research and ideas from neuroscientists and philosophers over the last fifty years but they view the integrated visual scene as resulting from a competition of coalitions of neurons. Blake & Logothetis (2002), DiLollo, Enns, & Rensink (2000), Tononi, Srinivasan, Russell, & Edelman (1998), and Dennett (1991) are representative of thinkers who believe cognitive awareness results from a kind of competition, much like Crick & Koch. Given the brain's vast assembly of neurons receiving electrochemical signals from other neurons and passing those on to other neurons, Dennett (1991) thinks that cognition takes the form of something like a pandemonium of competing bits of content, and the ones that win the competition are the ones that are conscious.

We are now in a position to specify what is meant by visual cognition. *Visual cognition* is the phenomenal representation of some object in the animal's visual field that is the result of the integration of modular visual information received from that object in association with iconic memory, attention, and the synchronous firing of neurons in the areas of the brain relevant to the processing of the visual percept. This definition is an attempt to point in the direction of a solution to the visual binding problem. These parts and processes may not comprise the sufficient condition for an overall coherently unified visual percept; this is to say, there may be some element or elements missing. However, the empirical evidence seems to indicate that such conditions are *necessary* for a coherent visual scene.

To recapitulate: visual cognition requires the integration of parallel pieces of information concerning form, depth, motion, and so forth from the what and the where unimodal areas (the modularity and integration criteria); these pieces of information must be held in mind for at least 250 milliseconds (the iconic memory criterion); the pieces of information are selected as relevant to a visual scene (the attention criterion); and neurons relevant to the processing of such information are firing at relatively the same time (the neural synchrony criterion). The end result is a coherently *bound* phenomenal visual scene of which an animal is cognitively aware when it *looks at* or *sees* something in its visual field.

It is important to note again that visual cognition need not be accompanied by consciousness. I agree with Roth (2000, p. 78) when he claims that cognition includes perception, learning, and memory as well as limited forms of imagination, thinking, expecting, and planning, *"whether accom-*

panied by consciousness or not [italics mine]" (also see Arp, 2007b, 2008b, 2008d). The above definition of cognition applies to all vertebrate species in the phylum Chordata, including mammals, birds, reptiles, amphibians, and fish. Roth correctly notes that consciousness comprises subjective awareness, experience, intentionality, indexicality, and self-reflexivity. These would be *additional* phenomenal states over and above visual cognition that humans with fully functioning nervous systems have to the fullest degree.

Several animal species engage in cognitive visual processing. They appear to *know* to some degree what is going on around them as well as being able to recall memories, make associations between objects in their visual field, and make associations between objects in their visual field and percepts stored in memory. Nevertheless, in comparison to the human mind, there is obviously some characteristic that is missing in the animal mind. What is it about the human mind that enables us to solve problems to a degree such that we can flourish, theorize, and dominate the earth? Humans have *conscious* visual experiences, as well as other conscious phenomenal states that other species (apparently) lack. As we will see in the next two chapters, my hypothesis of scenario visualization will be added to the list of conscious phenomenal states, the evolution of which has enabled humans to solve vision-related problems creatively, construct advanced tools and other products, and dominate the earth.

3.8   The Visual System and Environmental Information Exchange

In the first chapter, it was made clear that organisms exchange information with environments, that these environments can comprise interactions within the organism as well as interactions with the external world of the organism, and that environmental pressures can be described in terms of information that is exchanged within the organism and/or between environment and organism. Such exchanges with environments also affect the visual system. This is the last section of this chapter, and it acts as an important segue into the next chapter where I deal with the evolution of the visual system. This is so for two reasons: it is the *internal* environment of the cell related to genetic mutations in cell differentiation where evolution principally takes place, and, it is the *external* environment of the organism as a whole that acts as the *condition for the possibility of* the evolution of the visual system and scenario visualization. In this section, I describe first how the internal environment of the organism's processes and subsystems has an effect upon the visual system. Then, I describe the effects of the external environment upon the visual system.

The following examples all illustrate that the workings and interactions of the brain act as internal environmental pressures that affect the processes and functioning of the visual system. First of all, with the discovery of HOX genes it has been shown that much of an organism's phenotypic characteristics are under direct genetic control. For example, moving around, replacing, or taking out certain *Drosophila* (fruit fly) HOX genetic sequences produces mutated and monstrous results—antennae grow out of abdomens, appendages grow out of heads, or basic parts are missing (Nüsslein-Volhard & Wieschaus, 1980). The visual system is no exception to this rule, as researchers have been able to adjust gene sequences related to the visual systems of *Drosophila*, fish, amphibians, mice, and hedgehogs (Chitnis, 1999; Maconochioe, Nonchev, Morrison, & Krumlauf, 1996; Belloni et al., 1996; Goddard et al., 1996).

The important point to realize is that the experimenter's adjustments to the genetic code are directly analogous to the natural mutations that occur on a regular basis in the reproductive lives of organisms. During cell division and reproduction, genes go about their functioning in their own chemical environments of the cell. What takes place in those environments directly affects genetic formation in terms of mutant alleles (alternate forms of a particular gene). When neurons differentiate, there are natural genetic mutations that constantly occur because of chemical influences upon chromosomal chains. In fact, if it were not for the regular occurrence of mutant alleles, *every living thing would look exactly like everything else* (Mayr, 1976; Eldredge, 2001). The processes associated with mutant allele formation—rife with internal environmental pressures—account for the phenotypic diversity of living things. In the next chapter, before tracing the evolution of the brain and visual system, I talk more about genetic mutations in relation to the environments of organisms.

Another example illustrating the effect of internal environmental pressures upon the visual system has to do with *neurulation*, the successful positioning of the various kinds of neurons in their appropriate spots throughout certain developmental stages. Formation of the neural tube, some three weeks after conception in humans, depends on a fairly precise sequence of changes in the shape of individual cells, as well as the connections of cells to one another. Timing is a factor in the process, since neurulation must be coordinated with the ectoderm (outer layer of cells) and mesoderm (middle layer of cells) of the neural tube. At the molecular level, neurulation is dependent upon specific sequences of gene expression that are affected, to a large degree, by the positions and local chemical environment of the cell. For example, a deficiency of folate—a chemical found to be important in the healthy development of the neural tube— may cause a malformation of the retina, which develops out of the ecto- derm. This is one reason why doctors will ask women to take certain doses of folate during pregnancy.

A final example that illustrates the effect of internal environmental pres- sures upon the visual system has to do with the *neurotrophic theory*, that is, the idea that neurons compete for space in their own environment of the brain (Reichardt & Fariñas, 1997). It is well-known that the developing nervous system overproduces connections in great excess during develop- ment. Through programmed cell death, as well as through a competition for space, neuronal connections are pruned away as the nervous system continues to develop. Hubel & Wiesel (1962, 1968) coined the term *binocu- lar rivalry*, which has to do with the inputs from both eyes in layer IV competing for space (Myerson, Miezin, & Allman, 1981; Lumer, 2000). Interestingly enough, this internal environmental conflict is necessary for the appropriate development and functioning of the nervous system (Craig & Lichtman, 2001; cf. Lumer, Friston, & Rees, 1998; Zhang, Tao, Holt, Harris, & Poo, 1998). Other forms of visual competition have been docu- mented (e.g., Antonini & Stryker, 1993; Blake & Logothetis, 2002; DiLollo et al., 2000). Also cats, rats, and birds that have had their eyes occluded or removed in early development show evidence of synaptic competition for the unused visual space (Shatz & Stryker, 1978; Antononi & Stryker, 1993). It is important to note that overproduction and competition were the first two observations Darwin (1859) made concerning species in general that led to his formation of evolutionary theory.

There is a time frame in the development of the nervous system known as a *critical period*. During this critical period, it is important for the nervous system to receive information from the external world so as to aid in appropriate neuronal maturation and synapse formation. As Zigmond et al. (1999, p. 637) make clear: "During a critical period, the pathway awaits specific instructional information, encoded by impulse activity, to continue developing normally. This information causes the pathway to commit irreversibly to one of a number of possible patterns of connectivity. If appropriate experience is not gained during the critical period, the pathway never attains the ability to process information in a normal fashion and, as a result, perception or behavior is permanently impaired." It is widely agreed that a combination of *natural* genetic factors (nature) as well as environmental stimuli (nurture) are necessary for normal, healthy nervous system development. Notably, even though it is the genetic blueprint that acts as the formal guideline by which differentiated neurons move into position in development, there can be material factors in the environment of the neuron—like some kind of lesion or another mutated neuron—that prevent the neuron from achieving its blueprinted designation. It is not only the environment of the neuron but also the external environment of the organism that affect the development of the nervous system. For example, Bear et al. (2001) note that a lack of appropriate nutrition, socializing, and sensory stimulation can contribute to the malformation of dendritic spines, a key factor in mental handicaps.

The sensory pathways from one brain region to the next are organized in such a way that neighboring groups of neurons maintain the spatial relationship of sensory receptors in the periphery of the body. In fact, the olfactory, visual, and somatosensory systems share the common feature of topographic mappings of sensory surfaces, as well as parallel processing, cortical modules, multiple cortical representations, and synaptic relays in the dorsal thalamus. Topographical organization is an important way of conveying information about the world to the nervous system. In essence, the sensory pathways in the brain topographically reflect the spatial relationships of the environment (Kandel et al., 2000; Kosslyn, Thompson, Kim, & Alpert, 1995). What this suggests is that *the environment determines, to a great extent, what we cognize.* This has caused Sekuler & Blake (2002, p. 26) to claim that the "information picked up by the senses is not merely a series of unrelated, incoherent data. Instead, sensory information closely conforms to predictable, structured patterns. These patterns arise from the very nature of the physical world itself, the world our senses have evolved in." Sekuler & Blake (2002, p. 168) also claim: "Organization in perception mirrors the organization of real objects as they actually exist. The correspondence between perceptual experience and the objects represented in that experience is not accidental. After all, the visual system did evolve for a purpose, namely to inform one about the objects with which one needs to interact."

The Gestalt psychologists noted that the visual system has built-in mechanisms whereby the visual scene is grouped according to the following principles: *closure*, the tendency of the visual system to ignore small breaks or gaps in objects; *good continuation*, the tendency to group straight or smoothly curving lines together; *similarity*, the tendency to group objects of similar texture and shape together; and *proximity*, the tendency to group objects that are near to one another together.

Numerous studies have ratified these principles as reflective of the visual system (Wertheimer, 1912, 1923; Brunswik & Kamiya, 1953; Kanizsa, 1976, 1979; Peterhans & von der Heydt, 1991; Gray, 1999; Sekuler & Blake, 2002). These mechanisms can work *only if* the environment actually displays the features on which the visual system is capitalizing. There must be these kinds of regularities out there in the world, or else it seems these principles would not be able to be delineated. Over 100 years ago, James (1890, p. 4) noted that mind and world "have evolved together, and in consequence are something of a mutual fit," and the Gestalt principles underscore this mutual fit. Further, in reference to the second chapter, where I dealt with metaphysical and epistemological forms of emergence, this apparent mutual fit of mind and world underscores the argument from miracles. One might argue that it would certainly be miraculous for the Gestalt psychologists to delineate their principles if there were *not* this mutual fit between mind and some actually existing environment in which the mind finds itself.

It also has been shown that neuronal size and complexity—as well as numbers of glial cells—increase in the cerebral cortices of animals exposed to so-called enriched environments, that is, environments where there are large cages and a variety of different objects that arouse curiosity and stimulate exploratory activity (Diamond, 1988; Diamond & Hopson, 1989; Mattson, Sorensen, Zimmer, & Johansson, 1997; Receveur & Vossen, 1998). In these environments, it is important that animals be exposed to objects having a wide variety of shapes, colors, and sizes because there seems to be a close correlation between *seeing* these kinds of objects and brain development. From such data, we can infer that experiences in environments are reflected to some degree in the structure of our brains.

Add to this the most recent data suggesting that regions of the brain can be trained, through mental and physical exercises, to pick up tasks from other regions. The evidence for this comes from stroke patients who regain the ability to speak, musicians who relearn how to play an instrument after nerve damage, and cerebral palsy patients who learn to perform activities long thought impossible to perform (Holloway, 2003; van Praag, Kempermann, & Gage, 2000; Schwartz & Begley, 2002). Not only does this suggest that certain brain processes are highly malleable and flexible (Malenka & Siegelbaum, 2001; Singer, 1995) but it again points to the fact that the external environment exerts a causal influence upon the brain and visual system. As we will see in the next chapter, the implications of synapse strengthening from environmental stimuli, as well as the ability of neuronal processes to perform alternate functions, are integral to an evolutionary account of conscious visual processing and creative problem solving in humans.

In this chapter, I built upon work of the previous chapters and showed how the processes associated with vision in mammals comprise a hierarchically organized system exhibiting the same kinds of properties of information exchange, selectivity, and integration found in organisms in general. I distinguished four levels of visual processing in animals: a noncognitive visual processing, two cognitive/psychological forms of visual processing, and a conscious cognitive visual processing that occurs at the highest level of the visual hierarchy. Since in this project I am concerned mostly with the progression from cognitive visual processing to conscious cognitive visual processing, the relationship of these processes to one another, and, ultimately, how conscious cognitive visual processing evolved from cognitive visual processing, I showed that the visual systems of mammals function so as to produce visual cognition.

Visual cognition is the phenomenal representation of some object in the animal's visual field that is the result of the integration of modular visual information received from that object in association with iconic memory, attention, and the synchronous firing of neurons in the areas of the brain relevant to the processing of the visual percept. Special attention was paid to visual modularity, which refers to the fact that the visual system is made up of distinctly functioning and interacting modules or areas having evolved to respond to certain features of an object in typical environments, and visual integration, which refers to a neurobiological process or set of processes that bind together the relevant information gleaned from visual modules/areas into a coherent cognitive representation of some object, enabling an animal to negotiate typical environments. In the next chapter—which is really the heart of the book—I trace the evolution of the visual system from organisms that developed a light/dark sensitivity area to humans who are capable of the complex activities involved in scenario visualization, one form of conscious cognitive visual processing.

4 The Evolution of the Visual System and Scenario Visualization

4.1 Genetic Variability and Natural Selection

In the next chapter, I show how scenario visualization fits into the evolutionary psychologist's schematization of the mind to form a more complete picture of how it is that humans evolved the ability to solve vision-related problems creatively. In this chapter, I trace the evolution of the visual system beginning with organisms that developed a light/dark sensitivity area and culminating in the complex activities involved in an aspect of conscious cognitive visual processing that I call scenario visualization. I do this utilizing the anatomical evidence from fossils and living species thought to be homologous to ancient species. I also use evidence from ancient toolmaking techniques because, in my estimation, the evolution of tool types parallels the evolution from noncognitive visual processing, through cognitive visual processing, to scenario visualization, a form of conscious cognitive visual processing (also see Arp, 2006, 2007a, 2008c). The variety and complexity of tools discovered and dated by archeologists offer compelling evidence that the brain and visual system have evolved with the passage of time. Before tracing the evolution of the visual system, I first must say something about the general evolutionary principles of genetic variability and natural selection.

As was noted in the last section of the previous chapter, neural development is dependent upon genetic and environmental factors. Even though neurulation follows a genetic blueprint, the way in which neurons differentiate, localize, and ultimately perform depends upon the internal chemiconeural environment of nervous system processes as well as the interaction between the nervous system and the external environment. This neurobiological process is representative of the general evolutionary pattern that all processes of organisms follow. The evolutionary pattern consists of genetic variability and the natural selection of traits that are most fit given a particular environment.

Darwin's (1859) insights concerning evolution—ones that still hold today—are the following: (1) there is variation in organisms such that they differ from each other in ways that are inherited; (2) there is a struggle or competition for existence, since more organisms are born than can survive; (3) there is a natural selection of the traits that are most fit given a particular environment; (4) organisms fortunate enough to have the variation in traits that fit a particular environment will have an increased chance of surviving to pass those traits on to their progeny; and (5) natural selection leads to the accumulation of favored variants, which may produce new species or a segregated gene pool, given the right environmental conditions and a certain amount of time.

Since Darwin's time, we have been able to determine that a major source of variation in organisms has to do with genetic mutation. A *gene* is a functional segment of DNA located at a particular site on a chromosome in the nucleus of all cells. Basically, DNA is the template from which RNA copies are made that transmits genetic information concerning an organism's physical and behavioral traits (phenotypic traits) to synthesis sites in the cytoplasm of the cell. RNA takes this information to ribosomes in a cell where amino acids, and then proteins, are formed according to that information. The proteins are the so-called *building blocks* of life, since they ultimately determine the physical characteristics of organisms (Carroll, 2005; Audesirk et al., 2002; Strickberger, 1985, 2000; Dawkins, 1986; Mayr, 2001; Ruse, 2000; also see the relevant papers in Arp & Rosenberg, 2008; Arp & Ayala, 2008).

DNA and RNA are composed of nucleic acids. These nucleic acids specify the amino-acid sequences of all the proteins needed to make up the physical characteristics of an organism, much like a code or cryptogram. This code consists of specific sequences of nucleotides that are composed of a sugar (deoxyribose in DNA, ribose in RNA), a phosphate group, and one of four different nitrogen-containing bases, namely, adenine, guanine, cytosine, and thymine in DNA (uracil replaces thymine in RNA). These four bases are like a four-letter alphabet, and triplets of bases form three-letter words or *codons* that identify an amino acid or signal a function.

There are 64 possible permutations of the four bases, and if one of the nucleotides in a sequence is either deleted or substituted, or if an alternate nucleotide is inserted, then a mutation is said to occur. A *mutation* is nothing other than an alteration in the nucleotide sequence of a DNA or RNA molecule. Mutations can result from a variety of environmental sources, including certain chemicals, radiation from X rays, and ultraviolet rays in sunlight. Mutations also can occur spontaneously. However, the most common source of mutations occurs regularly in base pairing during replication, as a cell prepares for cell division. In other words, mutations are occurring all of the time, since cell division is occurring in organisms all of the time.

Now, the genetic makeup of an organism directly affects its phenotypic characteristics. Whether an animal will have all of its limbs, or be stronger than another member of its species, or look more appealing to the opposite sex—all of these phenotypic characteristics are under genetic control (Carroll, 2005; Strickberger, 1985, 2000; Mayr, 2001; Lewontin, 1992). The examples of the manipulations of HOX genes that result in monstrous animal forms I spoke about in the last section of the previous chapter should make this point clear.

When an organism exists in a particular environment, the chance of it being naturally selected to survive depends upon whether its genetic makeup happened to have produced the phenotypic characteristics necessary for optimal survival in that particular environment. To a certain extent, the randomness of a mutation makes the business of life a "crapshoot." If your wolf genes coded you to have three legs instead of four, then it is likely you will not survive in the wolf pack out in the forests of Colorado. And if your rabbit genes coded you to have poor eyesight, then it is likely you will not survive in the same forests of Colorado, where your eyesight is essential for avoiding such packs of wolves. The phenotypic effects of mutations need only be slight so that, for example, one wolf may be just a little stronger, or a little faster, or a little more aggressive than the rest of the pack. This small genotypic variation leads to a slight phenotypic benefit, giving the wolf an advantage in hunting, mating, and passing its genes on to future generations.

Natural selection is a mechanism of evolution by which the environment favors the reproductive success of individuals possessing desirable genetic variants with greater phenotypic fitness, increasing the chance that those genotypes for the phenotypic traits will predominate in succeeding generations. The evolutionary principles of genetic variation and the natural selection of the traits most fit in a particular environment are illustrated in figure 4.1. This illustration owes its genesis to productive conversations with my graduate school colleague at Saint Louis University, Kevin Decker, as well as with biologists such as Robert Wood, at Saint Louis University, and Charles Granger, at the University of Missouri—St. Louis. In this figure, I try to show how natural selection acts like a sieve that allows for a certain

Generic Variants

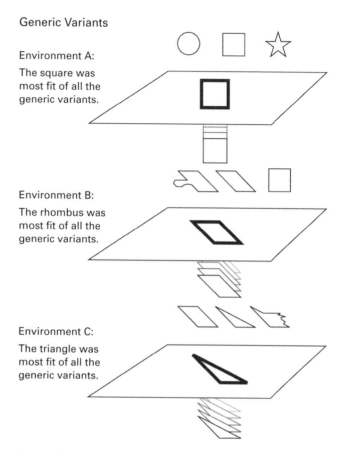

Environment A:
The square was
most fit of all the
generic variants.

Environment B:
The rhombus was
most fit of all the
generic variants.

Environment C:
The triangle was
most fit of all the
generic variants.

Figure 4.1
The evolutionary sieve

phenotypic characteristic to pass through to a subsequent generation. The various shapes represent organisms having certain phenotypic traits that are genetically controlled. The sieves themselves (the rectangular planes) represent the certain environments in which these organisms live. The preformed slot or hole represents the optimal survival of organisms possessing a desirable phenotypic trait in that particular environment.

The point of this illustration is to represent pictorially what biologists such as Audesirk et al. (2002) and Berra (1990) have claimed about genetic variability and natural selection. According to Audesirk et al. (2002, p. 175): "Mutations are essential for evolution, because these random changes in DNA sequence are the ultimate source of all genetic variation. New base sequences undergo natural selection as organisms compete to survive and reproduce. Occasionally, a mutation proves beneficial in the organism's interactions with its environment. The mutant base sequence may spread throughout the population and become common as organisms that possess it outcompete rivals that bear the original, unmutated base sequence." In Berra's (1990, p. 8) words: "Some genetic variants will be better adapted to their environment than others of their sort, and will therefore tend to survive to maturity and to leave more offspring than will organisms with less favorable variations. . . . The environment is the selecting agent, and because the environment changes over time and from one region to another, different variants will be selected under different environmental conditions."

Stated simply, the various species around us today are those organisms that have made it through one of these environmental sieves, the result of some fortunate mutation in combination with the traits that were most fit for some environment. As we will see, the human nervous system and human creative problem solving arose by the same evolutionary mechanisms.

4.2 The Evolution of the Nervous System

The information regarding the evolution of the nervous system derives from a variety of sources, including the comparison of anatomical features of fossils with living species thought closely to resemble such fossils. In this way, biologists and other researchers can study the nervous systems of living species in order to gain a picture of how the nervous systems of ancient creatures most likely had functioned. Accordingly, after I speak about the evolution of the cell, I trace the evolution of the nervous system in the following progression: euglena → hydra → worm → fish → reptile → mammal → primate. Thankfully, we have fossilized remains of creatures resembling each of these types of species—including what we take to be cells and protocells (Forterre, 2005; Pennisi, 2004; Margulis & Dolan, 2002; Berra, 1990)—making our inferences regarding the evolution of nervous systems reliable and probable.

Some 3.5 billion years ago, approximately 1 billion years after the earth was formed and 12 billion or so years after the Big Bang, rudimentary one-celled life forms—bacteria—appeared here on earth. Since the famous Stanley Miller experiment in 1953 where four amino acids, urea, and several fatty acids (all organic molecules) were synthesized from methane, ammonia, hydrogen, and water, numerous other laboratory experiments, thought experiments, and hypotheses have shown that it surely is possible to generate organic molecules from inorganic molecules (Forterre, 2005; Pennisi, 2004; Margulis & Dolan, 2002; Schopf, 2002; Line, 2002; Balter, 2000; Margulis & Sagan, 1986; Dawkins, 1976, 1986, 1996, 2005; DeDuve, 1995, 1996; Ball, 1999; Fry, 2000; Eigen, 1992; Fenchel & Finlay, 1994). Theorists postulate that amino acid chains, proteins, and then the organelles of the cell would have been the first things to evolve, in either a primordial soup or some crystalline formations (Pennisi, 2004; Margulis & Dolan, 2002; Margulis & Sagan, 1986; Mayr, 2001; Eldredge, 2001; Churchland, 1984). The cell is the first kind of thing that exhibits the four properties I have spoken of in the previous chapters, namely, internal–hierarchical data exchange, data selectivity, informational integration, and environmental–organismic information exchange.

However, added to these properties would be mechanisms of self-replication, protection, and Humphrey's (1983, 1992, 1998) distinction between *what is happening out there* (hereafter, OT) versus *what is happening in here* (hereafter, IH) mechanisms (also see Dawkins, 1996; Churchland, 1984). The DNA and RNA of cells act as the mechanism of self-replication, the cell wall acts as the mechanism of protection and encapsulation, and the processes of the organelles themselves engage in the exchange and control of information while interacting with environments. In light of the ideas already presented regarding genetic variation and natural selection, once RNA and DNA emerge, the mechanisms of evolution can do their work in cellular processes of organisms. Nervous systems came into being by the interplay of genetic mutation and environmental fitness, as generation after generation of RNA and DNA have replicated in cells over and over again.

The evolution of the nervous system really begins with microscopic organisms that developed a light/dark sensitivity area, most likely in primordial waters, some 3 billion years ago. In the first chapter, I spoke about the euglena, an algae that has an eyespot and uses its flagellum to move toward light in order to get food. This is not yet a nervous system; however, we witness the information exchange among the processes within the euglena, as well as the hierarchical organization of such processes that will be found in nervous systems. We also see the beginnings of Humphrey's distinction between OT and IH, since the euglena uses basic stimulus/response mechanisms to maneuver toward food and away from danger.

It is important to note that a kind of primitive visual system would appear to act as the catalyst for the evolutionary development of the nervous system. In fact, light/dark sensitivity emerged among a whole multitude of organisms in the protist and monera kingdoms (Febvre-Chevalier, Bilbaut, Febvre, & Bone, 1989). Further refinements of the light/dark sensitivity area can be found in animals, either in terms of stimulus/response mechanisms or various kinds of rudimentary and advanced visual systems (Cronly-Dillon, 1991; Blake & Truscianko, 1990; Horridge, 1987). For example, the photosensitive pigment cells in a worm's skin are responsive to light, as is the rudimentary pinhole eye of the nautilus. This speaks to the fact that an organism's ability to "see" is crucial for its survival, which makes sense given that the world is bathed in sunlight. Sunlight interacts in the world in such a way that organisms have taken advantage of this form of energy so as to optimally engage in forms of feeding, foraging, fleeing, fighting, and so forth.

The euglena is a one-celled organism. With the arrival of multicellular organisms having simple nervous systems came the possibility that a variety of cells could have a variety of functions. The hydra is a cnidarian that has a simple nervous system called a *nerve net*. This nerve net forms an undifferentiated network of sensory neurons, motor neurons, and interneurons (DeDuve, 1996; Bonner, 2000; Mackie, 1989). This was a crucial development in the evolution of the nervous system for at least three reasons. First, the electrochemical processes of the neuron, as well as the multiple axonal/dendritic neuronal connections, could aid in speeding up reactions to external stimuli, enabling the animal to be more efficient at hunting and/or avoiding being eaten.

Second, more complex and more efficient forms of communication within the animal could be achieved with the introduction of sensory neurons, motor neurons, and interneurons that are specialized in their functions. Sensory neurons deal with the *out there* of an animal, since they are located near the periphery of an animal's body and are concerned with relaying external environmental information to it. Motor neurons deal with the *in here* of an animal, since they aid in controlling the animal's bodily movements, as well as internal responses to external environmental stimuli. Interneurons connect sensory neurons to motor neurons and act as a kind of filter or buffer for the exchange of information between the two. Response times could be decreased by specialized neurons' performing specific tasks in parallel rather than having general-purpose neurons perform a variety of tasks. A neuron that has emerged to handle only one kind of problem likely will be able to handle that problem swiftly and efficiently because it has to handle only *that particular kind* of problem and no other one (also see Arp, 2008b). Further, many specialized neurons working on some problem together minimizes errors and allows systems to perform more optimally (cf. Culler & Singh, 1999; Bechtel & Abrahamsen, 2002; Feldman & Ballard, 1982). The parallel form of processing exhibited in the tripartite neuronal network made it through an evolutionary sieve because of its efficiency, and such a natural selection comports with the general evolutionary *principle of economy*, namely, whatever trait gives an organism a competitive advantage most likely will be naturally selected as fit for that organism and will be passed on to that organism's progeny. I will say more about specialized versus general-purpose processing in the next chapter.

Third, with the introduction of this tripartite neuronal system, Humphrey's distinction between IH and OT clearly comes into play. This is important for more evolved organisms that require part of the nervous system to be devoted to maintaining homeostasis within the organism (IH) while another part of the nervous system is attending to external stimuli (OT). Again, a nervous system having neurons of differing types devoted to specialized tasks could perform more efficiently than one having general-purpose neurons.

The next step in evolution was for sensory cells to cluster in the heads of simple animals like the worm. The body began to take on segmentation, and the movement of each segment came to be regulated by nerve cell bodies, or ganglia. A central cord of nerve fibers connected ganglia to each other and to the head. Also, a larger clustering of nerve cell bodies (a *cerebral ganglion*) appeared in the head, where a kind of brain-like command center for integrating sensory input and directing the body began to take shape. It makes sense that the clustering of nerve cells together in the head was selected for, since electrochemical information would not have as far to travel, thus allowing for conservation of energy and faster communication between neurons.

Fish evolved from worms, and, at first, there was just a brain-like bulge on top of the spine. Then, the nerves started to sort themselves into specialized modules—some became sensitive to certain molecules and formed smell modules, while others became sensitive to light and formed visual modules. The major evolutionary advance concerning fish has to do with the clear differentiation of the nervous system into the CNS and the peripheral nervous system (PNS). The CNS consists of the brain and spinal cord and is in constant two-way communication with the PNS, which consists of the somatosensory, afferent somatic, visceral, motor efferent, automatic (made up of the involuntary sympathetic and parasympathetic systems), and somatic (voluntary) systems. This is the general layout that is found in reptiles, amphibians, and mammals as well (Audesirk et al., 2002; Kandel et al., 2000).

The distinction between IH and OT is crucial in order to understand more complex vertebrate nervous system functioning and behavior. Parts of the CNS and PNS—like the hypothalamus and parasympathetic systems in mammals—are devoted to the internal homeostasis of the organism; these are the IH processes. Other parts of the CNS and PNS—like the LGN in the brain and the somatic system in mammals—are devoted to reaction to external stimuli around the organism; these are the OT processes. Ultimately, as we will see in the evolution of primates, some of the IH processes formed a kind of feedback loop, generating emotions and conscious thought. Instead of *merely* being directed toward the maintenance of OT and IH processes, the brain evolved abilities to feed back information within itself that is distinct from, but analogously related to, the processes of the CNS and PNS. It is arguable that this feedback of information allowed for the possibility of mental states such as emotion, reflection, and consciousness to emerge (Humphrey, 1992, 1998).

After fish came into being, the processes and systems of the brains of subsequent animals evolved at a rate that is disproportionate in relation to the rest of the body. The evolutionary story from here on out is more about the increasing size and complexity of the brain rather than that of the nervous system generally. Presumably, this is the case because the primary sensory mechanisms converge in the head of most animals, and the brain has become a kind of command center for both the CNS and PNS. There is an adaptive payoff to having a locus for information transfer and exchange. As this locus, the brain can go about its business of processing information quickly and efficiently, utilizing neurons that are cross-connected, working in parallel, and in close proximity to one another. Given the brain's ability to process information efficiently, it has been able to pass through one environment after another in the evolutionary sieve. At the same time, more parts and processes have been added to the brain because, to put it crudely, more parts mean more possibilities for efficient information exchange. However, it is not merely the addition of new parts to the brain that accounts for its efficient processing, and, later in this section, I will make some qualifications about how to understand the evolutionary addition of parts to the brain.

The evolutionary development of the brain from fish, through reptiles, to mammals and primates has been explained effectively in the famous works by MacLean (1967, 1991; cf. Sternberg, 1988; Kaas, 1987, 1993, 1995, 1996). According to MacLean's model, the primate brain is really a three-part brain having evolved the *neocortex* but retaining the *limbic system* found in mammals and the *brainstem core* found only in reptiles. The base of the primate brain is shared with reptiles and consists of the brainstem, reticular formation, and striate cortex. These areas are where the necessary command centers for living are located, namely, the control of sleep and waking, respiration, body temperature, basic automatic movements, and the primary way stations for sensory input.

Eventually, what MacLean calls the *paleomammalian* cortex evolved on top of the reptilian brainstem, allowing for more modules to develop: the thalamus, allowing sight, smell, and hearing to be used together; the amygdala and hippocampus, apparatuses for memory and emotions; and the hypothalamus, making it possible for the organism to react to more stimuli by refining, amending, and coordinating movements. The functioning of the *paleomammalian* and *reptilian* cortices are somewhat analogous to the functioning of a heart, pancreas, or kidney, since they are organized less for thought and more for automatic action and response. This makes sense from an evolutionary perspective. Reptiles, amphibians, and mammals out in the wild share the common problems of having to respond quickly to environmental stimuli so as to know whether to fight, flee, forage, or procreate in order to survive.

Finally, in the evolutionary history of primates what MacLean calls the *neomammalian* cortex (or cerebral cortex) evolved on top of the paleomammalian and reptilian brains. This area is responsible for the fine-tuning of lower functions, complex multimodular sensory associations, voluntary motor control, abstract thinking, planning abilities, and responsiveness to novel challenges. MacLean's model is powerful because it not only comports well with the fossil evidence but is consistent with experiments and studies performed on humans, other primates, mammals, reptiles, and fish (Harvey & Pagel, 1991; Kaas, 1987, 1993, 1995, 1996; Reiner, 1993; Karten & Shimazu, 1989; Jerison, 1973, 1991, 1997; Wise, 1996; Frith, 1996; Fuster, 1997; Sternberg, 1988; Northcutt & Kaas, 1995).

We must make at least one qualification regarding MacLean's model. It would be an oversimplification to claim *simply* that structures were added onto existing structures in the evolution of the brain. It is true in the evolution of primates that the brain expanded, thereby ultimately allowing for humans to do such things as invent tools, develop language, and contemplate Goldbach's conjecture. However, it is more accurate to say that with the increase of brain size came the addition of new brain structures to provide new functions, *as well as* a reorganization of the connections of existing brain structures to allow them to serve novel functions,

and the expansion of certain structures to augment particular abilities (Karten, 1998; Karten & Shimazu, 1989; Keverne, Martel, & Nevison, 1996).

For example, Deacon (1990) has put together a convincing case that the six-layered mammalian neocortex is not homologous to a single structure in a reptile but instead derives from the merger of the dorsal ventricular plate (or pallium) and the dorsal ventricular ridge of the reptile. Such a development would require the addition of new cortical material *and* the reorganization of existing cortical material (Rakic & Kornack, 2001; Kaas, 1987, 1993; Reiner, 1993). Also, Gannon, Holloway, Broadfield, & Braun (1998) and Gannon & Kheck (1999) have made a similar case regarding the evolution of Wernicke's area in humans as being homologous to the planum temporale and planum parietale in macaque monkeys and chimpanzees (cf. the recent research concerning Broca's area in Petrides et al., 2005).

4.3 The Evolution of the Brain

Thus far, I have given a general evolutionary account of the emergence of the primate brain from organisms that developed a light/dark sensitivity area. In order to explain the evolution of the primate visual system in particular—from which emerged the uniquely human, conscious ability to scenario visualize—it is necessary to narrow our focus further and trace the evolution of the brain from our insectivore ancestor of 65 million years ago (mya), through the primate missing link, to the emergence of *Homo sapiens* some 100,000 years ago (ya). This is the case for at least three reasons.

First, not only does the visual system utilize some 40% of the monkey's neocortex and some 15% of the human neocortex but the visual system makes further connections with other systems of the brain that are important in memory formation, emotions, planning, and motor control. Thus, it seems evident that the visual system evolved for important reasons. Second, the visual systems of the mammals from which primates evolved most likely were integral to the animal's survival. Primates ultimately evolved from archaic insectivores, and the insectivore needs to have acute vision in order to see in the dark when it feeds (Jerison, 1973, 1997; Allman, 1977; cf. Barlow, 1994). Third, the size of the brain in relation to the body of animals, in general, is an indicator of abilities to integrate and process pieces of sensory information (Roth, 2000; Jerison, 1997; Kaas, 1993; Armstrong & Falk, 1982). As the brain enlarged throughout primate

Geological Time Scale			
Millions of Years before the Present	Eras	Periods	Epochs
.01	Cenozoic	Quarternary	Holocene
2			Pleistocene
5		Tertiary	Pliocene
24			Miocene
37			Oligocene
58			Eocene
65			Paleocene
142	Mesozoic	Cretaceous	
206		Jurassic	
248		Triassic	
290	Paleozoic	Permian	
325		Pennsylvanian	
360		Mississippian	
417		Devonian	
443		Silurian	
495		Ordovician	
545		Cambrian	
545–4,550	Pre-Cambrian		

Figure 4.2
The geological time scale

evolution, the visual system evolved in complexity as well. In fact, as the brain increased in relative size, I explain this evolution as nothing short of the move from noncognitive visual processing, through cognitive visual processing, to conscious cognitive visual processing in terms of scenario visualization.

It is generally agreed that archaic primates have evolved from an early insectivore like *Purgatorius*, a mouse-sized, squirrel-looking mammal that spent its life on the ground foraging for insects in the evenings during the Cretaceous period (see the geological time scale in figure 4.2). From *Purgatorius*, all primates, tarsiers, lorises, and lemurs likely evolved. Although the exact phylogenic lines are sketchy, early primates known as *Aegyptopithecus* and *Proconsul* that lived during the Oligocene and Miocene epochs, respectively, likely are direct antecedents of modern human beings (Anapol,

German, & Jablonski, 2004; Fleagle, 1999; Mithen, 1996; Martin, 1990; Relethford, 1994).

Modern human beings are considered members of the species *Homo sapiens*. The following is a categorization of our hominin ancestry. Given the fact that fossilized skeletal remains of our hominin ancestors continually are being discovered in parts of the world, along with the fact that paleoclassification primarily occurs through comparisons of morphological traits, there are debates among scientists about the exact number and placement of our ancestors in the hominin family tree (or bush). It is most probably the case that several of the lineages represent lateral relatives, rather than direct ancestors. For example, it seems that *aethiopicus, bosei,* and *robustus* lived during the same time with *rudolfensis, habilis, ergaster,* and *erectus*, causing some scientists to classify the former three as in the genus *Paranthropus*, rather than classifying them all as in the genus *Australopithecus*. Simply put, the further back we go, the more likelihood there is for disagreement concerning hominin classification. So, the following classification is tentative and debatable but, nonetheless, represents the latest research as of the time I am writing this book.

Having said this, there is still a way to classify our hominin lineage(s), noting a few qualifications. Humans are members of the species *Homo sapiens*. The order *Primate* contains all prosimians, monkeys, apes, ape-men, and humans; the suborder *Anthropoidae* contains monkeys, apes, ape-men, and humans; the superfamily *Hominoidea* contains apes, ape-men, and humans; the family *Homininae* contains ape-men and humans; the subfamily *Homininae* contains humans; the genus *Homo* contains archaic and modern humans, of which there are seven extinct and one living species we are aware of at this time, namely, *Homo habilis, H. rudolfensis, H. ergaster, H. hiedelbergensis, H. erectus, H. neandertalensis, H. floresiensis,* and *H. sapiens* (modern humans). Some consider *habilis* to be an *Australopithecine*. Under the family *Homininae* and in the genus *Australopithecus* are included seven extinct species: the gracile *Australopithecines, Australopithecus anamensis, A. afarensis, A. africanus, A. garhi;* and the robust *Australopithecines, A. aethiopicus, A. bosei,* and *A. robustus*. Some classify the robust group as the separate genus *Paranthropus*. *Toumai Sahelanthropus tchadensis, Samburupithecus kiptalami, Orrorin tugenensis, Ardipithecus kadabba, Ardipithecus ramidus,* and *Kenyanthropus platyops* have been discovered and dated but have an even murkier classification than the species just mentioned (Stringer & Andrews, 2005; Cameron & Groves, 2004; White, 2003; Brunet et al., 2002; Hartwig, 2002; Kingdon, 2003; Tattersall, 2002; Stringer, 2002; Brown et al., 2004; Leakey et al., 2001; Johanson,

1996; McHenry, 1998; Abitbol, 1995; Johanson & Edgar, 1996; Wolpoff, 1999; Lieberman et al., 1996; Swisher, 1994; Wood, 1994; Mithen, 1996; Relethford, 1994).

The various hominin species are situated chronologically as follows:

Samburupithecus kiptalami: lived approximately 8.5–7.5 mya
Sahelanthropus tchadensis: 7–6 mya
Orrorin tugenensis: 6–5.8 mya
Ardipithecus kadabba: 5.8–5.3 mya
Ardipithecus ramidus: 4.7–4.4 mya
Australopithecus anamensis: 4.3–3.9 mya
Australopithecus afarensis: 3.9–2.9 mya
Kenyanthropus platyops: 3.5–3.1 mya
Australopithecus africanus: 3.1–2.4 mya
Australopithecus garhi: 2.7–2.4 mya
Australopithecus/Paranthropus aethiopicus: 2.7–2.3 mya
Australopithecus rudolfensis: 2.6–1.8 mya
Australopithecus/Paranthropus bosiei: 2.4–1.5 mya
Homo habilis: 2.3–1.7 mya
Homo rudolfensis: 2.3–1.9 mya
Australopithecus/Paranthropus robustus: 2–1.4 mya
Homo ergaster: 2–1.5 mya
Homo heidelbergensis: 1 mya–220,000 ya
Homo erectus: 800,000–100,000 ya
Homo neandertalensis: 370,000–80,000 ya
Homo floresiensis: 100,000–20,000 ya
Homo sapiens: 120,000 ya–present.

Again, we must keep in mind that it is most probably the case that several of the lineages represent lateral relatives rather than direct ancestors of *Homo sapiens*. The lineage leading to *Homo sapiens* is what is most significant for my project and, as of this time, can be traced as follows: *Ardipithecus kadabba* → *Australopithecus anamensis* → *Australopithecus afarensis* → *Homo habilis* → *Homo ergaster* → *Homo heidelbergensis* → *Homo sapiens*.

Interestingly enough, the earlier hominin species had brains that more closely resemble the size of a chimpanzee's brain, while the later species, like *Homo erectus*, had brains that were almost as big as ours. Brain sizes can be estimated from the internal volume of skulls. Typical modern adult humans have brains that are between 1,200 and 1,400 cm in volume. The *Australopithecines* all had a brain around 450 cm in volume. The *Homo* line shows a steady increase in size, with *Homo habilis* having a brain volume of around 700 cm, *Homo ergaster* having a brain volume of around 900 cm, and *Homo heidelbergensis* achieving the 1,200 cm status.

The brains of *Homo neandertalensis* actually got bigger than ours, but this is argued to be the result of a larger body mass (see Stringer & Andrews, 2005; Cameron & Groves, 2004; Roth, 2000). Not only did the *neandertals* die out but they also left no advanced signs of culture like that of ours, even though their brains were larger than ours (Mithen, 1996). This is puzzling. However, we must remember that brain size alone does not account for intellectual complexity or capacity to solve novel problems in environments. What accounts for such complexity and/or capacity has to do with the total number of synaptic connections, as well as the hierarchical organization of processes and systems in the brain. We can think of it another way. Elephants and blue whales have larger brains than humans because of their body mass, but this does not mean that they are more intelligent. Why? Because they do not have as many synaptic connections and the more advanced hierarchical arrangement of processes and systems that we do (see Aboitiz, 1996; Kappelman, 1996). To use a computer metaphor, it is not just bigger hardware that enables complex functioning; it is the amount of wiring in the hardware, and how that wiring is all hooked up, that makes the determination (see Jackendoff, 1987, 1992, 1994; Copeland, 1993; Sternberg, 2001).

4.4 The Evolution of the Visual System

So, how did this wiring come into existence? And how, ultimately, did it form into the complex wiring that comprises the human visual system, eventually enabling humans to solve vision-related, nonroutine problems creatively with the use of scenario visualization?

As noted earlier, organisms first developed a light/dark sensitivity area. We have already spoken about the euglena's eyespot, but hydras and worms also have light/dark sensitivity cells located in their outer epidermal layers. Eventually, a pinhole eyespot formed, which enabled even more complex processing of visual information. Of course, in order for this eyespot to have occurred, other parts of a rudimentary nervous system had to be in place, like the mass of neurons localized in one area, such as the head.

For example, the nautilus—one of the so-called *living fossils*, because it morphologically has not changed much since the Cambrian explosion—is representative of this next step in the evolution of the eye. The evolution of the visual system likely began with a general light sensitivity around the ventricle of the forebrain. These forebrain neurons were transformed in the course of evolution into an assemblage of neurons capable of analyzing strictly visual information, rather than other information carried to this area by other input neurons. The processed visual information was transferred through relay neurons (the future ganglion cells) to the contralateral part of the brain. In subsequent generations, this primordial retina evaginated (formed a cup-like hole) and eventually transformed into the lateral eyes of vertebrates (Cronly-Dillon, 1991).

Once this rudimentary eye developed, it took different directions in terms of its formation among the various species that have vision. There are all types of eyes falling into two broad categories: the compound eyes of insects, crabs, and arthropods that are composed of hundreds of cylindrical elements consisting of a lens, eight photoreceptor cells, and a sleeve of opaque pigment cells, and the vertebrate eyes of fish, reptiles, and mammals that all build upon the basic flatworm eye having a retina, ganglion cells, and projections to a brain. This divergence further ratifies the evolutionary principles of genetic variability and the natural selection of the fittest traits given a specific environment. The kind of eye that fortuitously developed, and then flourished, in the sand shark population under the sea will be different from the eye that fortuitously developed, and then flourished, in the black widow spider population on land, and so on.

As noted already, through investigation of the fossil endocasts of insectivores, Jerison (1973, 1991) has offered a convincing case that the ancestor of the primate was a small, nocturnal creature that prowled through trees and bushes on the lookout for insects, as some small primates do today. The eyes of this creature were close set and forward facing, indicating that it was a predator. Predators like owls, cats, and primates have close set, forward facing eyes with stereotopic vision, enabling them to more easily identify depths and distances while hunting their prey. Animals like rabbits and squirrels—the prey of predators like owls, cats, and some primates—have eyes on the sides of their heads with panoramic vision, enabling them to more easily identify predators from a variety of angles. The eyes of this insectivore would have had an abundance of rods and fewer cones to enable maneuverability in the dark. Insectivores had to forage on the ground and in the dark in order to steer clear of bigger reptiles, amphibians, and dinosaurs that would have preyed on them during that time.

However, when most of the dinosaurs and other larger predators were wiped out by an asteroid at the close of the Cretaceous, this allowed for the possibility of insectivores to occupy different niches. Eventually, some of the descendents of these creatures did their foraging during the day, while others took to life in the trees. Still others, like our primate ancestors, did both. By 20 mya, *Proconsul* had taken to life in the trees of Africa, most likely because such a life off of the ground made it easier to avoid predators lurking on the ground, as well as pounce upon prey that happened to be on the ground. This life in the trees is evidenced by their money-like and ape-like skeletons as well as their diet, which indicate a lifestyle not unlike that of present-day monkeys and apes (Groves, 2002; Hartwig, 2002; McGrew, 2004; Byrne & Whiten, 1988; Allman, 1982, 2000).

Life during the daytime and in the trees meant that a visual system, at the very least, would need to have evolved more cones, the capacity to distinguish colors, more memory-storage capacities, and facial recognition. More cones would be needed to be able to handle the brighter light of daytime living. A capacity to distinguish colors would be needed to determine what foods one could eat, as well as distinguish foreground from background while maneuvering through the trees. Rudimentary forms of long-term and short-term memory would be needed for a mental map of the area where this creature lived, as well as for distinguishing friend from foe. Finally, facial recognition would be needed to distinguish friend from foe, as well as to communicate various messages like "Leave me alone," "Back off," "It's o.k. to touch me," and the like to other members of one's social group or to enemies. On top of all of this, arboreal life required extremities more fit for grasping, jumping, launching, and other sorts of bodily maneuvering (Barton, 1998; Fleagle, 1999; Byrne, 1995, 2001; Rilling & Insel, 1998; Allman, 1977).

In order to do all of this, the connections between eye and brain, as well as those connections between other sensorimotor systems and brain, would need to be more complex. As Jerison (1973, 1997) and Kaas (1996) point out, the visual system of this early arboreal ancestor would have had a brain very similar to that of a lemur or a monkey. This being the case, at least three features of the brain and visual system would have needed to be in place in *Proconsul*.

First, referring back to MacLean's model, the reptilian, the paleomammalian, and *part* of the neomammalian brain would have to be present in *Proconsul*, since the amount of processing that such arboreal ancestors had to do required a brain larger than that of reptiles. The amount of processing that the visual system does alone would constitute a bigger brain. However, arboreal social life entailed the interaction of sensory modalities in combination with memory, emotion, planning, and motor function. All of this processing required a bigger brain, more synaptic connections, and more types of neural connections. In addition, the system must have been a hierarchical organization of processes and subsystems so that the right data could be selected and information could be integrated as *Proconsul* went about the business of negotiating its environment.

Second, in order to organize and coordinate information from the specialized visual modules and each of the other sensory modalities, integrative or association areas and systems had to evolve. Research by Kaas (1987, 1993, 1995, 1996), Bear et al. (2001), Uylings & van Eden (1990), Roberts, Robbins, & Weiskrantz (1998), and Hofman (2001) has shown that it is primarily the association areas of the brain that increase in the evolution of the mammal. The association areas show a marked increase when we compare the brains of rats, cats, macaque monkeys, and humans, in that order. On inspection, the visual, auditory, and sensorimotor areas of a rat basically butt up against one another with very little of the cortex—some 15%–20%—devoted to the association of these areas. Some 40%–50% of the frontal, parietal, and temporal lobes of the macaque monkey are devoted to association of sensorimotor information. Even more cortex— some 50%–60%—is devoted to association of sensorimotor information in humans.

Third, the visual areas would have needed to be linked up with the motor areas, so that visual information could be communicated to the brain and then translated into voluntary motion. The motor areas of primates receive inputs from the thalamic nuclei that relay information from the basal telencephalon and the cerebellum, and they send outputs to motor control neurons in the brain and spinal cord. The motor area is situated next to the somatosensory area, and both are located in the frontal lobe near the central sulcus at the parietofrontal junction of the brain. The sensorimotor area—along with the auditory and visual areas—send projections to association areas in the parietal and temporal cortices. From there, the projections are sent to the multimodal areas located in the parietotemporal, prefrontal, and limbic cortices (Kandel et al., 2000). These connections would have had to be in place in the brain of *Proconsul* so that it could have acted on visual information it received.

In the last chapter, I mentioned the idea put forward by the Gestalt theorists and William James that the mind and the world are "something of a mutual fit." This idea should be kept in mind here as we investigate the evolution of visual modules, along with the evolution of other sensory modules and mechanisms of selectivity and integration. Events in the physical environment are composed of materials that the human brain, complete with its specialized modules, has evolved to perceive and discriminate. These materials take forms ranging from specific chemicals, to mechanical energy, to electromagnetic radiation (light) and are discriminated by the different sensory modalities that are specifically attuned to these stimuli: taste and smell are specialized for processing concentrations of different chemicals, touch is specialized for processing mechanical deformations of the skin, hearing is specialized for the intake of sound waves, and vision is specialized for the intake of electromagnetic radiation. Thus, given the environment surrounding an animal, it makes sense that the CNS is a hierarchically organized system composed of specialized modules, as well as mechanisms of selectivity and integration, in order to process the myriad pieces of environmental information.

4.5 Tools and the Visual System

The hominin line diverged from the common ancestor of African apes some 6 mya. As was noted above, the brains of *Australopithecines* got no bigger than that of a chimpanzee. Therefore, from research on primates and monkeys, coupled with the archeological and geological data, we have an idea of what the brain and visual system of *Australopithecines* may have looked like and how they would have performed (Dunbar, 1988; see the articles in Berthelet & Chavaillon, 1993). The neurophysiology and lifestyle of Early *Australopithecines*, like *A. anamensis*, were probably similar to those of present-day chimps.

However, the climate in Africa slowly changed. Approximately 8 mya, present-day India (which was separate from Asia prior to this time) butted up against Asia and formed the Himalayan mountains, thereby robbing Africa of excess amounts of water. This climatic change caused eastern Africa to be transformed from predominantly forested environments, to savanna-like environments of forest and open range, to open range environments with little or no forestation (Calvin, 2001, 2004; Potts, 1996; Eldredge, 2001). Daly & Wilson (1999), Foley (1995), and Boyd & Silk (1997) have shown that the Pleistocene epoch did not consist of a single hunter–gatherer type of environment but was actually a constellation of environments that presented a host of challenges to the early hominin mind. The climate shift in Africa from jungle life to desert/savanna life forced our early hominins to come out of the trees and survive in totally new environments (Tattersall, 2001; Calvin, 2004; Aiello, 1997; Fleagle, 1999).

If the *Australopithecines* wanted to continue to live a life in the trees, they would have had to spend more time on the ground moving from tree to tree, so they must have had to utilize all four of their extremities more often. As Aiello (1997) notes, knuckle-walking and knuckle-running are quite taxing on a body. Ultimately, mutations coded for a semi-erect posture, and other mutations coded for an erect posture. Such fortuitous mutations would have been fitting for a savanna lifestyle where one could be more efficient at foraging, scavenging, and running away from predators if one were on two legs, freeing up the arms for other activities.

Along with bipedalism, it is generally agreed by biologists, anthropologists, archeologists, and other researchers that a variety of factors contributed to the evolution of the human brain. These factors include, but are by no means limited to, such things as diversified habitats, social systems, protein from large animals, higher amounts of starch, delayed consumption of food, food sharing, language, and toolmaking (Aboitiz, 1996; Aiello, 1996, 1997; Aiello & Dunbar, 1993; Allman, 2000; Byrne, 1995; Deacon, 1997; Donald, 1991, 1997; Gibson & Ingold, 1993; Lock, 1993; Calvin, 1998, 2001, 2004; Dawkins, 2005). It is not possible to get a complete picture of the evolution of the brain without looking at all of these factors, as brain development is involved in a complex coevolution with physiology, environment, and social circumstances. And, most obviously, the emergence of language in our species occupies a central place with respect to our ability to flourish and dominate the earth (Tallerman, 2005; Christiansen & Kirby, 2003; Deacon, 1997; Mithen, 1996; Aiello & Dunbar, 1993). However, I wish to focus on toolmaking as essential in the evolution of the brain and visual system. I do this for three reasons.

First, toolmaking is the mark of intelligence that distinguishes the *Australopithecine* species from the *Homo* species in our evolutionary past. *Homo habilis* was the first toolmaker, as the Latin name (*handy-man*) suggests. Second, tools offer us indirect—but compelling—evidence that psychological states emerged from brain states. In trying to simulate ancient toolmaking techniques, archeologists have discovered that certain tools only can be made according to *mental* templates, goal formations, and scenarios, as Pelegrin (1993), Isaac (1986), and Wynn (1979, 1981, 1991, 1993) have demonstrated. Finally, as I show, the evolution of toolmaking parallels the evolution of the visual system from noncognitive visual processing to conscious cognitive visual processing in terms of scenario visualization. Let me explicate these three points.

As was noted above, *Proconsul* most likely had a brain similar to that of a monkey. The *Australopithecine* brain was not much larger but probably had all of the same neural connections as that of a present-day chimpanzee. Thus, we can look to the chimpanzee and its usage of tools as an indicator of what *Australopithecine* tool usage may have been like. Chimps can strip leaves from branches and use these branches to fish for termites, knock fruit from a tree, or hit other chimps. They also use leaves to construct little makeshift baskets to carry food, protect themselves from rain, or scoop up water to drink. Further, they use stones to crack open nuts and other husks in order to extract food (McGrew, 2004; Byrne, 1995, 2001; Byrne & Whiten, 1988; Griffin, 1992; Stanford, 2000). It is likely that the *Australopithecines* did similar things.

The first stone artifacts, Oldowan stones, date to between 3 and 2 mya and usually are associated with *Homo habilis*. They consist of flakes, choppers, and bone breakers that likely were used to break open the bones of animals in order to get at the protein-rich marrow (Pelegrin, 1993; Isaac, 1986; Wynn, 1981; Wynn & McGrew, 1989; Mithen, 1996). Most probably, *Homo habilis* had to wait until other bigger animals killed their prey and feasted before they went in and scavenged what was left of the carcass. The key innovation has to do with the technique of chopping stones to create a chopping or cutting edge. Typically, many flakes and the like were struck from a single core stone, using a softer hammer stone to strike the blow.

Here, we have the first instance of *making* a tool to *make* another tool, and it is arguable that this technique is what distinguishes ape-men from apes. Another way to put this is that chimps and *Australopithecines* used the tools they made but did not use these tools they made *to make other tools*. Thus, the distinction is between a tool *user* who has made a certain tool A to serve some function (e.g., *Australopithecines* and chimps) and a tool*maker* who has made a certain tool A to serve the specific function of making another tool B to serve some function (e.g., *Homo habilis*).

Also, as has been noted, the brain of *Homo habilis* was approximately 700 cm in volume, almost twice the size of the *Australopithecine*'s brain. It is likely that this increase in brain size contributed to the move from tool usage to toolmaking. What this means is that, through the combined factors of genetic mutation and environmental pressures, the brain evolved the capacity for more complex connections and capacities, setting up the *conditions for the possibility of* toolmaking. Those hominins who were either lucky enough or resourceful enough to discover the benefits of toolmaking began to do so and survived to reproduce more "crafty" hominins like themselves.

The Acheulian tool industry consisted of axes, picks, and cleavers. It first appeared around 1.5 mya and usually is associated with *Homo erectus* or *Homo ergaster*. The key innovations include the shaping of an entire stone to a stereotyped tool form, as well as producing a symmetrical (bifacial) cutting edge by chipping the stone from both sides. It seems that the same tools were being used for a variety of tasks such as slicing open animal skins, carving meat, and breaking bones (Pelegrin, 1993; Isaac, 1986; Mithen, 1996; Wynn, 1979). Consistent with the increase in the complexity of toolmaking, the brain of *Homo erectus* increased to 900 cm in volume, up 200 cm from *Homo habilis*. The Oldowan and Acheulian industries are part of the time period commonly referred to as the Lower Paleolithic.

The Acheulian industry stayed in place for over a million years. The next breakthrough in tool technology was the Mousterian industry that arrived on the scene with the *Homo neandertalensis* lineage, near the end of the *Homo heidelbergensis* lineage, around 300,000 ya. Mousterian techniques (also called Levallois methods) involved a more complex three-stage process of constructing (1) the basic core stone, (2) the rough blank, and (3) the refined finalized tool. Such a process enabled various kinds of tools to be created, since the rough blank could follow a pattern that ultimately would become flake blades, scrapers, cutting tools, serrated tools, or lances. Further, these tools had wider applications as they were being used with other material components to form handles and spears, and they were being used as tools to make other tools, such as wooden and bone artifacts (Pelegrin, 1993; Isaac, 1986; Mithen, 1996; Wynn, 1981, 1991). Again, consistent with the increase in complexity of toolmaking, the brain of *Homo heidelbergensis* and *Homo neandertalensis* increased to 1,200 cm and 1,500 cm in volume, respectively, up 300 to 600 cm from *Homo erectus*. The Mousterian industry is part of the time period commonly referred to as the Middle Paleolithic.

By 40,000 ya, some 80,000 years after anatomically modern *Homo sapiens* evolved, we find instances of human art in the forms of beads, tooth necklaces, cave paintings, stone carvings, and figurines. This period in tool manufacture is known as the Upper Paleolithic industry, and it ranges from 40,000 ya to the advent of agriculture around 12,000 ya. Sewing needles and fish hooks made of bone and antlers first appear, along with flaked stones for arrows and spears, burins (chisel-like stones for working bone and ivory), multibarbed harpoon points, and spear throwers made of wood, bone, or antler (Pelegrin, 1993; Isaac, 1986; Mithen, 1996; Wynn, 1991). The human brain during this period was about the same size as it is today, between 1,200 and 1,400 cm in volume.

In the previous chapter, I distinguished four levels of visual processing. The first level is a *noncognitive* visual processing that occurs at the lowest level of the visual hierarchy associated with the eye, LGN, and primary visual cortex. The second level of visual processing is a *cognitive* visual processing that occurs at a higher level of visual awareness associated with the *what* and *where* visual unimodal areas. As I noted, the move from noncognitive visual processing to cognitive visual processing is a move from the purely neurobiological to the psychoneurobiological dimension of the brain. The third level of visual processing is a cognitive visual processing that consists of the integration of visual information in the visual unimodal association area. The fourth level of visual processing is a *conscious cognitive* visual processing that occurs at the highest level of the visual hierarchy concerned with the multimodal areas, frontal areas, and, most probably, the summated areas of the cerebral cortex.

The question now becomes this: What level of visual processing did these early hominins achieve in light of the size of their brains and the tools they constructed? Given the neural connections of present-day chimps, as well as the eye-socket formations and endocasts of *Australopithecines*, it is clear that both have (had) noncognitive visual processing. Also, given that chimps are aware of and attend to visual stimuli, it is likely that they, along with *Australopithecines*, have (had) cognitive visual processing. But can these species be said to have *conscious* cognitive visual processing? Possibly, to a certain extent. However, it is arguable that what counts against such species having *full* conscious cognitive visual processing is a lack of advanced forms of toolmaking, like those found in the Upper Paleolithic industry. There seems to be a direct connection between advanced forms of toolmaking and conscious visual processing. What exactly is that connection?

4.6   Scenario Visualization

I suggest that the advanced forms of toolmaking evidenced by early hominins beginning in the Upper Paleolithic industry require *conscious* visual processing. However, what exactly does this kind of conscious visual processing entail? Such an activity entails that a mind be able to *scenario visualize* the many different aspects of the toolmaking process. But then, what is scenario visualization? Scenario visualization is a conscious process that entails selecting pieces of visual information from a wide range of possibilities, forming a coherent and organized visual cognition, and then projecting that visual cognition into some suitable imagined scenario for the purpose of solving some problem posed by the environment in which one inhabits.

As an active mental process, scenario visualization would include the following steps: (1) reception of visual stimulus cues from the external environment, indicating that a problem is present; (2) identification of a goal to be achieved in terms of a solution to the problem encountered in some external environment; (3) selection of imagined visual images that appear to be relevant to the solution from several possible choices of imagined visual images; (4) integration of the visual images concerning possible scenarios into organized and coherent imagined visual scenes; (5) integration of the visual images concerning the imagined problem solving tool into an organized and coherent perception, vis-à-vis the imagined possible scenarios; (6) projection of visual images into imagined scenarios to judge the potential viability or appropriateness of a particular problem solving tool to a problem; (7) recollection of the particular goal of the project from memory; and (8) recognition that a particular problem solving tool is appropriate as a solution in the relevant environment that prompted the process of scenario visualization in the first place.

Figure 4.3 depicts the mental steps involved in the construction of a javelin by a member of the species *Homo sapiens* who lived out in the African savanna around 40,000 ya. This illustration is supposed to represent the intelligent processes associated with scenario visualization, so as to construct a certain kind of javelin in order to solve some adaptive problem. In this case, the problem to be solved has to do with easily and efficiently killing a large antelope for the purposes of skinning it and using its body parts for food and warmth during the approaching winter months. I ask you to imagine that this is the *very first instance* of one of our ancestors coming up with the idea of the javelin, with the intention of subsequently manufacturing it. At first, he has no prior knowledge of the javelin, but through the process of scenario visualization, he eventually "puts two and two together," and devises the mental blueprints for the manufacture of the javelin.

In the top panel of the figure, the hunter has separate visual images associated with antelope characteristics, the manufacture of the bifaced hand ax, as well as with how projectiles move through the air. The hunter also has visual images associated with all kinds of other pieces of information like the faces of the members of his group, a mental map of the immediate area, some intuitive sense of mechanics and biology, and so forth. In the second panel, scenario visualization is beginning as the hunter has not only identified the problem to be solved in the environment and is selecting imagined visual images that appear to be relevant to the solution from several possible choices of imagined visual images but also is integrating the visual images concerning possible scenarios into organized and coherent imagined visual scenes. In the third panel, the hunter is

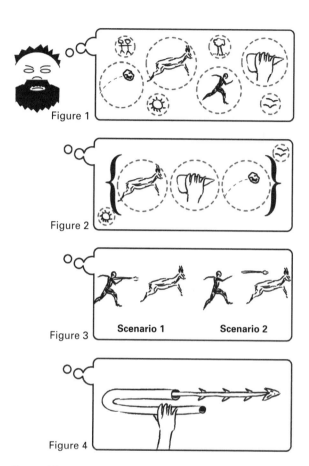

Figure 4.3
The construction of a javelin

integrating the visual images concerning the imagined problem solving tool into an organized and coherent perception, vis-à-vis the imagined possible scenarios, as well as projecting the visual images into imagined scenarios to judge the potential viability or appropriateness of a particular problem solving tool to a problem. In the fourth panel, the hunter has formed a coherent and organized image of a particular javelin that can be implemented in the actual production of the javelin and has recognized that a particular problem solving tool (this particular kind of javelin) is appropriate as a solution in this environment.

As an active, *conscious* process scenario visualization is more than merely the *cognitive* process of forming a visual image or recalling a visual image from memory; these activities can be performed by nonhuman primates, mammals, and possibly other animals. When my cat looks at me or the squirrel outside, she is forming a visual image. And when my cat sees me open the cabinet door, she most likely comes running because she recalls the visual image that inside the cabinet is where her treat is located. Such behaviors exhibited by my cat seem to indicate cognitive visual processing. However, the process of scenario visualizing requires something more than mere cognitive awareness of an object in a visual field or cognitive awareness of a memory. Forming a visual image is part of scenario visualizing; yet, this is not the full story. Further, depending upon what is being visualized, recalling a visual image from memory may be part of visualizing, but again, this is not the full story. Scenario visualization requires a mind that is more opportunistic, innovative, and creative in the *utilization* of visual images through the processes of selectivity, integration, and projection into future scenarios. It is not the having of visual images that is important; it is what the mind does in terms of actively selecting and integrating visual information for the purposes of solving some problem *relative to some environment* that really matters.

We are the only species that can visualize in this more complete way, and what I am suggesting is threefold: First, humans share with other animals the abilities to select among visual images, as well as integrate and organize visual information so as to form a coherent visual cognition. However, humans have the unique abilities to go beyond the present in order to project visual images into future scenarios, as well as transform the visual images within a variety of imagined environments so as to solve some vision-related problem creatively—this is scenario visualization. We construct novel tools to do work in some environment. We need some kind of environmental setting in which to construct an artifact precisely because the artifact, presumably, is going to *serve some purpose in some environment.* In order to survive in unstable and changing environments, hominins evolved a capacity to deal with this instability, whereby they could visually *anticipate* the kinds of tools—even novel tools—needed for a variety of settings.

Second, our capacity to scenario visualize is a *central feature* of conscious behavior, an idea that comports well with Sternberg's (2001) notion of consciousness's entailing the setting up of future goals, Carruthers' (2002) idea that humans are the only kinds of beings able to generate, and then reason with, novel suppositions or imaginary scenarios, and Crick & Koch's (1999, p. 324) claim that "conscious seeing" requires the brain's ability to "form a conscious representation of the visual scene that it then can use for many different actions or thoughts."

Third, scenario visualization emerged as a natural consequence of our evolutionary history, which includes the development of a complex nervous system in association with environmental pressures that occasioned the evolution of such a function. In attempts to recreate early hominin tools from the later Mousterian and Upper Paleolithic industries, archeologists like Mithen (1996, 2001) and Wynn (1979, 1981, 1991, 1993) have shown that the construction of such tools would require several mental visualizations, as well as numerous revisions of the material, so as to attain optimal performance of such tools. Such visualizations likely included the abilities to, at least, identify horizontal or vertical lines within a distracting frame, select an image from several possible choices, distinguish a target figure embedded in a complex background, construct an image of a future scenario, and project an image onto that future scenario, as well as recall from memory the particular goal of the project. If an advanced form of toolmaking acts as a mark of consciousness, then given the complex and changing Pleistocene environments, as well as the scenario visualization that is necessary to produce tools so as to survive these environments, what I am suggesting is that visual processing most likely was the primary way in which this consciousness emerged on the evolutionary scene (also see Arp, 2005a, 2006a, 2008c).

Scenario visualization is only one aspect of consciousness. There are several other aspects of consciousness, including self-awareness, intentionality, indexicality, and qualia-based, perceptual awareness (experience), to name just a few. Two paragraphs back, I mentioned Sternberg's (2001) idea that consciousness comprises the ability to form a belief or set up a goal that a human being can ultimately act upon. When one scenario visualizes in order to solve a problem, not only must one have some idea of the environment in which the solution to the problem presents itself but one must also have some idea of the *goal* to be achieved through solving the problem in that environment. My suggestion is that the aspect of conscious behavior regarding belief/goal formation works with the aspect of conscious behavior regarding scenario visualization in order to solve vision-related problems creatively. How do these two work together?

I believe these two aspects of conscious behavior mutually inform one another in a vision-related, problem solving process. In what follows, I elucidate elements of this conscious process. To start with, some visual cue causes one to form a belief regarding some goal to be achieved. The goal to be achieved then causes one to select visual images that *seem to be relevant* to the solution to the problem at hand. I say "seem to be relevant" because, at first, the images are not integrated or organized fully in one's mind. In other words, the solution utilizing the certain selected visual images is not seen clearly. This would be kind of like a *hunch* concerning the relevance of certain visual images to the solution of some problem. The integrative aspect of scenario visualization then goes to work, attempting a variety of possible visual scenarios through manipulating and adjusting the selected visual images. Again, this integration occurs against a backdrop of some kind of environment, since the solution to the problem must be believed to be relevant in some situation. Once a visual scenario comes into view clearly or is clarified in one's mind as being appropriate to solve some problem in an environment, the visual scenario then informs the goal that has been set up at the beginning of the entire process. A solution is then believed to be the accurate one to pursue, and the person sets out to actually solve the problem through constructing some tool, devising some plan, and so forth.

4.7   The Evolution of the Javelin and Scenario Visualization

In what follows, I trace the development of the multipurposed javelin from its meager beginnings as a stick, through the modification of the stick into the spear, to the specialization of the spear as a javelin equipped with a launcher. We need an example that illustrates the emergence of scenario visualization in our evolutionary past, and the development of this tool gives us concrete evidence of this emergence. The following story is meant to be presented as a plausible account of how it is that scenario visualization would have emerged in our early hominin past and, like all evolutionary stories, is not meant to be an account for which we have *decisive* evidence.

However, before proceeding, it is necessary to make some general points about the possibility of reconstructing early hominin environments and erecting hypotheses concerning hominin mental evolution. Researchers and thinkers doing work concerning the evolution of the human mind are in agreement with the fact that certain environmental selection forces were present in our early hominin past, and that these forces contributed to the mind's formation. Further, forming an accurate picture of what those selection forces were like is integral to our understanding of the mental mechanisms that have survived the process. At the same time, once we have an understanding of the environmental challenges faced by our early hominins, we can get a better picture of what our mental architecture has evolved to look like.

A common criticism leveled against thinkers who put forward accounts of the evolution of the human mind is that they too readily accept hypotheses concerning the adaptive pressures associated with our human mental architecture. As Gould & Vrba (1982) and Rose, Kamin, & Lewontin (1984) note, we must remember that a great deal of evolutionary hypothesizing comprises "just so" stories. Now, Laland & Brown (2002, p. 100) are correct to claim that "inventing evolutionary stories is a seductively easy exercise," and Barrett, Dunbar, & Lycett (2002, p. 10) are wise to point out that "we shouldn't extrapolate beyond the realms of our data." Nonetheless, these stories can become *well-informed* stories if we integrate several pieces of evidence and lines of inference from a variety of disciplines relevant to the mind and its evolution.

First, the geological evidence suggests that the environments in which our early hominin ancestors lived rapidly changed—*rapid* in the sense of hundred- or thousand-year intervals of wet, cold, hot, and dry climates as well as several combinations thereof.

Second, the archeological evidence of fossilized tools suggests that we had to have been able to do some fairly sophisticated problem solving in order to survive in these rapidly changing environments.

Third, the technological and psychological evidence associated with present-day human behavior indicates that we do some sophisticated problem solving in order to deal with novelty in our environments. One of the ways in which we deal with this novelty is through the construction of tools. If we are consistent in applying the Darwinian rule of common evolutionary heritage, then we can draw the inference—given the correlation between modern and fossilized tools—that our early hominins must have had to deal with novelty in their environments. Further, the variety and complexity of the tools used by certain early hominins suggests that they must have had a cognitive architecture similar to ours.

Fourth, we can make comparisons between human and primate brains and behaviors, and again, given the rule of common evolutionary heritage, we are justified in drawing certain conclusions about early hominin life.

Fifth, we can look to present-day peoples whose cultures, as far as we know, have not changed in hundreds or thousands of years and draw inferences concerning what our early hominin cultures might have been like. For example, it seems that the !Kung San peoples of the Kalahari desert, as well as the Australian Aborigines, exist in hunter–gatherer types of cultures that have been fairly stable for thousands of years (see Bahn, 1996). Further, Mithen (1996) and Oswalt (1976) document the Angmagsalik hunters of Greenland and their construction of harpoons utilized to hunt seals. Their harpoons are fairly complex, having a spearhead equipped with a line attached to a flotation device, as well as several other parts designed to make the harpoon sturdy, accurate, and easy to throw. These hunters are an interesting case because it is likely that their harpoon technology has not changed much in thousands of years; thus, their technology can be studied to get a sense of what some early hominin toolmaking may have been like.

The upshot is that we do not need to know *directly* what the early hominin environment looked like (obviously, we never will be able to!). Even though we are constrained by an inability to reconstruct such environments fully, we can get several clues from the combined input of biology, archeology, paleogeography, paleoanthropology, geology, evolutionary psychology, primatology, psychology, cognitive science, and neurobiology, to name just a few of the disciplines. However, we then must go about the business of presenting a coherent and systematic picture of these ancient worlds; thus, the well-informed storytelling. This is part of the business of offering a *philosophy* of biology, archeology, paleogeography, paleoanthropology, and so forth. After all, it is hypothesis formation that, in many ways, leads thinkers to discover new ideas, pieces of evidence, and ways to interpret data.

This having been said, I will now trace the development of the multipurposed javelin from its meager beginnings as a stick, through the modification of the stick into the spear, to the specialization of the spear as a javelin equipped with a launcher.

Step 1: The stick   As was noted already, we can take present-day chimpanzee activities to be representative of early hominin life, and we can see that chimps in their native jungle environments do indeed use tools. As was noted also, the chimps use rocks, leaves, and sticks to crack open nuts, carry items, fish for termites, and hit in self-defense or in attack. This is probably what our early hominins did while in the jungles of Africa as well.

The kind of activities chimps engage in when they use tools can be categorized as trial-and-error learning, or imitative learning. If we watch baby chimps, they try to imitate the actions of older chimps, including the usage of tools. Researchers have tried to get chimps to make tools to make other tools with cobbles and stones (the way in which early *Homo habilis* likely made tools to make tools) by flaking and edging, but they cannot do it (McGrew, 2004; Byrne, 1995, 2001; Tomasello et al., 1987, 1993). Thus, it seems that chimps form visual images and can even recall visual images from memory when they use tools. However, they clearly do not have the capacity to produce tools like those found in the Upper Paleolithic industry, let alone those found in the Mousterian, Acheulian, and Oldowan industries. Their tool *usage* merely is imitative and wholly lacking in innovation.

When the climate changed and our early hominins moved from the jungles to forage and kill food out on African savannas and other environments, they eventually constructed javelins that they could throw from a distance in order to kill prey. One could continue to hit prey or a predator with a stick until it dies, as was done in jungle environments. This may work for some prey and predators, but what about the ones that are much bigger than you? Imagine being stuck out on the savanna with a stick as your only tool of defense against wooly-mammoth-type and saber-toothed-tiger-type creatures. Stated simply, you would need to become more creative in your toolmaking just to survive. Calvin (2004, p. 25) asks a simple question related to the survival of our early hominins: "Could they innovate?" If the answer was *no*, then such hominins ultimately went the way of the dodo.

The progression from stick to thrown javelin went through its own evolution that is indicative of the advance from *cognitive* visual processing in terms of forming visual images to *conscious cognitive* visual processing in terms of scenario visualization. The kind of toolmaking that our early *Homo* ancestors engaged in was likely to be little more than trial-and-error or imitative learning that was passed on from generation to generation, the same way certain activities are passed on from one chimp generation to the next. Flakes were constructed. So too, sticks were constructed. Apparently, however, it never occurred to members of these species to place one of their flaked stones on the edge of a stick.

Step 2: The spear   By the end of the Mousterian industry, archaic *Homo heidelbergensis* and *Homo neandertalensis* were going through a three-step stone-forming process, allowing for the possibility that a variety of tools be constructed in the outcome. Also, such stone flakes were placed on the end of sticks as spears. The most basic step in constructing a stone tool has to do with simply striking a flake from a cobble. We have been able to get chimpanzees to imitate this behavior in captivity, but there is no evidence of apes in the wild performing this rudimentary procedure (McGrew, 2004; Griffin, 1992; Stanford, 2000).

Considering that our early hominin ancestors not only had to select certain materials that were appropriate to solve some problem but also engaged in a number of mental steps that resulted in the construction of a variety of tool types, it becomes apparent that a fairly advanced form of cognitive activity had to occur. The various steps in the process must be evaluated, and it may be the case that previous steps be seen in light of future steps. It does not seem that this kind of toolmaking could be performed by an animal with an inflexible and mechanical trial-and-error or imitative mental routine, because there are too many potential outcomes at every strike of the stone. Thus, Wynn (1993, pp. 396–397) claims that tool behavior "entails problem solving, the ability to adjust behavior to a specific task at hand, and, for this, rote sequences are not enough." This mental complexity has caused McNabb & Ashton (1995) to refer to our hominin toolmaking ancestors as "thoughtful flakers."

It is safe to say that the variety of tools constructed is evidence that these hominins were visualizing future scenarios in which these tools could be used; otherwise, *what would be the point of constructing a variety of tools in the first place?* Chimps use the same medium of sticks or rocks to either hit, throw, or smash. However, the construction of a variety of tools indicates that they have a variety of purposes. What is a purpose in this context, other than the formation of a visual image, the projection of that visual image onto some future scenario, and the intent to carry out or act on such a visualization? The variety of tools is the material result of purposive scenario visualization. Following Wynn, Mithen (1996, p. 36) notes that a mind with an ability to "think about hypothetical objects and events is absolutely essential for the manufacture of a stone tool like the hand axe. One must form a mental image of what the finished tool is to look like before starting to remove flakes from the stone nodule. Each strike follows from a hypothesis as to its effect on the shape of the tool."

Step 3: The javelin   Around 40,000 ya, some 80,000 years after the arrival of modern humans on the scene, we find evidence of a variety of types of javelins, spears, and javelin launchers. Archeologists like Mithen (1996) and Wynn (1979, 1981, 1991, 1993) have shown that the construction of a javelin would require several mental visualizations, as well as numerous revisions of the material, so as to attain optimal performance of such a tool. Different types of javelins with different shaped heads and shafts were constructed, depending upon the kind of kill or defense anticipated. If our early hominin ancestors tried simply to walk up to and hit a large animal, they likely would have been killed. In fact, this is probably what happened on more than one occasion to the early hominin who attempted to utilize a familiar problem solving solution in some totally new environment and subsequently failed. Eventually our ancestors, such as *Homo neandertalensis*, developed the spear; however, the evidence suggests that they could only develop spears and not javelins. *Homo sapiens* developed javelins, equipped with launchers, that could be used in creative ways to not only throw from a distance but also spear at close range, hack, and cut (Mithen, 1996; Wynn, 1991).

Again, when we consider that our early hominin ancestors not only had to select certain materials that were appropriate to solve some problem in a particular environment but utilized a diverse set of stone working techniques and went through a number of steps involving an array of stages that resulted in a variety of tool types, then it becomes apparent that a fairly advanced form of mental activity had to occur. Thus, the emergence of the javelin and its myriad uses would seem to indicate the presence of a different kind of mind that could creatively form, recall, readjust, select, and integrate visual scenes and scenarios for the purposes of producing tools that would enable one to survive and flourish in novel environments.

We must reiterate the importance of the effect that novel environments have on the brain. As I pointed out at the end of the third chapter, there is now solid evidence that the environment contributes to the formation and maintenance—even regrowth or co-opting—of neurons and neural processes in the brain. For example, it has been shown that neuronal size and complexity, as well as numbers of glial cells, increase in the cerebral cortices of animals exposed to so-called enriched environments, namely, environments where there are large cages and a variety of different objects that arouse curiosity and stimulate exploratory activity. Also, I noted that recent data suggest that regions of the brain can be trained, through mental and physical exercises, to pick up tasks from other regions.

The implications of synapse strengthening from environmental stimuli, as well as the ability of neuronal processes to perform alternate functions, are integral to an evolutionary explanation of conscious creative problem solving in humans. This so because the novel promotes unusual or extreme stimulation of cells, such stimulation of cells causes new connections to be made in the brain, new connections cause better response of the animal to external stimuli, and better response causes likelihood of survival so as to pass genes on to progeny.

Again, environment is only half of the two-sided biological coin that includes nurture (the environmental influence) *as well as* nature (the genetic influence). On the genetic side, chance mutations cause a trait—like the brain and consciousness that emerges from it—to come to be, this trait may be useful in some environment, the animal with that trait may survive to pass it on to its progeny, and this is an endless progressing cycle of genetic adjustment, readjustment, adjustment, readjustment, and so forth. It is wholly plausible that the mental properties necessary for creative problem solving evolved from this interplay of genes and a novel environment. Thus, Barlow (1994, p. 10) maintains: "Anything that improves the appropriateness and speed of learning must have immense competitive advantage, and the main point of this proposal is that it would explain the enormous selective advantage of the neocortex. Such an advantage, together with the appropriate genetic variability, could in turn account for its rapid evolution and the subsequent growth of our species to its dominant position in the world." This aforementioned information is significant to my hypothesis of scenario visualization because, given the novelty our early hominins dealt with in their environments, we can see how it would have been possible for newer connections between areas of the brain to have been made, as well as how wholly new connections could have arisen, acting as the neurobiological conditions for scenario visualization.

Given the concrete evidence of fossilized tools, Mithen (1996), Donald (1997), Sperber (1994), and Pinker (1997) speculate that *Homo sapiens* were clearly conscious, whereas *Australopithecines* clearly did not have consciousness. This is consistent with my claim that one aspect of consciousness involves scenario visualization and that such conscious cognitive visual processing emerged so as to enable the production of more complex tools.

Of course, our hominin ancestors were living in social groups, watching and learning from each other. I am not suggesting that scenario visualization occurs in some solipsistic vacuum. Just as with other primates, our ancestors would have learned a lot from trial and error, and various forms of imititative expression, in their social groups. At the same time, we can think of the proverbial "mad scientists" who might lock themselves away to work on some problem into which they have some insight. There are always those innovators who are present in some social group. My suggestion is that, somewhere between the close of the Mousterian and the beginning of the Upper Paleolithic industries, the brains of our hominin ancestors were fortunate enough, through genetic variability, to have the right connections in their neural hardware so as to allow for the possibility of scenario visualization. With these *neural* connections already in place, all that was needed was some environmental cue to prompt the *psychological* connections, inferences, and insights to be made. All it took was some psychologically creative "good trick" (to use the words of Dennett, 1995)— implemented, possibly, by even one hominin—to get the creative juices flowing, so to speak, and prompt scenario visualization in our hominin ancestry. I would imagine that there would have been a complex interplay of trial-and-error and creative learning and implementation occurring in our hominin lineage with respect to negotiating environments, just as there is today. Still, at some point, at least one of our hominin ancestors had to have broken from the trial-and-error mode of thinking so as to begin scenario visualizing.

To reiterate, through the fortunes of genetic variability and natural selection, the brains of our hominin ancestors would have had to have all the right neural connections in place to allow for the possibility of scenario visualization. In other words, the wiring was all there and hooked up, and the right switch just needed to be pulled. The hominins were living in social groups, learning from each other and implementing behaviors through trail-and-error and imitation. Some environmental cue prompted a psychological response that actually utilized the neural connections—a switch was pulled that allows for a response in terms of scenario visualization. This good trick was just that, a *useful device* for handling certain vision-related problems encountered by our ancestors, and the ones who could utilize it survived so as to pass their genes and memes (trial-and-error kinds as well as more innovative kinds) on to the next generation. And those of us in our species living today still retain this capacity.

4.8   Scenario Visualization: The Psychological Evidence

Thus far in this chapter, my primary aim has been to describe how it is that our early hominin ancestors evolved scenario visualization. However, since modern humans evolved from early hominins, it is important that I present evidence that this conscious activity occurs in our present-day species. Support for my suggestion that scenario visualization occurs in our species, and is a form of conscious behavior, comes from two broad areas of evidence. The first is psychological evidence derived from case studies, interviews, introspective reports, and biographical studies of people who either are involved in controlled problem solving experiments or who have exhibited creativity in terms of their livelihood as inventors, artists, theorists, and the like. The second is neurobiological evidence derived from studies on monkeys as they perform simple problem solving exercises and from PET and fMRI scans of humans performing simple mental tasks such as forming mental images, recalling images in memory, and engaging in future planning as well as performing more advanced problem solving exercises.

Many people report using visual images to answer questions and solve problems in controlled experiments. Answering a question as simple as, How many traffic lights are there at the end of your street? or solving a problem such as lining up balls on pegs, in a certain way, in the least amount of moves—as in the Tower of London test—can involve the utilization of mental pictures (see Tye, 1991; Shallice, 1988; Beveridge & Parkins, 1987). In fact, as Finke, Ward, & Smith (1992, p. 45) point out, "there is considerable evidence that much of our everyday thinking is based on the formation and transformation of visual images." This makes sense given the visual animals we are, and in the words of Tye (1991, p. 59), "Just as it is much easier to see whether three cities lie on a straight line by looking at a map than by performing calculations on a list of descriptions of their longitudes and latitudes, so too it is often much easier to construct and examine a mental map or quasi-picture than it is to proceed in any other way."

In one experiment put together by Shephard & Metzler (1971), people were shown 1,600 pairs of Rubik's-cubish-looking three-dimensional block figures and then asked whether they were congruent with one another or not (if you have ever taken a battery of IQ tests, then you may remember a similar spatial manipulation test). People reported that, in order to answer the question, they needed to form mental images of the block figures and then manipulate and rotate them around in a variety of scenarios against a variety of imagined backgrounds "in their minds" and/or "in their heads" (also see Shephard & Cooper, 1992; Kosslyn, 1980, 1996; Gregory, 1997).

The Tower of Hanoi puzzle was invented by the French mathematician Edouard Lucas in 1883 and has been used by researchers in problem solving experiments with humans (Simon, 1975). In the puzzle, the subject is given a tower of eight disks, initially stacked in increasing size on one of three pegs. The objective is to transfer the entire tower to one of the other pegs, moving only one disk at a time and never moving a larger disk onto a smaller one. Neth & Payne (2003) report that while subjects engaged in the Tower of Hanoi experiment, the moves were used to plan ahead, indicating that the subjects were visualizing possible scenarios. They noted that, rather than "learning by doing," subjects meticulously utilized "online planning" of one move to the next.

Further, when children begin to pretend, they set up visual scenarios and then suppose themselves to be in the scenario. They pretend that bananas are phones while an important business call is being made, or they simulate teatime occurring with stuffed animals all around a table

(Jarrold, Carruthers, Smith, & Boucher, 1994; Nichols & Stich, 2000; Harris, 2000). Also, the drawing of pictures to express situations, scenarios, and circumstances appears to be integral to the developing psyche of a child, and children instinctively will engage in such activity (Richert & Lillard, 2002). Picture drawing resonates with early hominin cave painting and other forms of pictorial representation (Eshleman, 2003).

As Arnheim (1969) makes clear, not only is visual imagery necessary for childhood development but it is arguable that the very elements of reasoning—thoughts, concepts, abstractions, and words—require visual imagery and the further use of that imagery in creative and imaginative ways. Kosslyn & Koenig (1995, p. 146) bolster this argument when they maintain that visual imagery is integral to reasoning and that "using imagery to reason involves not only inspecting objects and generating them, but also transforming objects in imagery and retaining images long enough to work with them." Reasoning itself can be viewed as the ability to either solve novel problems, manipulate several disparate concepts simultaneously, or deal adaptively with a complex and changing environment (see the papers in Sternberg, 1998, 1999, 2001; Sternberg & Frensch, 1991; Sternberg & Kaufmann, 2002). When viewed in this way, reasoning could require the use of visual images in a variety of ways, against a variety of imagined backgrounds, and in a variety of visually imagined scenarios.

Finke et al. (1992) recount a test utilized by McKim (1980) called the *monk problem*. In the problem, subjects are told that a monk walks a path to the top of a mountain to meditate, stays overnight, and then descends the mountain the next day. Subjects then are asked the question as to whether the monk was ever at the same place on his path, at exactly the same time of day, on both days. As Finke et al. (1992, p. 175) point out, the solution to the problem "becomes obvious by visualizing the monk simultaneously ascending and descending the mountain. Since there must be a point at which he would 'meet' himself, such a place must indeed exist."

McKim's problem along with the Tower of Hanoi puzzle and the experiment put together by Shephard & Metzler are examples that are representative of the various kinds of problem solving exercises people engage in on a regular basis either in think tanks, brainstorming sessions, analysis of problems on the GRE exam, even figuring out where to place a new couch in one's living room. People find themselves constantly constructing visual images and future scenarios—either in one's mind, or on paper, or on a chalkboard—and then transforming, moving, shifting, rotating, and/or manipulating the images around in order to visualize a solution to the problem (Huttenlocher, 1968; Meyer, 1989; Prince, 1970).

The scenario visualization hypothesis I have been putting forward comports well with what is known as the *pictorialist* approach, whereby mental images are understood as pictures in the mind. This approach to images has been put forward by Kosslyn (1980, 1983, 1996), Kosslyn et al. (2001), Marr (1983), Pinker (1984), and Finke & Pinker (1982). In their human studies, Finke & Pinker (1982) have argued that images are generated from three-dimensional representations of the spatial relationships and appearances of parts of objects in the visual field. Such images may be stored in one's memory, filed away like slides or photographs that can be recalled spontaneously or by certain stimulus cues, if necessary. We should note that the visual image that is immediately constructed in the visual field, as well as the memory of such an image, are both understood as pictorial representations. Tye (1991) traces this idea back to Aristotle (1941, 427b19): "For imagining lies within our power whenever we wish, e.g., we can call up a picture, as in the practice of mnemonics by the use of mental images." Kosslyn et al. (2001, p. 635) have referred to visual mental imagery as "giving rise to the experience of 'seeing with the mind's eye.'"

Someone may object at this point that not everyone visualizes when they solve problems, and/or that blind persons, who cannot visualize in the way I have defined the term, surely have the ability to solve problems. I will respond to these two points.

First, it seems implausible that no one *ever* visualizes when trying to solve a problem. There is a debate concerning whether people use visual images or some other form of semantic reasoning when they solve problems (e.g., Pylyshyn, 2003; Kosslyn, 1996; Tye, 1991). I am not suggesting that people *always* visualize or *never* use semantic forms of reasoning, or other forms of reasoning, when solving problems. I simply am pointing out that there exists this capacity to scenario visualize in our species as a whole and that, at times, people utilize it to solve problems in innovative ways. In fact, whether one utilizes scenario visualization most likely will depend upon the type of problem with which one is confronted. There are some problems—for example, certain mathematical problems—that can be solved without the use of scenario visualization. Other problems, like spatial relation or depth perception problems, may require scenario visualization. The kinds of problems with which our early hominin ancestors were confronted *most likely were of the spatial relation and depth relation types*, and so the capacity to scenario visualize would have been useful for their survival. Our early hominin ancestors were not solving math equations; they were negotiating environments primarily with the use of their visual systems.

Second, I am trying to give an account of how it is that *the human species as a whole, with their visual systems intact*, evolved the ability to solve *vision-related* problems. Thus, my account skirts the issue of a blind person's capacity to solve problems because such a person does not have an intact visual system and so does not solve vision-related problems. Blind persons assuredly have the capacity to solve problems in sophisticated and innovative ways. Louis Braille, the man who invented Braille as a means for blind persons to communicate information with the usage of bumps on pieces of paper, is a prime example (see Davidson, 1971). However, he obviously could not scenario visualize (maybe he could scenario *tactilize?*). The human species *as a whole* has evolved the capacity to engage in scenario visualization, even though *certain members* of our species do not have this capacity because of blindness. This makes sense, since humans, in general, are not coded genetically for blindness—they are coded for sight.

4.9 Scenario Visualization: The Neurobiological Evidence

Earlier, I noted that the neural wiring necessary for scenario visualization would had to have been in place in our species by 40,000 ya. The neurobiological evidence for scenario visualization begins with the fact that the brain is wired in such a way that this activity can occur. The visual system is intimately tied to memory, planning, and motor systems in the brain. Studies have shown that the prefrontal region contains a complete map of the contralateral visual field. This map can be used for visual short-term and working memory, as Finke (1986) and Goldman-Rakic (1996) have demonstrated (also see Smith, Jonides, & Koeppe, 1996; Smith & Jonides, 1997). Recall from the last chapter that iconic memory is necessary to hold a percept in our visual field long enough for the information it conveys to be processed by the visual system. Recordings from the dorsolateral prefrontal cortex of adult monkeys have shown that some neurons respond only when spatial information had to be stored, while other neurons responded only when visual-object information had to be maintained briefly, as Funahashi, Bruce, & Goldman-Rakic (1989) and Wilson et al. (1993) report.

Also, we know that visual attention requires subcortical structures such as the pulvinar, claustrum, and superior colliculus, as well as the prefrontal cortex (Farah, 1984; Kandel et al., 2000). Visual awareness and planning involve the frontal cortices, which receive projections from the higher, specialized visual areas, such as V4 and V5. The dorsolateral prefrontal cortex receives projections from the posterior parietal cortex (part of the *where* visual trajectory), and the ventrolateral prefrontal cortex receives projections from the IT cortex (part of the *what* visual trajectory). The dorsolateral prefrontal cortex integrates multimodal sensory information and is involved in the generation of hypotheses, planning, goal direction, and the deployment of strategies (Fuster, 1997; Passingham, 1993).

We know that areas of the brain involved in problem solving also involve the visual system. For example, Dehaene & Changeux (1989, 1991, 1997, 2000) have reported that damage to the dorsolateral and ventrolateral prefrontal areas associated with problem solving cause memory loss, delayed responses, and loss of attention. These same prefrontal areas receive projections from the *what* and the *where* visual systems. Thus, these patients can determine the *what* and the *where* of objects they are looking at, but they have problems utilizing these visual images in possible visual scenarios.

Further, the prefrontal cortex is part of the heteromodal association cortex, which includes part of the superior temporal and inferior parietal cortices. These regions are all linked in a cognitive network that controls executive functions, attention, social interaction, language, working memory, and future planning. They also link to limbic areas and so play a primary role in drive, mood, and personality. The prefrontal cortex is really the seat of all distinctively human characteristics and is the latest evolutionary installment (MacLean, 1967). Note that these areas are involved in memory and future planning. Again, such activities would require, at times, the formation of visual images and scenario visualization. It is arguable that future planning is nothing other than the generation of visual images, possibly from memory (which could take the cognitive form of another visual image), and the projecting of these images into possible visual scenarios for the purpose of achieving some goal, solving some problem, or negotiating some environment (Weisberg, 1995).

Kosslyn et al. (1999a, 1999b, 2001) used fMRI and transcranial magnetic stimulation tests to identify regions that were active during visual imagery. Subjects were shown a complex series of stimuli and then were asked to close their eyes to make judgments about what they had just seen. Kosslyn et al. found that V1, which is normally active during visual perception, is active during visual imagery as well. Imagining objects in the mind seems similar to inspecting an object in the world and *would appear to draw on the same underlying neurological processes*. Such results should not appear surprising, since imagery, like vision, can be a helpful guide in the world.

An animal that could visualize moves before actually making them could be in a much better position to succeed in feeding, fighting, mating, and so forth. As Sekuler & Blake (2002, p. 248) claim, "Imagery makes it possible for us to envision the consequences of some behavior without actually going through the motions."

The visual system interacts with many other parts of the brain and nervous system, making for a complex ensemble in which visual cognition and human action are linked. Many brain regions contribute to efficient behavior—toolmaking, socializing, or otherwise. The prefrontal cortex plays a major executive and supervisory role in the intelligent development of behavior (Joffe & Dunbar, 1997; Passingham, 1993; Fuster, 1997). The premotor cortex selects movement sequences that are contextually appropriate and, along with the basal ganglia, releases them through the primary motor cortex. The cerebellum handles the automatized and timed coordination of individual muscles. Sherwood et al. (2003) have argued that Meynert cells of the primary visual cortex and Betz cells of the primary motor cortex may have evolved together because their axons and dendrites make multiple synaptic connections and, hence, play an important role in the integration of sensorimotor information. This would make sense from an evolutionary perspective, since negotiation of space by an arboreal dweller, such as a monkey, requires the interaction of vision and manual dexterity. In the words of Churchland, Barlow, Ramachandran, & Sejnowski (1994, pp. 59–60): "Obviously visual systems evolved not for the achievement of sophisticated visual perception as an end in itself, but because visual perception can serve motor control and motor control can serve vision to better serve motor control, and so on. What evolution 'cares about' is who survives, and that means, basically, who excels in the four Fs: feeding, fleeing, fighting and reproducing."

The impression one gets when considering the relationship of the wiring of the visual system to other systems of the brain and nervous system is that it is one "big smear," to use the words of Calvin (1998, p. 64). Kandel et al. (2000, pp. 365–366) remind us that "no part of the nervous system functions in the same way alone as it does in concert with other parts. . . . It is unlikely, therefore, that the neural basis of any cognitive function— thought, memory, perception, and language—will be understood by focusing on one region of the brain without considering the relationship of that region to the others." It is true that the visual system makes direct and indirect connections with virtually every major area in the brain. *However, this only serves to bolster my point that visualizing is integral in the emergence of the most complex brain processes.* Whether one is constructing tools, rethinking how to handle the next interpersonal conflict better, plotting a route through the Rockies, or organizing a poster presentation, one has the potential to be scenario visualizing.

In this chapter, I traced the evolution of the visual system, beginning with organisms that developed a light/dark sensitivity area and culminating in the complex activities involved in an aspect of conscious visual processing that I call scenario visualization. I did this utilizing the anatomical evidence from fossils and living species thought to be homologous to ancient species. I also used evidence from ancient toolmaking techniques, since the evolution of tools and tool types would seem to parallel the evolution from noncognitive visual processing, through cognitive visual processing, to scenario visualization, a form of conscious cognitive visual processing. I defined scenario visualization as a conscious process that entails selecting pieces of visual information from a wide range of possibilities, forming a coherent and organized visual cognition, and then projecting that visual cognition into some suitable imagined scenario for the purpose of solving some problem posed by the environment that one inhabits.

Further, I traced the development of the multipurposed javelin from its meager beginnings as a stick, through the modification of the stick into the spear, to the specialization of the spear as a javelin equipped with a launcher. I did this because an explanation was needed of how scenario visualization emerged in our evolutionary past, and this tool is illustrative of this emergence that tells a concrete evolutionary story. Finally, I presented evidence that scenario visualization occurs at a conscious level in our present-day species. As I showed, support for my suggestion that scenario visualization occurs in our species, and is a form of conscious behavior, comes from two broad areas of evidence, namely, psychological and neurobiological evidence.

In the next chapter, I further explicate the notions of routine problem solving and nonroutine creative problem solving, as well as show how scenario visualization fits into the evolutionary psychologist's schematization of the mind to form a more complete picture of how it is that humans evolved the ability to solve vision-related, nonroutine creative problems.

5 Scenario Visualization, Creative Problem Solving, and Evolutionary Psychology

5.1 Routine and Nonroutine Forms of Problem Solving

The construction of novel tools, as much as language, characterizes our apparent human uniqueness among species in the animal kingdom. We are the only species that has evolved the ability to fashion Velcro, construct microchips, and send folks to the moon, all of which have involved solving vision-related problems in creative ways. In the previous chapter, I presented evidence of advanced forms of toolmaking in our hominin past—specifically, those that began at the end of the Mousterian industry—that require a mind having the capacity to scenario visualize. Considering that our early hominin ancestors not only had to select certain materials that were appropriate to solve some problem but also engaged in a number of mental steps that resulted in the construction of a variety of tool types, it becomes apparent that a fairly advanced form of cognitive activity had to occur. I suggested that advanced forms of toolmaking require scenario visualization, a conscious visual processing whereby visual images are selected and integrated, then subsequently transformed and projected in visual scenarios for the purposes of negotiating environments. I also suggested that scenario visualization emerged as a natural consequence of our evolutionary history, which includes the development of a complex nervous system in association with environmental pressures that occasioned the evolution of such a conscious activity. If an advanced form of toolmaking acts as a mark of conscious behavior, then given the complex and changing Pleistocene environments that our hominin ancestors inhabited, as well as the production of novel tools so as to survive these environments, visual processing most likely was the primary way in which this consciousness emerged on the evolutionary scene.

The toolmaking processes in which our early hominins were engaged—which researchers like Mithen, Wynn, and Pelegrin have been able to simulate—act as a microcosm example of the obstacles human beings face on a regular basis. Not only do human beings manufacture things but they successfully negotiate environments, invent, thrive, dominate the planet, and solve all kinds of vision-related problems in creative ways. Some of this problem solving is automatic and goes on unbeknownst to us. For example, we react quickly to, and at times successfully negotiate, certain situations where fighting or fleeing are called for. Many confrontations with bears have been avoided by campers in one of a variety of methods, either by waving their arms, hollering, banging canteens, curling up in the fetal position, or climbing up a tree (Kaniut, 1997). When asked about why they chose their particular method, these folks normally respond, "I don't know . . . it was automatic."

On the other hand, some of this problem solving is slower and more deliberate, requiring us to be consciously aware of the goal of our endeavor, the potential pitfalls, and the possible "plan Bs" that may have to be pursued. In the introduction to this text, I used Mayer's (1995) terms and drew a distinction between routine problem solving and nonroutine creative problem solving. In *routine* problem solving, a person recognizes many possible solutions to a problem, given that the problem was solved through one of those solutions in the past. People constantly perform routine problem solving activities that are concrete and basic to their survival such as pursue goals that have been established, form think tanks to troubleshoot regarding product placement, gather with their girlfriends at Starbucks to plan successful Halloween parties for their children, devise committees to update school curriculums, and meet with counselors to talk about how best to carry out an intervention.

We also can engage in activities that are more abstract and creative, such as invent new tools based upon mental blueprints, synthesize concepts that, at first glance, seemed wholly disparate or unrelated, and devise novel solutions to problems. If a person decided to pursue a *wholly new way* to solve a problem by, say, inventing some kind of tool, then we would have an instance of *nonroutine creative* problem solving. Nonroutine creative problem solving involves finding a solution to a problem that has not been solved previously. The invention of a tool would be an example of nonroutine creative problem solving because the inventor did not possess a way to solve the problem already. The significant question—the one to which I have been trying to respond throughout this book—becomes, How is it that humans are able to engage in vision-related forms of nonroutine creative problem solving?

In this chapter, I present the ideas and arguments put forward by evolutionary psychologists such as Cosmides, Tooby, and Mithen that the mind evolved certain capacities to solve problems creatively. Specifically, Cosmides & Tooby (1987, 1992, 1994) think that the complex activities in which the human mind can be engaged—such as those that result in complex problem solving, the construction of novel tools, artwork, and analogy—are the result of specified mental modules having evolved in our early hominin Pleistocene past to deal with the various and sundry problems a human may experience. Mithen (1996, 1999, 2001) shows the deficiency in this position and makes an advance upon Cosmides & Tooby's idea by arguing that problem solving, the novel construction of tools, artwork, and the like are possible because the mind has evolved *cognitive fluidity*, an ability to exchange information flexibly between and among the mental modules. In fact, according to Mithen, cognitive fluidity *is* what is meant by consciousness, our uniquely human ability.

While I agree with Mithen that cognitive fluidity acts as a necessary condition for vision-related, creative problem solving, I disagree that cognitive fluidity alone will suffice for such an activity. Cognitive fluidity allows for the flexible exchange of information among mental modules. However, since Mithen's description of the mind makes it out to be a passive thing, I transform Mithen's account by arguing that, while it may be true that the flexible exchange of information between and among mental modules is a feature of consciousness, conscious abilities to select, integrate, transform, and project information from mental modules into imagined visual scenarios—in terms of scenario visualization—are what account for vision-related, nonroutine creative problem solving. In essence, my hypothesis regarding scenario visualization is an advance upon Mithen's account of cognitive fluidity, which itself (Mithen's account) is an advance upon Cosmides & Tooby's model of the mind as being composed of encapsulated mental modules (also see Arp, 2005a, 2006a, 2008c).

5.2 Modularity and Evolutionary Psychology

In previous chapters, I noted that brains—as well as organisms in general—are hierarchically organized structures composed of components. These components are engaged in specialized processes that form subsystems, and these subsystems interact with one another at various levels in the organismic hierarchy, producing particularized and generalized homeostasis. Also, I endorsed the idea that these processes and subsystems function the way they do because of their role in the organization of the whole organism and the fact that they were selected for in their evolutionary past. From these realities of the brain concerning its hierarchical organization, specialized processing, and evolution, we can infer at least three things about human psychology.

First, psychological states are emergent properties that are the results of brain states; they may not be reducible to brain states, but they are certainly dependent upon brain state processes (Baars & Newman, 2001; Bisiach, 1999; Kim, 2000). If there is any doubt about this, one need only peruse any textbook or journal devoted to the human brain's workings and read about the effects of brain damage upon the psychology of a person. For example, without the normal functioning of the prefrontal cortex, individuals are not able to make plans, nor are they able to carry out the behavior necessary to fulfill those plans (Fuster, 1997; Passingham, 1993). Also, as Finke (1980) has demonstrated, damage to the prefrontal cortex causes a person to be unable to store short-term memories. Further, damage to the limbic system can cause certain autisms and other emotional dysfunctions (Bauman & Kemper, 1994).

Concerning my endorsement of psychological states as emergent properties of the brain, as I stated in the third chapter, just as the components at various levels of neurobiological and biological hierarchies—such as organelles, cells, tissues, and organs—cannot be reduced to the physicochemical parts of which they are composed, so too, various forms of visual cognition, although dependent upon neurobiological processes, are not reducible to such processes. Again, the main reason why psychological phenomena are nonreducible to neurobiological phenomena is the same reason why neurobiological and biological components are nonreducible to the physicochemical parts of which they are composed, namely, such components and phenomena emerge as a result of the way in which they are organized to do something directly related to generalized homeostasis of the organism. The psychological dimension associated with the brain's activities can be considered as another level of emergent phenomena added to the hierarchy. This is so because cognition appears to be organized in such a way as to aid an animal in discriminating information in environments so as to fight, flee, feast, forage, and so forth. However, the kind of end result or end product of cognition—although similar to other activities in the animal's hierarchy in having generalized homeostasis as the goal—is different in that such a product is a *psychological* phenomenon that aids in generalized homeostasis.

Second, given the localization and massive, specialized parallel processing of the brain, we can infer that there are a variety of specialized psychological states that are dependent upon these processes as well. Damage to certain areas of the brain yield specific psychological deficits. For example, damage to Wernicke's area causes one to be unable to comprehend language, damage to V5 causes one to be unable to perceive depth accurately, and damage to the IT cortex causes one to be unable to recognize faces. It may not be the case that *all* motor and cognitive abilities are localized, but we have evidence that many neurobiological processes, and the psychological phenomena that emerge from them, are dependent upon specific areas of the brain.

Third, given that the brain is an organ, it is subject to the same evolutionary principles as any other biological entity. The brain functions the way it does because of fortunate genetic mutations, in combination with environments, that occasioned its selection as a trait most fit for the animal. By inference, if psychological states are the results of brain states, and brain states are subject to evolutionary principles, then it is likely that psychological states are subject to evolutionary principles. The three points just mentioned are significant to the science of *evolutionary psychology*.

All evolutionary psychologists posit that evolution is responsible not only for human physiology and anatomy but also for certain human psychological and behavioral characteristics that evolved in our past to solve specific problems of survival (Buss, 1999; Cosmides & Tooby, 1992, 1994; Pinker, 1994, 2002; Shettleworth, 2000; Gardner, 1993; Sternberg, 1988; Wilson, 2003; Scher & Rauscher, 2003; Plotkin, 1997; Palmer & Palmer, 2002; also see the relevant papers in Arp & Ayala, 2008; Arp & Rosenberg, 2008). The logic here is straightforward and is consistent with the definition of function as a recent evolutionary development I endorsed in the second chapter, as well as with the evolutionary principles of genetic variability and natural selection mentioned in the previous chapter. Traits (e.g., organs, capacities, or behaviors) develop in evolutionary history to function as a result of chance mutations and the natural selection of the trait that is most fit, given the environment in which the trait exists. For example, eyes developed in order to see food, prey, mate, or predator; webbed appendages developed to allow an organism to swim more efficiently; and physiological systems in the body developed to serve each specific end—digestion, circulation, and so forth—with the greater and overall end of survival and reproduction. Just as other traits developed functions in some specified evolutionary history, so too, the human brain has developed the certain functions it performs in simply reacting to the information presented to it in an environment, as well as giving rise to a conscious feature that interprets, integrates, and makes decisions with respect to this information.

The brain, then, is envisioned as having evolved certain psychological *modules* (Fodor, 1983; Pinker, 1997, 2002), *intelligences* (Gardner, 1993), or *domains* (Cosmides & Tooby, 1992, 1994; Hirschfeld & Gelman, 1994) that, in the words of Cosmides & Tooby (1992, p. 34), are "specialized for solving evolutionary long-enduring adaptive problems and ... these mechanisms have content-specialized representational formats, procedures, cues, and so on." Some of these mental modules, like those associated with rudimentary phoneme and object recognition, are considered *domain specific*, since they are devoted to solving one particular kind of adaptive problem. Other modules—or possibly, just one huge module—are considered *domaingeneral*, since they are devoted to solving any number of adaptive problems. *General intelligence* is the term used most often to describe the domain-general feature of the mind. According to Wheeler & Atkinson (2001, p. 242), *adaptive problems* are "problems that are specifiable in terms of evolutionary selection pressures, i.e., recurring environmental conditions that affect, or have affected, the reproductive success of individual organisms." Thus, Pinker (1997, p. 27) claims that the mind "is not a single organ but a system of organs, which we can think of as psychological faculties or mental modules ... intelligent behavior is learned successfully because we have innate systems that do the learning"—such systems having evolved to deal with adaptive problems in our early hominin past.

These psychological modules/domains/intelligences are caused by, but not wholly reducible to, modules or areas of the brain. Here, we must keep in mind the distinction between a *psychological* or *mental* module that is caused by, but not reducible to, a *neurophysiological* or *brain-process* module or area. Thankfully, researchers will use the term *area* when specifically referring to a neurophysiological process, as opposed to a psychological process (Hermer & Spelke, 1996; Kaas, 1993; Karmiloff-Smith, 1992; Shallice, 1997; Bruno & Cutting, 1988).

According to evolutionary psychologists, the brain is represented as a host of modules, some of which are located in a single area (e.g., Broca's area for grammar–usage), while others are dispersed over the entire cortex. Brain-process modules can be viewed as nested within hierarchies, whereby larger modules coordinate information from smaller modules, which themselves coordinate information from still smaller modules, and so forth. The *what* system I spoke about in the third chapter works this way. We can think of this system as one big module made up of smaller modules; V1 is the smaller module responsible for initial visual processing, V2 is the smaller module responsible for stereo vision, and V4 is the smaller module responsible for color. In this way, as Marr (1983) intimates, early vision is a distinct *capital-M* module made up of *smaller-m* modules.

It is at the higher ends of certain brain-process modular hierarchies—for example, the dorsolateral prefrontal cortex, which integrates multimodal sensory information and is involved in the generation of hypotheses, planning, goal direction, and the deployment of strategies—where the psychological modules *clearly* have emerged. Because of brain-process and psychological modules interacting with environments for thousands— perhaps even millions—of years, evolutionary psychologists think that psychological modules specialized in their particular performances to deal with the various challenges posed by the environments in which our hominin ancestors lived.

5.3 Narrow Evolutionary Psychology and the Emergence of Modularity

However, there is a debate among evolutionary psychologists as to (1) the type and number of mental modules the human mind contains, (2) the exact time period or time periods when these mental modules were solidi- fied in the early hominin psyche, and (3) whether these mental modules have arisen directly through adaptation, or indirectly as an evolutionary side effect/by-product through exaptation (as in Gould & Vrba's, 1982, *spandrels*), or even through some form of cultural evolution.

Scher & Rauscher (2003) and Wilson (2003) have drawn a distinction between what they call *narrow* evolutionary psychology (NEP) and *broad* evolutionary psychology (BEP). Advocates of NEP follow the groundbreak- ing work of Cosmides & Tooby (1987, 1992, 1994), arguing that the mind is like a Swiss Army knife loaded with specific mental *tools* that evolved in our Pleistocene past to solve specific problems of survival, such as face recognition, mental mapping, intuitive mechanics, intuitive biology, kinship, language acquisition, mate selection, and detection of cheaters (the list could be longer or shorter; cf. Palmer & Palmer, 2002; Buss, 1999; Pinker, 1994, 1997, 2002; Gardner, 1993; Shettleworth, 2000).

In response to (1)–(3), adherents to NEP argue that (1) the mind is a host of specialized, domain-*specific* mental modules, (2) the Pleistocene epoch is *the* time period in which the basic psychological structure of the modern human mind was solidified in our genetic makeup, and (3) these modules have arisen directly through *specific adaptive problems* that early hominins faced.

In contrast to NEP, advocates of BEP consider alternative approaches to Cosmides & Tooby's Pleistocene-epoch-forming, Swiss Army knife model of the mind and want to argue that (1) the mind probably does not contain the myriad of specialized, domain-specific mental modules that the NEPers would have us believe but relies more upon domain-*general* mental capacities that have evolved to handle the various and sundry problems a human faces (Samuels, 1998; Wheeler & Atkinson, 2001; Laland & Brown, 2002), (2) although the Pleistocene epoch is a significant time period in our evolutionary past, it is by no means a *single* environment, nor is it the *only* environment that has shaped the modern mind (Foley, 1995; Boyd & Silk, 1997; Daly & Wilson, 1999), and (3) this mental architecture probably has evolved through adaptive, *as well as* exaptative and cultural forms of evolutionary processes (Barrett, Dunbar, & Lycett, 2002; Laland & Brown, 2002; Otto, Christiansen, & Feldman, 1995; Buller, 2005).

All evolutionary psychologists are in agreement with the fact that certain environmental selection forces were present in our early hominin past and that these forces contributed to the mind's formation. It seems, then, that forming an accurate picture of what those selection forces were like is integral to our understanding of the mental mechanisms that have survived the process. At the same time, once we have an understanding of the environmental challenges faced by our early hominins, we can get a better picture of what our mental architecture has evolved to look like.

Part of what I will do in this chapter is to try and adjudicate between NEP and BEP by utilizing Mithen's idea of cognitive fluidity and my account of scenario visualization that is rooted in problem solving tasks our early hominins would have faced in their environments (also see Arp, 2006a, 2007a). After a presentation of Cosmides & Tooby's NEP approach, as contrasted with one BEP approach put forward by Mithen, I will develop my account of scenario visualization further so as to get a more accurate picture of our mental architecture and the conditions that occasioned its evolution.

The fossil and paleogeographic evidence suggests that speciation (the formation of new species) occurs at times of rapid, *punctuated* environmental change, rather than during periods of relative stability (Gould, 1977, 2002; Eldredge, 2001; Calvin, 1998, 2001, 2004; Potts, 1996). Advocates of NEP wager that primate evolution is no different and took place against a rapidly changing climatic and geographic background. Global climates have changed greatly during the past 60 my, and especially in the past 20 my. Overall, the world's climate has become cooler and more seasonal, with less forestation, more deserts, and more ice on its surface. The key period of climatic change that occasioned the evolution of mental modularity was around 2.5 mya, just prior to the Pleistocene epoch, when there was a global shift from warm and wetter to cooler and drier conditions. The climate during the time period just prior to the Pleistocene exhibited more unpredictability than it had in the past, "flip-flopping"—a term Calvin (1996) uses—from warm, to hot, to cool, to dry, to warm and dry, to cool and dry, and so forth. In Africa, Europe, Asia, and North America, given the newer environmental niches, species of animals and plants appeared in bursts (Dawkins, 2005; Eldredge, 2001; Calvin, 1998).

In the midst of all of the climate change, new food sources, and different species emerging on the scene, Cosmides & Tooby (1994, p. 90) tell us that "simply to survive and reproduce, our Pleistocene ancestors had to be good at solving an enormously broad array of adaptive problems—problems that would defeat any modern artificial intelligence system." The analogy to a computer is appropriate. Generalized computer programs equipped with step-by-step algorithmic processing perform slowly and fail to perform the simplest of tasks that even earthworms can perform, like negotiating a maze. However, parallel processing computer mechanisms fare much better in terms of learning and negotiating environments (see Cziko, 1995; French & Sougne, 2001; Lek & Guegan, 2000; Lerman & Rudolph, 1994).

In their experiments comparing general-purpose computational mechanisms and parallel processing computational mechanisms, Rumelhart & McClelland (1985) have shown that the rate at which general-purpose mechanisms process multiple pieces of disparate information is much slower than that of parallel processing mechanisms. This is so because the general-purpose mechanisms have to work longer and harder at cataloguing, categorizing, and then storing the disparate pieces of information, whereas the parallel units are composed of processors that are specialized to recognize a particular piece of information and work simultaneously (thus, the *parallel* processing) to store information (also see Roosta, 1999; Copeland, 1993; Searle, 1992; Fodor, 2001; Churchland, 1986; McFarland & Bosser, 1993). Further tests performed by Connell (1989), Brooks (1991), and Franceschini, Pichon, & Blanes (1992) have shown that parallel processing robotic mechanisms have a quicker and easier time of collecting Coke cans from around MIT labs or navigating to some light source than do general-purpose kinds of robotic mechanisms. In the words of Culler & Singh (1999, p. 4), "whatever the performance of a single processor at a given time, higher performance can, in principle, be achieved by utilizing many such processors."

Evolutionary psychologists reason similarly that a single calculating mechanism with the same set of rules, meant to cover a multitude of tasks, would have processed information slowly and led to many errors. To use an example from Buss (1999), if our early ancestors had a generalized rule like "have sexual intercourse with any partner you can," then, in terms of the ultimate goal of propagating genes, such a rule would be beneficial with respect to nonkin but would backfire with respect to kin. A parallel processing, modular kind of mind would fare much better because it would have more specialized routines designed to handle a variety of situations. In other words, an individual module that has emerged to handle only one kind of problem likely will be able to handle that problem swiftly and efficiently because it has to handle only *that particular kind* of problem, and no other one.

In essence, modularity minimizes errors and allows systems to perform optimally. We should not underestimate the importance of this kind of reasoning on the part of NEPers. A speedy response and the minimization of error grant the system a competitive advantage—hence, the likelihood of such specified, parallel processing mechanisms being selected for in our early hominin mental architecture (see Arp, 2008b). This comports with the general evolutionary *principle of economy*, recognized by every evolutionist since Darwin, namely, whatever trait gives an organism a competitive advantage most likely will be naturally selected as fit for that organism in relation to an environment and likely will be passed on to that organism's progeny.

It appears that the parallel kind of processing has been selected for with respect to at least *some* of our mental architecture. As I intimated above and in the third chapter, there is ample evidence that the visual system is considered as a suite of coordinated physiological or brain-process modules engaged in the parallel processing of visual information. So too, Broca's area and Wernicke's area in the human brain are engaged in the parallel processing of grammar–usage and language comprehension, respectively. Further, the face-recognition area in the IT cortex works in parallel with other areas of the IT cortex, and other areas of the brain, to help someone distinguish faces from other objects.

Numerous studies on infants, children, and adults seem to confirm the fact that people have innate mental modules seemingly designated for specific tasks. For example, Chomsky (1964) has argued convincingly that there must be some innate capacity for language, since young children from any culture can pick up language easily, as well as being able to learn any language (see also Jackendoff, 1987, 1992, 1994). This makes sense from the NEP perspective, since Pleistocene hominins formed social groups and eventually communicated with one another through language during that time (Aiello, 1996; Aiello & Dunbar, 1993). Spelke (1991) has demonstrated that children as young as two years old have an apparent innate understanding of physical properties of objects like solidity, gravity, and inertia (see also Pinker, 1994). This also makes sense from the NEP perspective, since Pleistocene hominins constructed and handled a variety of tools in a variety of ways during that time. Palmer & Palmer (2002) demonstrate how people have mental modules attuned to certain fears, detection of cheaters, empathizing, and spatial reasoning (cf. Adolphs, Tranel, Damasio, & Damasio, 1995; Nesse & Abelson, 1995). Gardner's (1993) list of multiple intelligences of the mind is accepted by so many psychologists and educators that it forms the basis for the curricula of many primary and middle schools (Gardner, 1999). Pinker's (2002) list includes an intuitive knowledge of physics, biology, engineering, psychology, spatial sense, number sense, probability, economics, logic, and language. Kandel et al. (2000, p. 412) tell us simply, "A newborn's mind is not blank." According to NEPers, all of these capacities—language, intuitive physics, automatic knee-jerk responses to snakes and spiders, detection of cheaters, and so forth—most likely were solidified in our species' psyche during the Pleistocene epoch.

According to advocates of NEP, the adaptive problems in the Pleistocene environments occasioned the emergence of psychological modules *designed* to handle the various and sundry problems of such environments. Several basic components of our present-day psyches were solidified back then and, in the words of Cosmides & Tooby (1987, p. 34), "the complex architecture of the human psyche can be expected to have assumed approximately modern form during the Pleistocene . . . and to have undergone only minor modification since then." We must remember that the claim NEPers make regarding the solidification of our mental architecture occurs over a period of many years, since the Pleistocene epoch spans approximately 2 mya to 10,000 ya. There are more than 65,000 generations of one family line of one population *alone* that lived during that time! Thus, given this vast amount of time, it is not wholly implausible and, in fact, it is very possible that our human psyche was formed during this time period. In other words, given what we know about laws of probabilities in relation to genetic variability and natural selection, prima facie the hypothesis is not that outlandish.

Evolutionary psychologists speak of these modules as domains of specificity. What this means is that a module handles only one kind of adaptive problem to the exclusion of others. Modules are encapsulated in this sense and do not share information with one another (Fodor, 1983, 1985). For example, my cheater-detection module evolved under a certain set of circumstances and has no direct connection to my fear-of-snakes module, which evolved under a different set of circumstances. Like the various kinds of tools in a Swiss Army knife, the various mental modules are supposed to solve the various problems that arise in circumstances; however, they do so to the exclusion of each other. The scissors of the Swiss Army knife are not *directly* functionally related to the Phillip's-head screwdriver, which is not directly functionally related to the toothpick, and so forth.

This kind of encapsulation works best for environments where the responses need to be quick and routine—such developments enabled these organisms to respond efficiently and effectively in their environments. This being the case, the modules could perform quite well as long as the environments remained relatively unchanged and typical. In fact, most of this modular processing in mammals occurs at the unconscious level. It is arguable that since this processing occurs at the unconscious level and, further, since information can become memorized, mammals quickly are able to respond to the pressures associated with fighting, fleeing, eating, mating, and so forth (Fodor, 1983, 1985; Hermer & Spelke, 1996; Cosmides & Tooby, 1992; Shettleworth, 2000).

However, there seems to be a fundamental limitation in the NEPers' reasoning, especially if the environment in which the domain-specific module has been selected is supposed to have remained fairly stable. Cosmides & Tooby (1994) note that these domain-specific modules have evolved "for solving *long-enduring* [my italics] adaptive problems," and Hirschfeld & Gelman (1994, p. 21) characterize a module as a "stable response to a set of *recurring* [my italics] and complex problems faced by the organism." Now Daly & Wilson (1999), Foley (1995), and Boyd & Silk (1997) have shown that the Pleistocene did not consist of a single hunter–gatherer type of environment but was actually a constellation of environments that presented a host of challenges to the early hominin mind. Thus, the first problem for advocates of NEP has to do with the possibility of the environment in which a particular module evolved being *stable enough* for the module to have evolved. In other words, Daly et al.'s criticism of NEP is that the environments in which our Pleistocene ancestors lived were *too* varied and *too* erratic for the Swiss Army knife blades to be solidified in our genetic makeup.

We need only reflect on the kind of circumstances one experiences through the course of the proverbial *bad day* to see that one is bombarded constantly with novel pieces of information. Throughout this bad day, one finds oneself in a repertoire of novel *mini*-environments, from waking up to discover your toilet has overflowed, to locating a bus schedule and then riding a bus to work because you discovered your car broke down, to searching for some twine in your cubicle at work so that you can hold your pants up because in the rush out the door you forgot to wear a belt, and so forth. All of this was *a*typical of your normal day.

In fact, as Crick & Koch (1990) and Kosslyn & Koenig (1995) note, novel scenes are being presented to the visual system regularly. Everyday objects and circumstances in our visual field constantly are obscured, occluded, or observed from different angles: "There are an almost infinite number of possible, different objects that we are capable of seeing. . . . The combinatorial possibilities for representing so many objects at all different values of depth, motion, color, orientation and spatial location are simply too staggering" (Crick & Koch, 1990, p. 268). Today, I made a turn onto Main Street and looked down the block to see Mr. Jones' oak tree bathed in sunlight; yesterday, I made the same turn in the pouring rain but had to squint through the rain-soaked glass of my car to see the same tree darkened by the storm. Also, as I move around my cat teasing her with a ball of string, her body contorts into a variety of positions, and I experience her shape anew with every different angle.

Even if we tempered Daly et al.'s claims regarding the multitude of environments faced by our ancestors and grant that the Pleistocene consisted of a more unitary Stone Age, hunter–gatherer, life-out-on-the-savanna kind of existence—like the one Cosmides & Tooby would have us believe—then we have the further problem of the possibility of some stable and routine module being able to handle the *un*stable and *non*routine events occurring in some environment. When routine perceptual and knowledge structures fail, or when atypical environments present themselves, it is *then* that we need to be innovative in dealing with this novelty. If mental modules are encapsulated and are designed to perform certain *routine* functions, how can this modularity account for *novel* circumstances? The problem for NEP can be phrased in the form of a disjunction: either (1) the environment was not stable enough to occasion the emergence of domain-specific modules, as is part of the thrust of Daly et al.'s criticism, or (2) the environment was stable, allowing for domain-specific mental modules to emerge, but then the environment changed, making it such that the modules specified for the old environment would no longer be helpful in the new environment.

Now, imagine the Pleistocene epoch. The climate shift in Africa from jungle life to desert/savanna life forced early hominins to come out of the trees and survive in totally new environments. Given a fortuitous genetic code, some hominins readapted to new African landscapes, and some migrated to new places like Europe and Asia, but most died out. This environmental shift had a dramatic effect on modularity, since now the specific content of the information from the environment in a particular module was no longer relevant. *The information that was formerly suited for life in a certain environment could no longer be relied upon in the new environmental niches.* Appeal to modularity alone would have led to certain death and extinction of many mammalian species. In fact, countless thousands of mammalian species did become extinct, as fossil data indicate (Novacek, 2002; Dingus, 1990). Elsewhere, I have called mental disruptions of this nature *cognitive dissonance* (see Arp, 2004a, 2004b).

The successful progression from typical kinds of environments to other atypical kinds of environments would have required some other kind of mental capacity to emerge in our hominin ancestors that creatively could handle the new environments. Mere mental associations, or trial-and-error kinds of mental activities, would not be enough, since the environments in which these hominins found themselves were *wholly new*, and there would have been no precedent by or through which one could form mental associations utilizing past information. Mental associations deal with the familiar. What is one to do when encountering the wholly unfamiliar? Although important, modules have their limitations, since they do all of their associative work in routine environments. What happens if an environment radically changes, making the information that a particular module characteristically selects in a familiar environment no longer relevant in a wholly new environment? A radical readaptation and readjustment would be needed, one that transcends the limitations of the routine.

Recall that nonroutine creative problem solving involves finding a solution to a problem that has not been solved previously. The invention of a new tool would be an example of nonroutine creative problem solving because the inventor did not possess a way to solve the problem already. This totally new environment would require that we be *creative* or *innovative* in order to survive. But how is it that we can be creative? The significant question becomes, then, this: How is it that humans evolved the ability to engage in forms of nonroutine creative problem solving, especially given either that the Pleistocene environment in which early hominins existed was really a *constellation of ever-changing environments* (Daly et al.'s criticism) or that any *one* environment was filled with a myriad of nonroutine problems that seem only to be able to be handled creatively?

5.4 One BEP Response: Mithen's Cognitive Fluidity

This is where Mithen (1996, 1999, 2001) has made an advance upon the NEPers by introducing *cognitive fluidity*, an idea that serves the purpose of enabling one to respond creatively to nonroutine problems in environments. After explaining Mithen's idea of cognitive fluidity, I show the merits and limitations of his idea and argue that it is really the evolution of scenario visualization—in terms of the selection, integration, and utilization of visual images from mental modules in visual scenarios—that was necessary for solving vision-related problems creatively in the ever-changing environments of the Pleistocene.

Mithen's idea has merit because, as he notes, he is an archeologist who is applying the hard evidence of evolutionary theory, fossils, and toolmaking to psychology. Not only is he speculating about the mind but he has the archeological evidence to support his speculations. Fodor (1998), Calvin (2004), and Stringer & Andrews (2005) praise Mithen's idea of cognitive fluidity as being a significant hypothesis, as well as consistent with archeological and neurobiological evidence. As a philosopher of mind and biology, I applaud Mithen's hypothesis as well (see Arp, 2005a, 2005b, 2006a, 2007a, 2008c).

Mithen (1996) sees the evolving mind as going through a three-step process. The first step begins prior to 6 mya when the primate mind was dominated by what he calls a *general intelligence*. This general intelligence consisted of an all-purpose, trial-and-error learning mechanism that was devoted to multiple tasks. All behaviors were imitated, associative learning was slow, and there were frequent errors made, much like what would be expected of the mind of the chimpanzee.

The second step coincides with the evolution of the *Australopithecine* line and continues all the way through the *Homo* lineage to *Homo neandertalensis*. In this second step, multiple *specialized intelligences*, or modules, emerge alongside general intelligence. Associative learning within these modules was faster, and more complex activities could be performed. Compiling data from fossilized skulls, tools, foods, and habitats, Mithen concludes that *Homo habilis* probably had a general intelligence as well as modules devoted to social intelligence (because they lived in groups), natural history intelligence (because they lived off of the land), and technical intelligence (because they made tools). *Neandertals* and *Homo heidelbergensis* would have had all of these modules, including a primitive language module, because their skulls exhibit bigger frontal and temporal areas. According to Mithen, the *neandertals* and members of *Homo heidelbergensis* would have had the Swiss Army knife mind that the NEPers speak about.

At this point, we note a criticism Mithen makes about the NEPers who think that the essential ingredients of mind evolved during the Pleistocene epoch. This is a general criticism that has been leveled against NEP by advocates of BEP (e.g., see the articles in Scher & Rauscher, 2003; Buller, 2005). It concerns the simple fact that modern-day humans deal with a whole different set of problems to overcome than did our Pleistocene ancestors. We can look back to the environment of the Pleistocene and note how certain cognitive features emerge, and become part of, the normal genetic makeup of the human. However, as Mithen (1996, pp. 45–46) asks, "How do we account for those things that the modern mind is very good at doing, but which we can be confident that Stone Age hunter–gatherers never attempted, such as reading books and developing cures for cancer"? This concern is a correlate to my concern regarding the changing environment and the feasibility of the Swiss Army knife mind's being able to handle the change. If the environment changes suddenly, the animal may be left with inflexible behaviors appropriate to the environment that originally shaped its evolution but quite nonfunctional under the new condition.

The emergence of distinct mental modules *during the Pleistocene* that evolutionary psychologists like Cosmides, Tooby, and Pinker speak about as being adequate to account for learning, negotiating, and problem solving *in our world today* cannot be correct. For Mithen, the potential variety of problems encountered in generations subsequent to the Pleistocene is too vast for a much more limited Swiss Army knife mental repertoire; there are just too many situations for which *nonroutine creative problem solving* would have been needed in order not only to simply survive but also to flourish and dominate the earth. Pinker (2002) thinks that there are upwards of fifteen different domains, and various other evolutionary psychologists have their chosen number of mental domains (e.g., Buss, 1999; Shettleworth, 2000; Gardner, 1993; Plotkin, 1997; Palmer & Palmer, 2002). However, there are potentially an *infinite number* of problems to be faced on a regular basis by animals as they negotiate environments. It does not seem that there would be a way for fifteen, twenty, twenty-five—or even a thousand—domains to handle all of these potential problems. That we negotiate environments so well shows that we have some capacity to handle the various and sundry *potential nonroutine* problems that arise in our environments.

Here is where the third step in Mithen's (1996) evolution of the mind comes into play, known as *cognitive fluidity*. In this final step, which coincides with the emergence of modern humans, the various mental modules are working together with a *fluid* flow of knowledge and ideas between and among them. The information and learning from the modules can now influence one another, resulting in an almost limitless capacity for imagination, learning, and problem solving. The working together of the various mental modules as a result of this cognitive fluidity *is* consciousness for Mithen and represents the most advanced form of mental activity.

Mithen uses the schematization of the construction of a medieval cathedral as an analogy to the mind and consciousness. Each side chapel represents a mental module. The side chapels are closed off to one another during construction but allow people to have access from the outside to attend liturgies, much like mental modules are closed off to one another (encapsulated) and have specified input cues. Once the cathedral chapels have been constructed and the central domed super-chapel is in place, the doors of all of the chapels are opened and people are allowed to roam freely from chapel to chapel. Analogously, modern humans have evolved the ability to allow information to be freely transmitted between and among mental modules, and this cognitive fluidity comprises consciousness.

Mithen goes on to note that his model of cognitive fluidity accounts for human creativity in terms of problem solving, art, ingenuity, and technology. His idea has initial plausibility, since it is arguable that the *neandertals* died off because they did not have the conscious ability to readapt to the changing environment. It is also arguable that humans would not exist today if they did not evolve consciousness to deal with novelty (Bogdan, 1994; Cosmides & Tooby, 1992; Gardner, 1993; Humphrey, 1992; Pinker, 1997). It is no wonder, then, Crick (1994, p. 20) maintains that "without consciousness, you can deal only with familiar, rather routine situations or respond to very limited information in new situations." Also, as Searle (1992, p. 109) observes, "one of the evolutionary advantages conferred on us by consciousness is the much greater flexibility, sensitivity, and creativity we derive from being conscious." Modular processes can be used to explain how the mind functions in relation to routinely encountered features of environments. However, depending on the radicalness of a novel environmental feature, *inter*modular processes (Mithen's cognitive fluidity) may be required to deal effectively and, at times, creatively with the problem.

Mithen's idea resonates with what researchers refer to as *bissociative creativity* and creative problem solving. It is important here to elaborate further upon the distinction between routine problem solving and nonroutine creative problem solving. We already know that routine problem solving deals with the recognition of many possible solutions to a problem, given that the problem was solved through one of those solutions in the past. Here, we can link routine problem solving to the kind of trial-and-error strategizing and calculation that animals other than human beings typically engage in, although humans engage in routine problem solving as well. In this sense, routine problem solving entails a mental activity that is stereotyped and wholly lacking in innovation, because there are simply perceptual *associative* connections being made by the mind of an animal. Images in perception or memory are associated with one another and/or with some environmental stimuli so as to learn some behavior, or produce some desired result. If that result is not achieved, an alternate route is pursued in a trial-and-error fashion.

For example, Olton & Samuelson (1976) showed that rats are able to associate routes in a maze with food acquisition. In these experiments, food was placed at the end of each arm of an eight-arm radial maze, and a rat was placed in the center of the maze and was kept in the maze until all the food was collected. At first, the rat did not associate a certain path with the food, but after trial and error, the rat eventually got all of the food. In subsequent tests, the food was placed in the same spot in the maze, and the same rat was able to more quickly and efficiently associate the correct pathway with the acquisition of food.

Associative learning tests have been performed on humans and animals numerous times (Zentall et al., 1990; Rescorla, 1988; Macphail, 1996, 1998; Mackintosh, 1983, 1995; Hall, 1994, 1996). In his famous *delayed matching to sample* tests, Hunter (1913) demonstrated that rats, raccoons, and dogs are able to associate memories of a stimulus with the same stimulus perceived by the animal so as to solve some problem. Wright (1989, 1997) has shown that pigeons and monkeys can perform similar associations. A typical battery of IQ tests will have several association tests whereby people are asked to solve routine problems, such as linking a word to a picture and/or linking pictures to one another in a familiar sequence (Sternberg, 1996, 1998, 2001).

Concerning nonroutine creative problem solving, we already know that this entails pursuing a wholly new way to solve a problem that has not been solved previously and that the problem solver did not possess a way to solve the problem already. Here, however, we can draw a distinction between solving a nonroutine problem *through imitation with another's help* and solving a nonroutine problem *on one's own*. Some animals appear to have the capacity to solve nonroutine problems, once the solutions have been shown to them or imitated for them.

Consider the following cases that demonstrate an animal's ability to solve a problem creatively through imitation with another's help. An octopus studied by Fiorito et al. (1990) has been documented as being able to unpop the cork on a jar to get at food inside. Initially, the octopus could see the food in the jar but was unable to unpop the cork of the jar to get at the food. The next time, Fiorito et al. unpopped the cork while the octopus was watching, resealed the jar, and gave it to him in his tank. The octopus was able to associate the unpopping of the cork with the acquisition of food, remembered what Fiorito et al. had shown him, and unpopped the cork himself to get at the food.

Also, we have documented chimps trying a couple of different ways to get at fruit in a tree—like jumping at it from different angles or jumping at it off of tree limbs—before finally using a stick to knock it down. Scientists also document young chimps watching older chimps do the same thing (Tomasello, 1990; Tomasello et al., 1987, 1993; Byrne, 1995; Savage-Rumbaugh & Boysen, 1978; Whiten et al., 1996, 1999). Like the octopus's problem solving ability, this seems to be a form of nonroutine creative problem solving by use of another's help.

In fact, several observations have been made of various kinds of animals engaged in imitative behaviors: Whiten & Custance (1996), Whiten et al. (1996, 1999), Tomasello et al. (1987, 1993), and Abravanel (1991) have documented imitative behaviors in chimpanzees and children; Parker (1996), Miles, Mitchell, & Harper (1996), Call & Tomasello (1994), and Russon & Galdikas (1993, 1995) have witnessed young orangutans imitating older orangutans using sticks and rocks to gather food, as well as throwing sticks and rocks at other orangutans in self-defense; Yando, Seitz, & Ziqler (1978), Mitchell (1987), and Moore (1992) report mimicry and imitation in birds; and Heyes & Dawson (1990) and Heyes, Jaldon, & Dawson (1992) note evidence of imitative behaviors in rats.

However, the number of possible solution routes is limited in these examples of routine problem solving. If either the octopus's corked jar was sealed with Crazy Glue, or there were no sticks around, or there were no other older chimps or researchers around to show younger chimps how to use sticks, the octopus and chimpanzees in the above cases likely would starve to death. The possible solution routes are limited because the mental repertoires of these animals are environmentally fixed, and their tool usage (if they have this capacity) is limited to stereotypical kinds of associations.

Bitterman (1965, 1975, 2000) tested the intelligence levels of fish, turtles, pigeons, rats, and monkeys with a variety of tasks, including pushing paddles in water, pecking or pressing lighted disks, and crawling down narrow runways. Although such animals improved their abilities to perform these tasks as time went on, Bitterman found that these species only could perform a limited number of associative learning tasks. These data, along with the data concerning the octopus, chimps, orangutans, rats, and birds, support the idea that these animals are engaged in mostly habitual, stereo-typed forms of associative thinking and learning (cf. the new research concerning crows and other birds in Weir, Chappell, & Kacelnik, 2002; Emery & Clayton, 2004; Reiner, Perkel, Mello, & Jarvis, 2004).

Unlike routine problem solving, which deals with associative connec-tions within familiar perspectives, nonroutine creative problem solving entails an innovative ability to make connections between wholly unre-lated perspectives or ideas. Again, this kind of problem solving can occur as a result of imitation through another's help—as in the above octopus and chimpanzee examples—as well as on one's own. A human seems to be the only kind of being who can solve nonroutine problems *on his or her own, without imitation or help*. This is not to say that humans do not engage in solving nonroutine problems through imitation; in fact, nonroutine problem solving by imitation occurs all of the time, especially in the earlier years of a human's life. This is just to say that humans are the only animals who have the potential to consider wholly new routes to problem solving.

Koestler (1964) referred to this quality of the creative mind as a *bissocia-tion of matrices*. When a human bissociates, that person puts together ideas, memories, representations, stimuli, and the like in wholly new and unfa-miliar ways *for that person*. Echoing Koestler, Boden (1990, p. 5) calls this an ability to "juxtapose formerly unrelated ideas." Thus, Dominowski (1995, p. 77) claims that "overcoming convention and generating a new understanding of a situation is considered to be an important component of creativity."

When animals associate, they put together perceptions, memories, rep-resentations, stimuli, and the like in familiar ways. For example, my cat associates my loud voice with her being in trouble for knocking the plant over and runs away, the rat associates a route with food, and the octopus associates corked-jar-experiment B with corked-jar-experiment A and more quickly can unpop the cork on the jar to get at the food in subse-quent tests. As far as we know, animals can associate *only*, so they always go for solutions to problems that are related to the environment or situation in which they typically reside. Humans bissociate and are able to ignore normal associations and try out *novel* ideas and approaches in solving problems. Such an ability to bissociate accounts for more advanced forms of problem solving, whereby the routine or habitual associations are the kinds of associations that precisely *need to be avoided, ignored, or bracketed out* as irrelevant to the optional solution (Finke et al., 1992). Bissociation also has been pointed to as an aid in accounting for risibility; hypothesis formation; art; technological advances; and the proverbial "ah-hah," creative insight, eureka moments humans experience when they come up with a new idea, insight, or tool (Koestler, 1964; Boden, 1990; Holyoak & Thagard, 1989, 1995; Terzis, 2001; Davidson, 1995; Arp, 2005a, 2008c).

Thus, when we ask how it is that humans can be creative, part of what we are asking is how they bissociate, namely, *juxtapose formerly unrelated ideas in wholly new and unfamiliar ways for that person.* To put it colloquially, humans can take some idea found "way over here in the left field" of the mind and make some coherent connection with some other idea found "way over here in the right field" of the mind. Humans seem to be the only species that can engage in this kind of mental activity, principally with visual images and ideas.

Mithen's idea of cognitive fluidity helps to explain our ability to bissociate because the potential is always there to make innovative, previously unrelated connections between ideas or perceptions, given that the information between and among modules has the capacity to be mixed together or intermingle. Thus, in essence, cognitive fluidity accounts for bissociation, which accounts for human creativity in terms of problem solving, art, ingenuity, and technology. This is not to say that the information *will in fact* mix together and then be bissociated by an individual. This is just to say that there is always the *potential* for such a mental process to occur in our species. In the words of Finke et al. (1992, p. 2), "people can generate original images that lead to insight and innovation or commonplace images that lead nowhere, depending on the properties of those images."

5.5   Scenario Visualization as an Active Feature of the Conscious Mind

However, Mithen's model of consciousness and its relationship to problem solving remain incomplete. In what follows, I transform Mithen's account by speaking about the role of scenario visualization as an active feature of the conscious mind necessary for solving vision-related, nonroutine problems creatively. Doing so will draw upon the information and arguments from previous chapters, making for a coherent picture of my project as a whole.

Consciousness probably is the essential mystery of the universe, arguably more mysterious than notions of the divine. Consequently, it is incredibly difficult to define. Roth (2000) gives a list of the party-line features of consciousness including everything from being awake, to self-awareness, experience, intentionality, and indexicality. Sternberg (1996, 2000) thinks consciousness comprises the ability to coherently form a belief or set up a goal that a human being ultimately can act upon, through selectivity and filtering of information. Chalmers (1996, pp. 6–11) generates a list of conscious experiences, noting that the "phenomenal feel," "qualia," or "what it is like" (all meaning the same thing) of our psychological experiences is what is meant by consciousness (also see Jackson, 1982; Arp, 2007b, 2008d). Chalmers claims that consciousness has many elements, from nonsensory aspects such as volition, emotion, memory, and thought to sensory experiences such as audition, bodily sensation, and vision.

Our visual perceptions are integral to our conscious experience of ourselves and the world around us. This is one reason Crick & Koch (1998, p. 98) give as to why they study the visual system in trying to understand consciousness and its neural correlates: "Humans are very visual animals and our visual percepts are especially vivid and rich in information." This is also why Logothetis (1999) titles his article in *Scientific American* "Vision: A Window on Consciousness." Further, this is why, after a lengthy discussion regarding the relationship between the visual system and consciousness, Damasio (2003, p. 208) has claimed that "without mental images, the organism (viz., a human) would not be able to perform in timely fashion the large-scale integration of information critical for survival, not to mention well-being."

As I have noted already, one way to understand conscious activity is in terms of scenario visualization. This feature of consciousness comes to light most clearly when humans engage in vision-related forms of problem solving. I am not suggesting that people *always* visualize or *never* use semantic forms of reasoning, or other forms of reasoning, when solving nonroutine problems. Nonetheless, it seems implausible that no one *ever* visualizes when trying to solve problems creatively. I simply am pointing out that there exists this capacity to scenario visualize in our species as a whole and that, at times, people utilize it to solve problems creatively. In fact, as I noted in the previous chapter, whether one utilizes scenario visualization most likely will depend upon the type of problem with which one is confronted. There are some problems—for example, certain mathematical problems—that can be solved without the use of scenario visualization. Other problems, like spatial relation or depth perception problems, may require scenario visualization. As noted earlier, the kinds of problems with which our hominin ancestors were confronted most likely were of the spatial relation and depth relation types, and so the capacity to scenario visualize would have been useful for their survival. Scenario visualization has been and still continues to be relevant for *vision-related* forms of creative problem solving.

Mithen's account of cognitive fluidity allows for the free movement of information between and among modules. I think this is important as a *precondition* for mental activities, like imagination, requiring the simultaneous utilization of several modules. Thus, for example, Mithen would think that totemic anthropomorphism associated with animals in, say, a totem pole made up of part-human/part-animal figures derives from the free flow of information between a natural history module dealing specifically with animals and their characteristics and a social module dealing specifically with people and their characteristics. A totem carved out of wood is the *material* result of the free flow of information between the natural history and social modules that has occurred in the mind of the artist. Another example would be conceiving of talking bananas, which entails the merger of a language module and a natural history module associated with food (I am thinking of the kid's show called "Bananas in Pajamas").

Mithen's model is unsatisfactory, however, because he makes consciousness out to be a passive phenomenon. On his account, consciousness is just a flexible fluidity, a free flowing of information between and among mental modules. This does not seem to be the full account of consciousness. When we are engaged in conscious activity, we are *doing* something. The fundamental insight derived from Kant (1929), and reiterated by numerous philosophers, psychologists, and neuroscientists, is that consciousness is an active process (e.g., Rock, 1984; Crick & Koch, 2003; Cziko, 1992; Singer, 2000; Sigala & Logothetis, 2002; Arp, 2005a, 2005b, 2006a).

Kandel et al. (2000, p. 412) bolster Kant's insight when they claim that perception "organizes an object's essential properties well enough to let us handle the object." Drawing directly on Kant's insights, they claim further that our perceptions "are constructed internally according to constraints

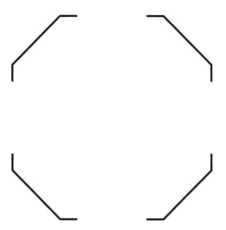

Figure 5.1
A fill-in-the-blank octagon

imposed by the architecture of the nervous system and its functional abilities." Consider figure 5.1. We immediately recognize the space in the middle as an octagon. However, the reason why we can do so seems to be because our visual perception is constructive. The mind brings something to the diagram and *fills in the blank* (literally!) in generating the image of the octagon.

I want to proffer Kant's fundamental insight and suggest that scenario visualization involves conscious mental activities of selecting and integrating visual information from mental modules for the purposes of negotiating environments *and* that Mithen's account of cognitive fluidity acts as a precondition for the possibility of the information contained in these modules to intermix. Thus, on the one hand, Mithen is correct about the possibility of information between and among mental modules as intermixing, and, contrary to NEPers, he is correct that cognitive fluidity probably is a better description of our mental architecture, given the early hominin ability to survive in the ever-changing Pleistocene environments. On the other hand, I am transforming Mithen's account by arguing that possible intermixing of modular information is not the full story of conscious, vision-related, creative problem solving. I am arguing for scenario visualization, and this form of conscious visual processing is not merely an intermixing of visual information from mental modules but involves the active selection and integration of that information for the purposes of solving some nonroutine problem creatively in an environment that a human inhabits.

Further, in light of the first and third chapters, I am suggesting that these psychological properties of selectivity and integration are similar to the properties that other neurobiological and biological processes exhibit. In other words, I want to argue that this conscious capacity shares an analogous affinity with neurobiological processes of selectivity and integration in the visual system, namely, processes that enable animals to select relevant information from environmental stimuli and to organize this information in ways useful for the problem solver. For example, visual processes actively select and integrate the information concerning the lines and spaces in figure 5.1 so as to produce a coherent picture of the octagon. So too, the conscious activity of scenario visualization—which is a psychological phenomenon that has emerged from neurobiological processes— actively selects and integrates visual information from mental modules so as to produce coherent imagined pictures. Further, similar processes of selectivity and integration can be found in the activities of organisms in general. I will say more about this psychological–neurobiological–biological continuum later in this chapter.

Mithen thinks that the kinds of unique behaviors we engage in are the result of a free flow of information between and among modules. This cannot be the full story. My claim is that scenario visualization emerged as a conscious property of the brain to act as a kind of metacognitive process that selects and integrates relevant visual information from psychological modules, in performing vision-related, creative problem solving tasks in environments. More accurately, we scenario visualize, that is, we selectively attend to visual information from certain modules, and actively integrate that visual information from those modules so as to solve some problem. If this kind of conscious activity were *merely* free flow of information, there would be no mental coherency; the information would be chaotic and directionless, and not really *informative* at all. It would be more like meaningless data that free floated around. However, as was noted in the first and third chapters, data must be segregated and integrated so that they can become informative for a system or a cognizer. Just as other neurobiological and biological processes engage in selectivity and integration of information relevant to their specific levels, so too, the most complex psychological processes involved in problem solving engage in selectivity and integration of information relevant to its level. Selectivity and integration of visual information from mental modules are two of the jobs of scenario visualization.

For example, that the visual images in the social module pertaining to human behaviors and the visual images in the natural history module pertaining to animal behaviors are put together in anthropomorphic animal totemism (the material result of which might be a totem pole fashioned out of wood) means that these images had to be *selected out from* or *segregated from* other visual images as relevant. Other modular visual images would be bracketed out as irrelevant, as the images in these two modules would be focused upon. However, it is not just *that* channels have been opened between these modules, so that their specified and selected information can intermix. Cognitive fluidity is necessary; however, something more active needs to occur when the idea of anthropomorphic animal totemism is brought to mind. The modules pertaining to such an idea must be integrated so that a coherent imagined product results. Another way to say this is that the visual information from both modules is synthesized, allowing for something sublimated (to use a Hegelian notion) or innovative to emerge anew as a result of the process. While speaking about Mithen's idea of cognitive fluidity, Fodor (1998, p. 159) expresses a similar claim about integration: "Even if early man had modules for 'natural intelligence' and 'technical intelligence,' he couldn't have become modern man just by adding what he knew about fires to what he knew about cows. The trick is in thinking out what happens when you put the two together; you get *steak au poivre* by *integrating* [my italics] knowledge bases, not by merely summing them."

Finally, the entire process requires that one be able to form, recall, and utilize visual images: from the image formation of human characteristics in one module, and the animal characteristics in another module; to the selective attention of these images in short-memory, or the recollection of these images in working memory; to the projecting of these images together in some future scenario where they are shifted, transformed, and finally integrated, in the coherent picture of the animal totem.

5.6   Scenario Visualization at Work in the Early Hominin Mind

Next we consider two diagrams that have to do with the construction of a harpoon and the generation of a piece of artwork. These schematizations are supposed to represent the slower, intelligent processes associated with two of our early hominin ancestors' abilities to consciously select and integrate the free flow of visual information between mental modules, as well as transform and manipulate these visual images against a backdrop of environments in scenarios, so as to solve some problem and imagine a novel piece of art.

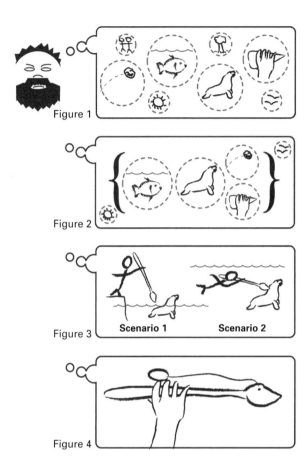

Figure 5.2
The construction of a harpoon

The first diagram (figure 5.2) is based upon information gathered from Mithen (1996) and Oswalt (1976) regarding the Angmagsalik hunters of Greenland and their construction of harpoons utilized to hunt seals. Their harpoons are fairly complex, having a spearhead equipped with a line attached to a flotation device, as well as several other parts designed to make the harpoon sturdy, accurate, and easy to throw. These hunters are an interesting case because it is likely that their harpoon technology has not changed much in thousands of years; thus, their technology can be studied to get a sense of what early hominin toolmaking may have been like.

In the schematization, I ask you to imagine that the problem to be solved has to do with throwing a projectile at a seal from a distance, for the purposes of killing it, skinning it, and using its body parts for food and warmth during the approaching winter months. I also ask you to imagine that this is the *very first instance* of some hominin coming up with the idea of the harpoon. At first, this particular hominin has no prior knowledge of the harpoon, but through the process of scenario visualization, he eventually "puts two and two together" and devises the mental blueprints for the harpoon. In other words, this is supposed to be a schematization of vision-related, nonroutine creative problem solving at work in the early hominin mind.

In the first step, the hunter has separate visual images associated with seal characteristics, the properties of objects in water, the manufacture of the bifaced hand ax, and projectiles moving through the air. Consistent with Mithen's idea of cognitive fluidity, the visual information among these mental spheres has the potential to intermix and is represented by the dotted-line bubbles. Further, consistent with the data presented by developmental and evolutionary psychologists, there are several mental modules (dotted-line bubbles) that make up a person's mind. In the second step, scenario visualization is beginning as the animal, biological, technological, and intuitive physics modules are bracketed off or segregated from the other mental modules. In the third step, the process of visualization is continuing because the hominin is manipulating, inverting, and transforming the images as they are projected into a future imagined scenario. In the fourth step, these modules are actively integrated so that a wholly new image is formed that can become implemented in the actual production of the harpoon.

The next diagram (figure 5.3) concerns the construction of fish–human figurines discovered by archeologists at the site of Lepenski Vir on the Danube and dated to about 7,000 ya (Mithen, 1996). These are considered pieces of artwork, probably constructed for some religious significance. Like problem solving and toolmaking, producing a novel piece of art follows a similar process of scenario visualization. As with the harpoon, I ask you to imagine that this is the *very first instance* of some hominin coming up with the idea of the fish–human figurine.

In the first step, the artist has separate visual images of human and animal morphology and behavior; however, the information between the two spheres has the potential to intermix and is represented by the dotted-line bubbles. In the second step, scenario visualization is beginning as the human and animal modules are bracketed off or segregated from the other modules. In the third step, scenario visualization is continuing as the artist is transforming, adjusting, and reconfiguring the information

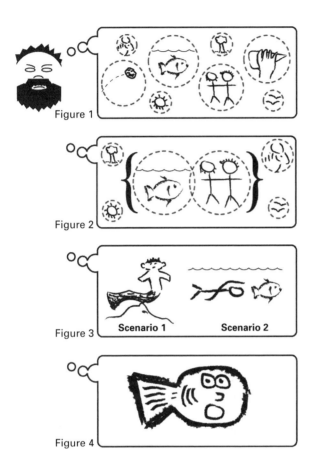

Figure 5.3
The construction of a fish-human figurine

regarding fish and human characteristics in some imagined future visual scenario. In the fourth step, the information regarding fish and humans has been integrated, and something wholly new—the fish–human—has been formed. The fourth panel in the schematization is based upon one of the figurines found at Lepenski Vir (poorly, given my lousy drawing abilities). These figurines are significant because they are some of the first pieces of art constructed by hominins whereby it could be said that the artist did not already possess an image of *that particular kind of finished product* in his or her mind. There have been fish figurines and human figurines found that predate these figurines, but never specifically *fish–human* figurines.

5.7   Scenario Visualization and the Psychological–Neurological–Biological Continuum

In this section, I want to bring my analysis of scenario visualization in this book around full circle, so to speak, and connect the conscious processes entailed in scenario visualization with similar neurobiological and biological processes spoken about in previous chapters. In the first chapter, I noted that biological processes of organisms exhibit the properties of environmental information exchange, selectivity, and integration. Even at the level of the cell, we see these properties being exhibited in the various functions of the organelles, including endocytosis, exocytosis, and nucleic control. Also, we saw that the property of internal–hierarchical data exchange in an organism manifests upward causation, whereby the lower levels of the hierarchy exhibit causal influence over the higher levels. Likewise, the dual properties of data selectivity and informational integration manifest downward causation, whereby the higher levels of the hierarchy exhibit causal influence over the lower levels, in terms of control. I asked the reader to think of the complex upward and downward causal relations taking place when the human body simply gets up out of bed. Put crudely, the brain must exhibit downward causation, as a necessary condition, upon its own neurochemical constituents in order to cause the body to get up, while the neurochemical constituents must exhibit upward causation, as a necessary condition, for movement to occur in the first place. Further, in the third chapter, I presented evidence that at higher levels of the visual hierarchy, the systems and processes therein segregate relevant from irrelevant data and integrate visual modules so as to produce a coherent visual picture.

My claim is that just as biological processes, in general, exhibit selective and integrative functions, and just as visual integration performs the function of selecting and integrating visual module areas, so too, a certain form of consciousness emerged as a property of the brain to act as a kind of metacognitive process that scenario visualizes, namely, selects and integrates relevant visual information from psychological modules for the purpose of solving vision-related problems in environments creatively (also see Arp, 2005b). I think that by envisioning this feature of conscious activity as a biologically emergent activity performing similar kinds of activities of selection and integration found at other levels in the biological hierarchy, the case for consciousness playing an active role in the solving of nonroutine, creative forms of problem solving can be made more fortifiable.

The idea that a conscious activity like scenario visualization is a biologically emergent phenomenon involving both the selectivity and integration of visual information comports well with neurobiological data from a variety of sources. First, several neuroscientists point to attention as a primary mechanism for consciousness (e.g., Desimone, 1992; Desimone et al., 1994; Desimone & Duncan, 1995; Treisman, 1977, 1988). In the third chapter, I noted that attention is like a selective mechanism in the visual system, segregating relevant from irrelevant information. When one is said to be conscious of something, say a patch of red in one's visual field or a memory of a roller-coaster ride, one is obviously attentive to that something. One is focusing in on that piece of information to the exclusion of other nonrelevant pieces of information.

Second, several philosophers, neuroscientists, and other researchers think that integration of information is essential for a unified conscious percept (e.g., Baars, 1988, 1997; Baars & Newman, 2001; Lumer, 2000; Singer, 1999, 2000; Singer & Gray, 1995; Cziko, 1992, 1995; Damasio, 2000; Fauconnier & Turner, 2002; Goguen & Harrell, 2004). This is really the issue of binding that is present at various levels of the psychophysical hierarchy. As Gray (1999, p. 31) notes, "Binding isn't a problem for nervous systems, as evolution has sculpted their organization to solve the problem efficiently and effectively. It is just a problem for those of us trying to understand how the nervous system achieves the task." Gray basically is admitting that integration is a fundamental feature of the mind, despite our ignorance of the exact mechanisms by which it occurs. Tononi & Edelman (1998) and Velmans (1992) specify integration as the essential feature of consciousness. When we are conscious of the tree outside our window blowing in the wind, we must be able to integrate several visual modalities so as to attain a coherent picture of what we are experiencing. Likewise, as a form of conscious visual processing, scenario visualization enables one to integrate several other *mental* modules of visual information that, in turn, integrate several other *brain-process* modules.

Thus, we must not think that consciousness is some kind of entity existing *completely* on its own, like some thing totally detached from the processes and functions of the brain. I am trying to put forward a view of consciousness as an emergent metacognitive *process*, one that utilizes several areas of the brain concerned with the visual system, memory, planning, and voluntary movements. To think that consciousness is some kind of entity completely divorced from the processes of the brain catapults one into what is known as *the problem of the homunculus*, a problem that is faced most directly by metaphysical dualists in the philosophy of mind (see

Dennett, 1986, 1987, 1991; Lycan, 1995; Baars & Newman, 2001). The problem of the homunculus is the idea that consciousness is a "little person inside the head" who perceives the world through the senses, as well as thinks, plans, and executes voluntary motions. The homunculus is used by some thinkers to explain how it is that the mind is able to bind together or integrate relevant information so as to generate a coherent picture or experience of the world. Dennett's (1991) notion of the *Cartesian theater*, whereby a person (representing consciousness) sits in a theater observing pictures on a screen (representing mental representations, volitions, emotions, etc.), is another expression of the homunculus idea.

Unfortunately, if one holds the homunculus view, a few problems result. First, there is the problem of consciousness being a thing that is too disassociated from the workings of the brain. If consciousness is a thing too disassociated from the brain, then we run into the further problems of (1) explaining how it is that consciousness, which presumably would exist on a nonbiological level, can interact with a brain that exists on the biological level (Jackson, 1982; McGinn, 1982; Baars, 1997), (2) specifying what the objective laws associated with consciousness would be if they are not biological, physical, chemical, or otherwise scientific laws (McGinn, 1982; Kim, 2000), (3) *third man* kinds of arguments whereby our mental life is (not really) explained by consciousness, which is explained by consciousness2, which is explained by consciousness3, and so forth, ad infinitum, (4) making consciousness out to be a "spooky" thing (Churchland, 1997; Heil, 2004a, 2004b) too removed from empirical, objectifiable, third-person evidence.

Thankfully, my account of consciousness as dependent upon biological processes skirts a lot of the problems just listed, although, of course, there may be a host of other problems that become evident. Some of these problems just mentioned are avoided because consciousness is an emergent phenomenon subject to the same laws as any other neurobiological and biological phenomena, although it is not reducible to such phenomena (also see Arp, 2008d). Provided that we switch the terms "constituted of" with "dependent upon, but not reducible to" in his definition of consciousness, Sperry (1980, p. 204) has stated the position succinctly: "Consciousness is a functional property of brain processing, constituted of neuronal and physicochemical activity, and embodied in, and inseparable from, the active brain." The psychological realm, although not reducible to these realms, is an extension of the neurobiological and biological realms, and all three of these realms are subject to evolutionary principles. Just as cellular process exhibit internal–hierarchical data exchange, data selectivity, and informational intregration, so too, neurobiological and psychological processes exhibit the same kinds of properties.

Scenario visualization is a form of conscious cognitive visual processing that enables one to select visual information while bracketing out irrelevant visual information. It also allows us to transform and project visual images into future scenarios, as well as coordinate and integrate visual information, so that the perceiver has a coherent picture of both the imagined and real worlds. This feature of the conscious mind—scenario visualization in terms of selectivity and integration—is a psychological process that has emerged from neurobiological processes exhibiting the same kinds of features, and subject to the same evolutionary principles, as any biological process. Another way to say this is that the mental and neurobiological processes of selectivity and integration are really analogous extensions of similar general biological processes. The upshot of my hypothesis is a biologically based account of vision-related, creative problem solving whereby the most complex psychological phenomena and processes are explained as emerging from neurobiological phenomena and processes, which, in turn, are explained as emerging from general biological phenomena and processes—all phenomena and processes being subject to evolutionary principles.

In this chapter, I presented the ideas and arguments put forward by evolutionary psychologists such as Cosmides, Tooby, and Mithen that the mind evolved certain capacities to creatively problem solve. I tried to respond to some of the debates in which evolutionary psychologists are engaged concerning our human mental architecture and the early hominin environments that have occasioned its evolution. We saw that Cosmides & Tooby think that the complex activities in which the human mind can be engaged are the result of specified mental modules having evolved during our Pleistocene past to deal with the various and sundry problems early humans had experienced. We also saw that Mithen shows the deficiency in this position and makes an advance upon Cosmides & Tooby's idea by arguing that problem solving is possible because the mind has evolved cognitive fluidity. I agreed with Mithen that cognitive fluidity acts as a necessary condition for creative problem solving, but I disagreed that cognitive fluidity alone will suffice for such an activity. I transformed Mithen's account by arguing that, while it may be true that the flexible exchange of information between and among mental modules is a feature of consciousness, conscious abilities to segregate, integrate, transform, and project visual information from mental modules—in terms of scenario visualization—are what have accounted for the possibility of vision-related, nonroutine creative problem solving in Pleistocene environments. As I have shown, my hypothesis regarding scenario visualization is an advance upon Mithen's account of cognitive fluidity, which itself (viz., Mithen's account) is an advance upon Cosmides & Tooby's model of the mind as being composed of encapsulated mental modules.

Further, I suggested that by envisioning this feature of consciousness as a psychologically emergent activity performing similar kinds of activities of segregation and integration found at other levels in the neurobiological and biological hierarchies, the case for consciousness's playing an active role in the solving of nonroutine, creative forms of problem solving can be made more fortifiable. Scenario visualization is a psychological process that has emerged from neurobiological processes exhibiting the same kinds of features, and subject to the same evolutionary principles, as any biological process. My intention has been to produce a coherent account of scenario visualization envisioned as part of a psychological–neurobiological–biological continuum that is subject to evolutionary history.

In the introduction to this book, I noted that I am a philosopher of mind and biology, and, insofar as this is the case, I am concerned with two principle questions concerning human nature, namely, What are humans, in essence, that distinguishes them from the rest of reality? and How did we get this way? The hypothesis of scenario visualization and its emergence in an evolutionary history are my small attempts to answer these fundamentally philosophical questions. Obviously, I have not answered these questions *completely*. But I hope that I have offered a plausible hypothetical "piece to the puzzle" that will inform and enliven the discussion and research concerning our mental architecture and its evolution.

References

Abeles, M. (1991). *Corticonics: Neural circuits of the cerebral cortex*. New York: Cambridge University Press.

Abitbol, M. (1995). Reconstruction of the STS 14 (*A. africanus*) pelvis. *American Journal of Physical Anthropology, 96*, 143–158.

Aboitiz, F. (1996). Does bigger mean better? Evolutionary determinants of brain size and structure. *Brain, Behavior and Evolution, 47*, 225–245.

Abravanel, E. (1991). Does immediate imitation influence long-term memory for observed actions? *Journal of Experimental Child Psychology, 21*, 614–623.

Achinstein, P. (1977). Function statements. *Philosophy of Science, 44*, 341–367.

Adolphs, R., Tranel, D., Damasio, H., & Damasio, A. (1995). Fear and the human amygdala. *Journal of Neuroscience, 15*, 5879–5891.

Aiello, L. (1996). Hominine preadaptions for language and cognition. In P. Mellars & K. Gibson (Eds.), *Modeling the early human mind* (pp. 121–137). Cambridge, UK: McDonald Institute Monograph Series.

Aiello, L. (1997). Brain and guts in human evolution: The expensive tissue hypothesis. *Brazilian Journal of Genetics, 20*, 141–148.

Aiello, L., & Dunbar, R. (1993). Neocortex size, group size and the evolution of language. *Current Anthropology, 34*, 184–193.

Allen, C., Bekoff, M., & Lauder, G. (1998). Introduction. In C. Allen, M. Bekoff, & G. Lauder (Eds.), *Nature's purposes: Analyses of function and design in biology* (pp. 1–26). Cambridge, MA: MIT Press.

Allman, J. (1977). Evolution of the visual system in the early primates. In J. Sprague & A. Epstein (Eds.), *Progress in psychobiology and physiological psychology* (pp. 1–53). New York: Academic Press.

Allman, J. (1982). Reconstructing the evolution of the brain in primates through the use of comparative neurophysiological and neuroanatomical data. In E. Armstrong & D. Falk (Eds.), *Primate brain evolution: Methods and concepts* (pp. 13–28). New York: Plenum Press.

Allman, J. (2000). *Evolving brains*. New York: Scientific American Library.

Allman, J., & Kaas, J. (1971). A representation of the visual field in the caudal third of the middle temporal gyrus of the owl monkey (*Aotus trivirgatus*). *Brain Research*, *31*, 84–105.

Alston, W. (1996). *A realist conception of truth*. Ithaca, NY: Cornell University Press.

Amundson, R. (1994). Two concepts of restraint: Adaptationism and the challenge from developmental biology. *Philosophy of Science*, *61*, 556–578.

Anapol, F., German, R., & Jablonski, N. (Eds.), (2004). *Shaping primate evolution: Form, function and behavior*. Cambridge, UK: Cambridge University Press.

Annas, J. (1981). *An introduction to Plato's Republic*. Oxford: Oxford University Press.

Antonini, A., & Stryker, M. (1993). Rapid remodeling of axonal arbors in the visual cortex. *Science*, *260*, 1819–1821.

Ariew, A., Cummins, R., & Perlman, M. (Eds.), (2002). *Functions: New essays in the philosophy of psychology and biology*. Oxford: Oxford University Press.

Aristotle. (1941). *De Anima*. In R. McKeon (Ed.), *The basic works of Aristotle* (pp. 535–606). New York: Random House.

Armstrong, E., & Falk, D. (1982). *Primate brain evolution: Methods and concepts*. New York: Plenum Press.

Arnhart, L. (1998). *Darwinian natural right*. Binghamton, NY: SUNY Press.

Arnheim, R. (1969). *Visual thinking*. Berkeley: University of California Press.

Arp, R. (1998). Hume's mitigated skepticism and the design argument. *American Catholic Philosophical Quarterly*, *72*, 539–558.

Arp, R. (1999). The *quinque viae* of Thomas Hobbes. *History of Philosophy Quarterly*, *16*, 367–394.

Arp, R. (2002). Re-thinking Hobbes's materialistic and mechanistic projects. *Hobbes Studies*, *15*, 3–31.

Arp, R. (2004a). Husserl and the penetrable spheres of the transcendental and the mundane. *Human Studies*, *27*, 115–136.

Arp, R. (2004b). Husserl, the transcendental, and the mundane. *The Journal of the British Society for Phenomenology*, *35*, 127–142.

Arp, R. (2005a). Scenario visualization: One explanation of creative problem solving. *Journal of Consciousness Studies*, *12*, 31–60.

Arp, R. (2005b). Selectivity, integration, and the psycho–neuro–biological continuum. *Journal of Mind and Behavior*, *6* & *7*, 35–64.

Arp, R. (2005c). The pragmatic value of Frege's Platonism for the pragmatist. *Journal of Speculative Philosophy*, *19*, 22–41.

Arp, R. (2005d). Frege, as-if Platonism, and pragmatism. *Journal of Critical Realism*, *9*, 1–27.

Arp, R. (2006a). The environments of our hominin ancestors, tool usage, and scenario visualization. *Biology & Philosophy*, *21*, 95–117.

Arp, R. (2006b). Evolution and two popular proposals for the definition of function. *Journal for General Philosophy of Science*, *37*, 2–12.

Arp, R. (2007a). Resolving conflicts in evolutionary psychology with cognitive fluidity. *Southwest Philosophy Review*, *35*, 91–101.

Arp, R. (2007b). Awareness and consciousness: Switched-on rheostats. *Journal of Consciousness Studies*, *14*, 101–106.

Arp, R. (2007c). Vindicating Kant's morality. *International Philosophical Quarterly*, *7*, 5–22.

Arp, R. (2008a). Life and the Homeostatic Organization View of biological phenomena. Cosmos and History: the Journal of Natural and Social Philosophy, in press.

Arp, R. (2008b). Biological versus computational approaches to creative problem solving. *Theoria et Historia Scientiarum*, in press.

Arp, R. (2008c). Scenario visualization and the evolution of art. *Arts and Neurosciences*, in press.

Arp, R. (2008d). *An integrated approach to the philosophy of mind*. Cambridge, UK: Cambridge University Press, in preparation.

Arp, R., & Ayala, F. (Eds.), (2008). *Contemporary debates in philosophy of biology*. Malden, MA: Blackwell Publishers.

Arp, R., & Rosenberg, A. (Eds.), (2008). *Philosophy of biology: An anthology*. Malden, MA: Blackwell Publishers.

Audesirk, T., Audesirk, G., & Beyers, B. (2002). *Biology: Life on earth*. Upper Saddle River, NJ: Prentice Hall.

Audi, R. (1993). *The structure of justification*. Cambridge, MA: Cambridge University Press.

Ayala, F. (1972). Frequency-dependent mating advantages in *Drosophila*. *Behavioral Genetics*, *2*, 85–91.

Ayala, F. (1982). *Population and evolutionary genetics: A primer*. Menlo Park, CA: Benjamin Cummings.

Ayala, F. (1998). Teleological explanations in evolutionary biology. In C. Allen, M. Bekoff, & G. Lauder (Eds.), *Nature's purposes: Analyses of function and design in biology* (pp. 29–49). Cambridge, MA: MIT Press.

Baars, B. (1988). *A cognitive theory of consciousness*. Cambridge, UK: Cambridge University Press.

Baars, B. (1997). *In the theater of consciousness: The workspace of the mind.* New York: Oxford University Press.

Baars, B., & Newman, J. (Eds.), (2001). *Essential sources in the scientific study of consciousness.* Cambridge, MA: MIT Press.

Bahn, P. (Ed.), (1996). *The Cambridge illustrated history of archeology.* Cambridge, UK: Cambridge University Press.

Ball, P. (1999). *The self-made tapestry: Pattern formation in nature.* Oxford: Oxford University Press.

Balter, M. (2000). Evolution on life's fringes. *Science, 289,* 1866–1867.

Barlow, H. (1994). What is the computational goal of the neocortex? In C. Koch & J. Davis (Eds.), *Large-scale neuronal theories of the brain* (pp. 1–22). Cambridge, MA: MIT Press.

Barrett, N., Dunbar, R., & Lycett, J. (2001). Human cortical processing of colour and pattern. *Human Brain Mapping, 13,* 213–225.

Barrett, L., Dunbar, R., & Lycett, J. (2002). *Human evolutionary psychology.* Princeton: Princeton University Press.

Barto, A. (1985). Learning by statistical co-operation of self-interested neuron-like computing elements. *Human Neurobiology, 4,* 229–256.

Barton, R. (1998). Visual specialization and brain evolution in primates. *Proceedings of the Royal Society of London, 1409,* 1933–1937.

Batterman, R. (2001). *The devil in the details: Asymptotic reasoning in explanation, reduction, and emergence.* Oxford: Oxford University Press.

Bauman, M., & Kemper, T. (Eds.), (1994). *The neurobiology of autism.* Baltimore, MD: The Johns Hopkins University Press.

Bear, M., Connors, B., & Pardiso, M. (2001). *Neuroscience: Exploring the brain.* New York: Lippincott Williams & Wilkins.

Beason-Held, L., et al. (1998). PET reveals occipitotemporal pathway activation during elementary form perception in humans. *Visual Neuroscience, 15,* 503–510.

Bechtel, W. (1989). Functional analyses and their justification. *Biology and Philosophy, 4,* 159–162.

Bechtel, W., & Abrahamsen, A. (2002). *Connectionism and the mind: Parallel processing dynamics and evolution.* New York: Blackwell.

Belloni, E., et al. (1996). Identification of *Sonic Hedgehog* as a candidate gene responsible for holoprosencephaly. *Natural Genetics, 14,* 353–356.

Belot, G., & Earman, J. (1997). Chaos out of order: Quantum mechanics, the correspondence principle and chaos. *Studies in the History and Philosophy of Modern Physics, 2,* 147–182.

Berra, T. (1990). *Evolution and the myth of creationism.* Stanford: Stanford University Press.

Berthelet, A., & Chavallion, J. (Eds.), (1993). *The use of tools by human and non-human primates.* Oxford: Oxford University Press.

Beveridge, M., & Parkins, E. (1987). Visual representation in analogue problem solving. *Memory and Cognition, 15,* 230–237.

Bigelow, J., & Pargetter, R. (1998). Functions. In C. Allen, M. Bekoff, & G. Lauder (Eds.), *Nature's purposes: Analyses of function and design in biology* (pp. 241–259). Cambridge, MA: MIT Press.

Bisiach, E. (1999). Understanding consciousness: Clues from unilateral neglect and related disorders. In N. Block, O. Flanagan, & G. Güzeldere (Eds.), *The nature of consciousness* (pp. 237–276). Cambridge, MA: MIT Press.

Bitterman, M. (1965). The evolution of intelligence. *Scientific American, 212,* 92–100.

Bitterman, M. (1975). The comparative analysis of learning. *Science, 188,* 699–709.

Bitterman, M. (2000). Cognitive evolution: A psychological perspective. In C. Heyes & L. Huber (Eds.), *The evolution of cognition* (pp. 61–79). Cambridge, MA: MIT Press.

Black, J., & Greenough, W. (1986). Induction of pattern in neural structure by experience: Implications for cognitive development. In M. Lamb (Ed.), *Advances in developmental psychology* (pp. 1–50). Mahwah, NJ: Lawrence Erlbaum Associates.

Blake, A., & Truscianko, T. (Eds.), (1990). *A. I. and the eye.* New York: Wiley.

Blake, R., & Logothetis, N. (2002). Visual competition. *Nature Reviews Neuroscience, 3,* 13–21.

Bliss, T., & Lømo, T. (1973). Long-lasting potentiation of synaptic transmission in the dentate area of the anaesthetized rabbit following stimulation of the perforant path. *Journal of Physiology, 232,* 331–356.

Block, N. (1980). Introduction: What is functionalism? In N. Block (Ed.), *Readings in philosophy and psychology* (pp. 171–184). Cambridge, MA: Harvard University Press.

Bogdan, R. (1994). *Grounds for cognition: How goal-guided behavior shapes the mind.* Hillsdale, NJ: Lawrence Erlbaum Associates.

Bonner, J. (2000). *First signals: The evolution of multicellular development.* Princeton: Princeton University Press.

Boorse, C. (2002). A rebuttal on functions. In A. Ariew, R. Cummins, & M. Perlman (Eds.), *Functions: New essays in the philosophy of psychology and biology* (pp. 63–112). Oxford: Oxford University Press.

Born, R. (Ed.), (1987). *Artificial intelligence: The case against.* London: Croom Helm.

Boyd, R. (1991). Realism, anti-foundationalism and the enthusiasm for natural kinds. *Philosophical Studies, 91,* 127–148.

Boyd, R., & Silk, J. (1997). *How humans evolved.* New York: Norton.

Brandom, R. (1994). *Making it explicit: Reasoning, representing and discursive commitment.* Cambridge, MA: Harvard University Press.

Brandon, R. (1984). On the concept of environment in evolutionary biology. *Journal of Philosophy, 81,* 613–665.

Brandon, R. (1992). Environment. In E. Keller & E. Lloyd (Eds.), *Keywords in evolutionary biology* (pp. 81–86). Cambridge, MA: Harvard University Press.

Brefczynski, J., & DeYoe, E. (1999). A physiological correlate of the "spotlight" of visual attention. *Nature Reviews Neuroscience, 2,* 370–374.

Brooks, R. (1991). Intelligence without reason. *Proceedings of the Twelfth International Joint Congress on Artificial Intelligence, San Mateo, California, 12,* 569–595.

Brown, P., et al. (2004). A new small-bodied hominin from the Late Pleistocene of Flores, Indonesia. *Nature, 408,* 708–713.

Brunet, M., et al. (2002). A new hominid from the upper Miocene of Chad. *Nature, 418,* 145–151.

Bruno, N., & Cutting, J. (1988). Minimodularity and the perception of layout. *Journal of Experimental Psychology, 117,* 161–170.

Brunswik, E., & Kamiya, J. (1953). Ecological cue-validity of proximity and other Gestalt factors. *American Journal of Psychology, 66,* 20–32.

Buckner, R., et al. (1995). Functional anatomical studies of explicit and implicit memory retrieval tasks. *Journal of Neuroscience, 15,* 12–29.

Buller, D. (1999). Natural teleology. In D. Buller (Ed.), *Function, selection, and design* (pp. 1–27). Binghamton, NY: SUNY Press.

Buller, D. (2005). *Adapting minds: Evolutionary psychology and the persistent quest for human nature.* Cambridge, MA: MIT Press.

Buss, D. (1999). *Evolutionary psychology: The new science of the mind.* Boston: Allyn and Bacon.

Butler, A., & Hodos, W. (1996). *Comparative vertebrate neuroanatomy: Evolution and adaptation.* New York: Wiley.

Byrne, R. (1995). *The thinking ape: Evolutionary origins of intelligence.* Oxford: Oxford University Press.

Byrne, R. (2001). Social and technical forms of primate intelligence. In F. DeWaal (Ed.), *Tree of origin: What primate behavior can tell us about human social evolution* (pp. 145–172). Cambridge, MA: Harvard University Press.

Byrne, R., & Whiten, A. (Eds.), (1988). *Machiavellian intelligence: Social expertise and the evolution of intellect in monkeys, apes and humans.* Oxford: Clarendon Press.

Call, J., & Tomasello, M. (1994). The social learning of tool use by orangutans (*Pan pygmaeus*). *Human Evolution, 9,* 297–313.

Calvert, G. (2001). Crossmodal processing in the human brain: Insights from functional neuroimaging studies. *Cerebral Cortex, 11,* 1110–1123.

Calvin, W. (1996). *The cerebral code: Thinking a thought in the mosaics of the mind.* Cambridge, MA: MIT Press.

Calvin, W. (1998). The great climate flip-flop. *Atlantic Monthly, 28,* 47–64.

Calvin, W. (2001). Pumping up intelligence: Abrupt climate jumps and the evolution of higher intellectual functions during the Ice Ages. In R. Sternberg & E. Grigorenko (Eds.), *Environmental effects on cognitive abilities* (pp. 97–115). Mahwah, NJ: Lawrence Erlbaum Associates.

Calvin, W. (2004). *A brief history of the mind: From apes to intellect and beyond.* Oxford: Oxford University Press.

Cameron, D., & Groves, C. (2004). *Bones, stones and molecules: "Out of Africa" and human origins.* Burlington, MA: Elsevier Academic Press.

Campbell, N., & Reece, M. (1999). *Biology.* Menlo Park, CA: Benjamin Cummings.

Carroll, S. (2005). *Endless forms most beautiful: The new science of Evo Devo and the making of the animal kingdom.* New York: Norton.

Carruthers, P. (1993). Eternal thoughts. In H. Sluga (Ed.), *Meaning and ontology in Frege's philosophy* (pp. 223–243). New York: Garland.

Carruthers, P. (2002). Human creativity: Its evolution, its cognitive basis, and its connections with childhood pretence. *British Journal for the Philosophy of Science, 53,* 1–29.

Cartwright, N. (1999). *The dappled world: A study of the boundaries of science.* New York: Cambridge University Press.

Casagrande, V., & Kaas, J. (1994). The afferent, intrinsic, and efferent connections of primary visual cortex in primates. In A. Peters & K. Rockland (Eds.), *Cerebral cortex: Vol. 10. Primary visual cortex in primates* (pp. 201–259). New York: Plenum Press.

Castalo-Branco, J., et al. (1998). Synchronization of visual responses between the cortex, lateral geniculate nucleus, and retina in the anesthetized cat. *Journal of Neuroscience, 18,* 6395–6410.

Chalmers, D. (1996). *The conscious mind: In search of a fundamental theory.* New York: Oxford University Press.

Chellapilla, K., & Fogel, D. (2001). Evolving an expert checkers playing program without using human expertise. *IEEE Transactions on Evolutionary Computation, 5,* 422–428.

Chitnis, A. (1999). Control of neurogenesis—Lessons from frogs, fish and flies. *Current Opinions in Neurobiology, 9,* 18–25.

Chomsky, N. (1964). *Current issues in linguistic theory.* The Hague: Mouton.

Christiansen, M., & Kirby, S. (Eds.), (2003). *Language evolution.* New York: Oxford University Press.

Churchland, P. M. (1984). *Matter and consciousness: A contemporary introduction to the philosophy of mind.* Cambridge, MA: MIT Press.

Churchland, P. M. (1989). *A neurocomputational perspective: The nature of mind and the structure of science.* Cambridge, MA: MIT Press.

Churchland, P. M. (1995). *The engine of reason, the seat of the soul: A philosophical journey into the brain.* Cambridge, MA: MIT Press.

Churchland, P. S. (1986). *Neurophilosophy: Toward a unified science of the mind-brain.* Cambridge, MA: MIT Press.

Churchland, P. S. (1993). The co-evolutionary research ideology. In A. Goldman (Ed.), *Readings in philosophy and cognitive science* (pp. 745–767). Cambridge, MA: MIT Press.

Churchland, P. S. (1997). Can neurobiology teach us anything about consciousness? In N. Block, O. Flanagan, & G. Güzeldere (Eds.), *The nature of consciousness* (pp. 127–140). Cambridge, MA: MIT Press.

Churchland, P. S., Barlow, H., Ramachandran, V., & Sejnowski, T. (1994). A critique of pure vision. In C. Koch & J. Davis (Eds.), *Large-scale neuronal theories of the brain* (pp. 23–60). Cambridge, MA: MIT Press.

Clarke, D. (1992). Descartes' philosophy of science and the scientific revolution. In J. Cottingham (Ed.), *The Cambridge companion to Descartes* (pp. 258–285). Cambridge, MA: Cambridge University Press.

Clayton, N., & Krebs, J. (1994). Hippocampal growth and attrition in birds affected by experience. *Proceedings of the National Academy of Sciences, 91,* 7410–7414.

Collier, J. (2000). Autonomy and process closure as the basis of functionality. In J. Chandler & G. van de Vijver (Eds.), *Closure: Emergent organizations and their dynamics* (pp. 280–291). New York: Annals of the New York Academy of Sciences.

Collier, J., & Hooker, C. (1999). Complexly organized dynamical systems. *Open Systems and Information Dynamics, 6,* 241–302.

Collins, H. & Pinch, T. (1993). *The golem: What everyone should know about science.* Cambridge: Cambridge University Press.

Connell, J. (1989). A colony architecture for an artificial creature. *MIT AI Lab Memo,* 1151.

Copeland, J. (1993). *Artificial intelligence.* Cambridge, MA: Blackwell.

Corazza, E. (2002). Temporal indexicals and temporal terms. *Synthese, 130,* 441–460.

Cosmides, L., & Tooby, J. (1987). From evolution to behavior: Evolutionary psychology as the missing link. In J. Dupre (Ed.), *The latest on the best: Essays on evolution and optimality* (pp. 27–36). Cambridge, MA: Cambridge University Press.

Cosmides, L., & Tooby, J. (1992). The psychological foundations of culture. In J. Barkow, L. Cosmides, & J. Tooby (Eds.), *The adapted mind* (pp. 19–136). New York: Oxford University Press.

Cosmides, L., & Tooby, J. (1994). Origins of domain specificity: The evolution of functional organization. In L. Hirschfeld & S. Gelman (Eds.), *Mapping the mind: Domain specificity in cognition and culture* (pp. 71–97). Cambridge, MA: Cambridge University Press.

Cowey, A., & Stoerig, P. (1995). Blindsight in monkeys. *Nature, 373,* 247–249.

Craig, A., & Lichtman, J. (2001). Synapse formation and maturation. In W. Cowan (Ed.), *Synapses* (pp. 571–612). Baltimore: The Johns Hopkins University Press.

Crane, T. (2001). *The elements of mind.* Oxford: Oxford University Press.

Craver, C. (2001). Role functions, mechanisms, and hierarchy. *Philosophy of Science, 68,* 53–74.

Crick, F. (1994). *The astonishing hypothesis.* New York: Simon & Schuster.

Crick, F., & Koch, C. (1990). Towards a neurobiological theory of consciousness. *Seminars in the Neurosciences, 2,* 263–275.

Crick, F., & Koch, C. (1998). Consciousness and neuroscience. *Cerebral Cortex, 8,* 97–107.

Crick, F., & Koch, C. (1999). The problem of consciousness. In A. Damasio (Ed.), *The Scientific American book of the brain* (pp. 311–324). New York: Lyons Press.

Crick, F., & Koch, C. (2003). A new framework for consciousness. *Nature Reviews Neuroscience, 6,* 119–126.

Cronly-Dillon, J. (1991). *Evolution of the eye and visual system.* Boca Raton, FL: CRC Press.

Csányi, V. (1996). Organization, function, and creativity in biological and social systems. In J. Boulding & K. Khalil (Eds.), *Evolution, order and complexity* (pp. 146–181). London: Routledge.

Culler, D., & Singh, J. (1999). *Parallel computer architecture: A hardware/software approach.* San Francisco: Morgan Kaufmann.

Cummins, R. (1975). Functional analyses. *Journal of Philosophy, 72,* 741–765.

Cummins, R. (1983). *The nature of psychological explanation.* Cambridge, MA: MIT Press.

Cummins, R. (2002). Neo-teleology. In A. Ariew, R. Cummins, & M. Perlman (Eds.), *Functions: New essays in the philosophy of psychology and biology* (pp. 157–172). Oxford: Oxford University Press.

Cziko, G. (1992). Purposeful behavior as the control of perception: Implications for educational research. *Educational Researcher, 21,* 10–18.

Cziko, G. (1995). *Without miracles: Universal selection theory and the second Darwinian revolution.* Cambridge, MA: Cambridge University Press.

Daly, M., & Wilson, M. (1999). Human evolutionary psychology and animal behaviour. *Animal Behaviour, 57,* 509–519.

Damasio, A. (2000). A neurobiology for consciousness. In T. Metzinger (Ed.), *Neural correlates of consciousness* (pp. 111–120). Cambridge, MA: MIT Press.

Damasio, A. (2003). *Looking for Spinoza: Joy, sorrow, and the feeling brain.* New York: Harcourt.

Darwin, C. (1859/1999). *The origin of species by natural selection: Or, the preservation of favored races in the struggle for life.* New York: Bantam Books.

Davidson, J. (1995). The suddenness of insight. In R. Sternberg & J. Davidson (Eds.), *The nature of insight* (pp. 7–27). Cambridge, MA: MIT Press.

Davidson, M. (1971). *Louis Braille: The boy who invented books for the blind.* New York: Scholastic.

Dawkins, R. (1976). *The selfish gene.* New York: Oxford University Press.

Dawkins, R. (1986). *The blind watchmaker.* New York: Norton.

Dawkins, R. (1996). *Climbing mount improbable.* New York: Norton.

Dawkins, R. (2005). *The ancestor's tale: A pilgrimage to the dawn of evolution.* New York: Mariner Books.

Deacon, T. (1990). Rethinking mammalian brain evolution. *American Zoologist, 30,* 629–705.

Deacon, T. (1997). *The symbolic species: The co-evolution of language and the brain.* New York: Norton.

DeDuve, C. (1995). *Vital dust: Life as a cosmic interpretive.* New York: Basic Books.

DeDuve, C. (1996). The birth of complex cells. *Scientific American, 106,* 36–40.

Dehaene, S., & Changeux, J. (1989). A simple model of prefrontal cortex function in delayed response tasks. *Journal of Cognitive Neurobiology, 1,* 244–261.

Dehaene, S., & Changeux, J. (1991). The Wisconsin card sorting test: Theoretical analysis and modeling in a neuronal network. *Cerebral Cortex, 1,* 62–79.

Dehaene, S., & Changeux, J. (1997). A hierarchical neuronal network for planning behavior. *Proceedings of the National Academy of Sciences: Neuroscience, 94,* 13293–13298.

Dehaene, S., & Changeux, J. (2000). Reward-dependent learning in neuronal networks for planning and decision making. *Progress in Brain Research, 126,* 217–229.

Dennett, D. (1986). *Content and consciousness.* London: Routledge.

Dennett, D. (1987). *The intentional stance.* Cambridge, MA: MIT Press.

Dennett, D. (1991). *Consciousness explained.* Boston: Little, Brown.

Dennett, D. (1995). *Darwin's dangerous idea: Evolution and the meanings of life.* New York: Simon & Schuster.

Desimone, R. (1992). Neural circuits for visual attention in the primate brain. In G. Carpenter & S. Grossberg (Eds.), *Neural networks for vision and image processing* (pp. 343–364). Cambridge, MA: MIT Press.

Desimone, R., Albright, T., Gross, C., & Bruce, C. (1984). Stimulus-selective properties of inferior temporal neurons in the macaque. *Journal of Neuroscience, 4,* 2051–2062.

Desimone, R., Chelazzi, L., & Duncan, J. (1994). The interaction of neural systems for attention and memory. In C. Koch & J. Davis (Eds.), *Large-scale neuronal theories of the brain* (pp. 61–74). Cambridge, MA: MIT Press.

Desimone, R., & Duncan, J. (1995). Neural mechanisms of selective visual attention. *Annual Review of Neuroscience, 18,* 193–222.

Desimone, R., & Ungerleider, L. (1989). Neural mechanisms of visual processing in monkeys. In F. Boller & J. Grafman (Eds.), *Handbook of neuropsychology* (pp. 267–299). New York: Elsevier.

Devitt, M. (1997). *Realism and truth.* Princeton: Princeton University Press.

Dewey, J. (1929a). *The quest for certainty.* New York: Minton, Balch.

Dewey, J. (1929b). *Experience and nature.* Minneola, MN: Dover.

Dewey, J. (1941). Propositions, warranted assertibility, and truth. *The Journal of Philosophy, 38,* 169–186.

Dewey, J. (1951). *The influence of Darwinism on philosophy.* New York: Peter Smith.

Dewey, J. (1982). *Logic: Theory of inquiry.* New York: Irvington.

DeYoe, E., Felleman, D., van Essen, D., & McClendon, E. (1994). Multiple processing streams in occipitotemporal visual cortex. *Nature, 371,* 151–154.

DeYoe, E., Trusk, T., & Wong-Riley, M. (1995). Activity correlates of cytochrome oxidase-defined compartments in granular and supragranular layers of primary visual cortex of the macaque monkey. *Visual Neuroscience, 12,* 624–639.

Diamond, M. (1988). *Enriching heredity.* New York: The Free Press.

Diamond, M., & Hopson, J. (1989). *Magic trees of the mind.* New York: Dutton Press.

Dickstein, M. (Ed.), (1998). *The revival of pragmatism*. Durham, NC: Duke University Press.

DiLollo, V., Enns, J., & Rensink, R. (2000). Competition for consciousness among visual events: The psychophysics of reentrant visual processes. *Journal of Experimental Psychology, 129,* 481–507.

Dingus, L. (1990). Systematics, stratigraphy and chronology for mammalian fossils. *PaleoBios, 48,* 37–54.

Dominowski, R. (1995). Productive problem solving. In S. Smith, T. Ward, & R. Finke (Eds.), *The creative cognition approach* (pp. 73–96). Cambridge, MA: MIT Press.

Donald, M. (1991). *Origins of the modern mind*. Cambridge, MA: Harvard University Press.

Donald, M. (1997). The mind considered from a historical perspective. In D. Johnson & C. Erneling (Eds.), *The future of the cognitive revolution* (pp. 355–365). New York: Oxford University Press.

Dummett, M. (1978). *Truth and other enigmas*. London: Duckworth.

Dummett, M. (1982). Realism. *Synthese, 52,* 55–112.

Dunbar, R. (1988). *Primate societies*. London: Chapman and Hall.

Duncan, D., Burgess, E., & Duncan, I. (1998). Control of distal antennal identity and tarsal development in *Drosophila* by *Spineless-aristapedia*: A homolog of the mammalian dioxin receptor. *Genes & Development, 12,* 1290–1303.

Duns Scotus, J. (1995). The science of metaphysics. In W. Frank & A. Wolter (Eds.), *Duns Scotus: Metaphysician* (pp. 18–21). West Lafayette, IN: Purdue University Press.

Dupré, J. (1993). *The disorder of things: Metaphysical foundations of the disunity of science*. Cambridge, MA: Harvard University Press.

Eagle, M. (1959). The effects of subliminal stimuli of aggressive content upon conscious cognition. *Journal of Personality, 27,* 578–600.

Edelman, G., & Tononi, G. (2000). Reentry and the dynamic core: Neural correlates of conscious experience. In T. Metzinger (Ed.), *Neural correlates of consciousness* (pp. 139–156). Cambridge, MA: MIT Press.

Eigen, M. (1992). *Steps toward life*. New York: Oxford University Press.

Eimer, M., & van Velzen, J. (2002). Cross-modal interactions between audition, touch, and vision in endogenous spatial attention: ERP evidence on preparatory states and sensory modulations. *Journal of Cognitive Neuroscience, 14,* 254–271.

Eldredge, N. (1993). History, function and evolutionary biology. In M. Hecht, W. Steele, & B. Wallace (Eds.), *Evolutionary biology* (pp. 33–49). New York: Plenum Press.

Eldredge, N. (1995). *Reinventing Darwin: The great debate at the high table of evolutionary theory*. New York: Wiley.

Eldredge, N. (2001). *The triumph of evolution and the failure of creationism*. New York: Henry Holt.

Emery, N., & Clayton, N. (2004). The mentality of crows: Convergent evolution of intelligence in corvids and apes. *Science, 306*, 1903–1907.

Emmeche, C., Køppe, S., & Stjernfelt, F. (2000). Levels, emergence, and three versions of downward causation. In P. Andersen, C. Emmeche, N. Finnemann, & P. Christiansen (Eds.), *Downward causation: Minds, bodies and matter* (pp. 13–34). Aarhus: Aarhus University Press.

Engel, A., Kreiter, A., König, P., & Singer, W. (1991). Synchronization of oscillatory neuronal responses between striate and extrastriate visual cortical areas of the cat. *Proceedings of the National Academy of Sciences, USA, 88*, 6048–6052.

Erdmann, B. (1892). *Logik*. Halle: M. Niemeyer.

Eshleman, C. (2003). *Juniper fuse: Upper Paleolithic imagination and the construction of the underworld*. Middletown, CT: Wesleyan University Press.

Farah, M. (1984). The neurobiological basis of mental imagery: A computational analysis. *Cognition, 18*, 245–272.

Farah, M. (1990). *Visual agnosias*. Cambridge, MA: MIT Press.

Farah, M. (1997). Visual perception and visual awareness after brain damage: A tutorial overview. In N. Block, O. Flanagan, & G. Güzeldere (Eds.), *The nature of consciousness* (pp. 203–236). Cambridge, MA: MIT Press.

Fauconnier, G., & Turner, M. (2002). *The way we think: Conceptual blending and the mind's hidden complexities*. New York: Basic Books.

Febvre-Chevalier, J., Bilbaut, A., Febvre, J., & Bone, Q. (1989). Membrane excitability and motile responses in the protozoa, with particular attention to the heliozoan *Actinocoryne contractilis*. In P. Anderson (Ed.), *Evolution of the first nervous systems* (pp. 237–254). New York: Plenum Press.

Feduccia, A. (1996). *The origin and evolution of birds*. New Haven, CT: Yale University Press.

Feldman, J., & Ballard, D. (1982). Connectionist models and their properties. *Cognitive Science, 6*, 205–254.

Felleman, D., & van Essen, D. (1991). Distributed hierarchical processing in the primate cerebral cortex. *Cerebral Cortex, 1*, 1–47.

Fenchel, T., & Finlay, B. (1994). The evolution of life without oxygen. *American Scientist, 5*, 21–30.

Fink, G. (2003). In search of one's own past: The neural bases of autobiographical memories. *Brain, 126*, 1509–1510.

Fink, G., et al. (1996). Where in the brain does visual attention select the forest and the trees? *Nature, 382,* 626–628.

Finke, R. (1980). Levels of equivalence in imagery and perception. *Psychological Review, 87,* 113–132.

Finke, R. (1986). Mental imagery and the visual system. *Scientific American, 160,* 88–95.

Finke, R., & Pinker, S. (1982). Spontaneous imagery scanning in mental extrapolation. *Journal of Experimental Psychology: Learning, Memory and Cognition, 2,* 142–147.

Finke, R., Ward, T., & Smith, S. (1992). *Creative cognition: Theory, research and applications.* Cambridge, MA: MIT Press.

Fiorito, G., et al. (1990). Problem solving ability of *Octopus vulgaris* Lamark (*mollusca, cephalopodo*). *Behavior and Neural Biology, 53,* 217–230.

FitzPatrick, W. (2000). *Teleology and the norms of nature.* New York: Garland.

Fleagle, J. (1999). *Primate adaptation and evolution.* San Diego: Academic Press.

Fodor, J. (1983). *The modularity of mind.* Cambridge, MA: MIT Press.

Fodor, J. (1985). Précis of "The Modularity of Mind." *The Behavioral and Brain Sciences, 8,* 1–42.

Fodor, J. (1998). *In critical condition: Polemical essays on cognitive science and the philosophy of mind.* Cambridge, MA: MIT Press.

Foley, R. (1995). The adaptive legacy of human evolution: A search for the environment of evolutionary adaptedness. *Evolutionary Anthropology, 4,* 192–203.

Forterre, P. (2005). The two ages of the RNA world, and the transition to the DNA world: A story of viruses and cells. *Biochimie, 87,* 793–803.

Franceschini, N., Pichon, J., & Blanes, C. (1992). From insect vision to robot vision. *Philosophical Transactions of the Royal Society B, 337,* 283–294.

Frank, E., & Wenner, P. (1993). Environmental specification of neuronal connectivity. *Neuron, 10,* 779–785.

Frege, G. (1964). *The basic laws of arithmetic.* M. Furth (Trans.). Berkeley: University of California Press.

Frege, G. (1966). On sense and reference. In P. Geach & M. Black (Eds.), *Translations from the philosophical writings of Gotlob Frege* (pp. 3–33). Oxford: Basil Blackwell.

Frege, G. (1977). Thoughts. In P. Geach (Ed.), *Logical investigations* (pp. 1–30). Oxford: Basil Blackwell.

Frege, G. (1979). Logic. In H. Hermes, F. Kambartel, & F. Kaulbach (Eds.), *Posthumous writings* (pp. 18–39). Chicago: University of Chicago Press.

French, R., & Sougne, J. (2001). *Connectionist models of learning, development and evolution.* Liege: Springer-Verlag.

Freud, S. (1964). *The future of an illusion*. W. Robson-Scott (Trans.). New York: Anchor Books.

Fries, P., Roelfsema, P., Engel, A., König, P., & Singer, W. (1997). Synchronization of oscillatory responses in visual cortex correlates with perception in interocular rivalry. *Proceedings of the National Academy of Sciences, USA, 94*, 12699–12704.

Frith, C. (1996). Brain mechanisms for "having a theory of mind." *Journal of Pharmacology, 10*, 9–15.

Fry, I. (2000). *The emergence of life on earth: A historical and scientific overview*. Brunswick, NJ: Rutgers University Press.

Fumerton, R. (2002). *Realism and the correspondence theory of truth*. New York: Rowman & Littlefiled.

Funahashi, S., Bruce, C., & Golman-Rakic, P. (1989). Mnemonic coding of visual space in the monkey's dorsolateral prefrontal cortex. *Journal of Neurophysiology, 61*, 331–349.

Fuster, J. (1997). *The prefrontal cortex: Anatomy, physiology, and neuropsychology of the frontal lobe*. New York: Lippincott-Raven.

Gannon, P., Holloway, R., Broadfeld, D., & Braun, A. (1998). Asymmetry of chimpanzee *planum temporale*: Humanlike pattern of Wernicke's brain language area homolog. *Science, 279*, 220–222.

Gannon, P., & Kheck, N. (1999). Primate brain "language" area evolution: Anatomy of Heschl's gyrus and *planum temporale* in hominids, hylobatids and macaques and of *planum parietale* in *Pan troglodytes*. *American Journal of Physical Anthropology, 28*, 132–133.

Gardner, H. (1993). *Multiple intelligences: The theory in practice*. New York: Basic Books.

Gardner, H. (1999). *Intelligence reframed: Multiple intelligences for the 21st century*. New York: Basic Books.

Geschwind, N. (1979). Specializations of the human brain. *Scientific American, 241*, 180–199.

Gibson, K., & Ingold, T. (Eds.), (1993). *Tools, language and cognition in human evolution*. Cambridge, UK: Cambridge University Press.

Glennan, S. (1996). Mechanisms and the nature of causation. *Erkenntnis, 44*, 49–71.

Goddard, J., Rossel, M., Manley, M., & Capecchi, M. (1996). Mice with targeted disruption of *Hoxb-1* fail to form the motor nucleus of the VIIth nerve. *Development, 122*, 3217–3228.

Godfrey-Smith, P. (1993). Functions: Consensus without unity. *Pacific Philosophical Quarterly, 74*, 196–208.

Godfrey-Smith, P. (1994). A modern history theory of functions. *Nous, 28,* 344–362.

Godfrey-Smith, P. (1996). *Complexity and the function of mind in nature.* Cambridge, UK: Cambridge University Press.

Goguen, J., & Harrell, D. (2004). Style as a choice of blending principles. In S. Argamon, S. Dubnov, & J. Jupp (Eds.), *Style and meaning in language, art, music and design* (pp. 49–56). New York: American Association for Artificial Intelligence Press.

Goldman-Rakic, P. (1996). Regional and cellular fractionalism of working memory. *Proceedings of the National Academy of Sciences, USA, 93,* 13473–13480.

Goodale, M., et al. (1994). Separate neural pathways for the visual analysis of object shape in perception and prehension. *Current Biology, 4,* 604–606.

Goodale, M., & Murphy, K. (2000). Space in the brain: Different neural substrates for allocentric and egocentric frames of reference. In T. Metzinger (Ed.), *Neural correlates of consciousness* (pp. 189–202). Cambridge, MA: MIT Press.

Gordon, D. (1992). Phenotypic plasticity. In E. Keller & E. Lloyd (Eds.), *Keywords in evolutionary biology* (pp. 255–262). Cambridge, MA: Harvard University Press.

Gould, S. (1977). *Ever since Darwin.* New York: Norton.

Gould, S. (1980). The evolutionary biology of constraint. *Daedalus, 109,* 39–53.

Gould, S. (2002). *The structure of evolutionary theory.* Cambridge, MA: Belknap Press.

Gould, S., & Vrba, E. (1982). Exaptation: A missing term in the science of form. *Paleobiology, 8,* 4–15.

Graves, R., & Jones, B. (1992). Conscious visual perceptual awareness versus nonconscious spatial localization examined with normal subjects using possible analogs of blindsight and neglect. *Cognitive Neuropsychology, 9,* 487–508.

Gray, C. (1999). The temporal correlation hypothesis of visual feature integration: Still alive and well. *Neuron, 24,* 31–47.

Gray, C., Knig, P., Engel, A., & Singer, W. (1989). Oscillatory responses in cat visual cortex exhibit inter-columnar synchronization which reflects global stimulus properties. *Nature, 338,* 334–337.

Gregory, R. (1997). *Eye and brain: The psychology of seeing.* Princeton: Princeton University Press.

Griffin, D. (1992). *Animal minds.* Chicago: University of Chicago Press.

Griffiths, P. (1992). Adaptive explanation and the concept of a vestige. In P. Griffiths (Ed.), *Trees of life: Essays in philosophy of biology* (pp. 111–131). Dordrecht: Kluwer Academic.

Griffiths, P. (1993). Functional analysis and proper function. *British Journal for the Philosophy of Science, 44,* 409–422.

Griffiths, P. (1996). The historical turn in the study of adaptation. *British Journal for the Philosophy of Science, 47*, 511–532.

Groves, C. (2002). *Primate taxonomy.* Washington, DC: Smithsonian Press.

Gupta, A. (2001). Truth. In L. Goble (Ed.), *The Blackwell guide to philosophical logic* (pp. 90–114). London: Blackwell.

Habermas, J. (1984). *The theory of communicative action.* T. McCarthy (Trans.). Boston: Beacon Press.

Hall, G. (1994). Pavlovian conditioning: Laws of association. In N. Mackintosh (Ed.), *Animal learning and cognition* (pp. 15–43). San Diego: Academic Press.

Hall, G. (1996). Learning about associatively activated stimulus representations: Implications for acquired equivalence and perceptual learning. *Animal Learning and Behavior, 24*, 233–255.

Hardcastle, V. (1999). Understanding functions: A pragmatic approach. In V. Hardcastle (Ed.), *Where biology meets psychology* (pp. 27–43). Cambridge, MA: MIT Press.

Harris, P. (2000). *The work of the imagination.* Oxford: Blackwell.

Hartwig, W. (Ed.), (2002). *The primate fossil record.* Cambridge, UK: Cambridge University Press.

Harvey, P., & Pagel, M. (1991). *The comparative method in evolutionary biology.* Oxford: Oxford University Press.

Hasker, W. (1999). *The emergent self.* Ithaca: Cornell University Press.

Hastings, A. (1998). *Population biology: Concepts and models.* New York: Springer.

Hatfield, G. (1999). Mental functions as constraints on neurophysiology: Biology and psychology of vision. In V. Hardcastle (Ed.), *Where biology meets psychology* (pp. 251–271). Cambridge, MA: MIT Press.

Hebb, D. (1949). *The organization of behavior: A neuropsychological theory.* New York: Wiley.

Hebb, D. (1966). *A textbook of psychology.* Philadelphia: Saunders Press.

Heil, J. (2004a). *Philosophy of mind: A contemporary introduction.* London: Routledge.

Heil, J. (Ed.), (2004b). *Philosophy of mind: A guide and anthology.* Oxford: Oxford University Press.

Hellman, G. (1999). Reduction (?) to what (?): Comments on Sklar's "The reduction of thermodynamics to statistical mechanics." *Philosophical Studies, 95*, 200–213.

Hempel, C. (1965). *Aspects of scientific explanation.* New York: The Free Press.

Hendry, R. (1999). Molecular models and the question of physicalism. *Hyle, 5*, 143–160.

Hermer, L., & Spelke, E. (1996). Modularity and development: The case of spatial reorientation. *Cognition, 61,* 195–232.

Heyes, C., & Dawson, G. (1990). A demonstration of observational learning in rats using a bidirectional control. *Quarterly Journal of Experimental Psychology, 42B,* 59–71.

Heyes, C., Jaldon, E., & Dawson, G. (1992). Imitation in rats: Initial responding and transfer evidence from a bidirectional control procedure. *Quarterly Journal of Experimental Psychology, 45B,* 229–240.

Hirschfeld, L., & Gelman, S. (1994). Toward a topography of mind: An introduction to domain specificity. In L. Hirschfeld & S. Gelman (Eds.), *Mapping the mind: Domain specificity in cognition and culture* (pp. 3–35). Cambridge, UK: Cambridge University Press.

Hodges, W. (2001). Classical logic I: First-order logic. In L. Goble (Ed.), *The Blackwell guide to philosophical logic* (pp. 9–32). London: Blackwell.

Hofman, M. (2001). Evolution and complexity of the human brain and some organizing principles. In G. Roth & M. Wullimann (Eds.), *Brain, evolution and cognition* (pp. 501–522). Cambridge, UK: Cambridge University Press.

Hoffman, K., & McNaughton, B. (2002). Coordinated reactivation of distributed memory traces in primate neocortex. *Science, 297,* 2070–2073.

Holloway, M. (2003). The mutable brain. *Scientific American, 289,* 78–85.

Holyoak, K., & Thagard, P. (1989). Analogical mapping by constraint satisfaction. *Cognitive Science, 13,* 295–355.

Holyoak, K., & Thagard, P. (1995). *Mental leaps: Analogy in creative thought.* Cambridge, MA: MIT Press.

Honda, M., Wise, S., Weeks, R., Deibel, M., & Hallett, M. (1998). Cortical areas with enhanced activation during object-centered spatial information processing. *Brain, 121,* 2145–2158.

Horan, B. (1989). Functional explanations in sociobiology. *Biology & Philosophy, 4,* 131–158.

Horridge, G. (1987). Evolution of visual processing and the construction of seeing systems. *Proceedings of the Royal Society of London: Series B, Biological Sciences, 230,* 279–292.

Hubel, D., & Wiesel, T. (1962). Receptive fields, binocular interaction and functional architecture in the cat's visual cortex. *Journal of Physiology, 160,* 106–154.

Hubel, D., & Wiesel, T. (1968). Receptive fields and functional architecture of monkey striate cortex. *Journal of Physiology, 195,* 215–243.

Humphrey, N. (1983). *Consciousness regained: Chapters in the development of mind.* Cambridge, MA: Harvard University Press.

Humphrey, N. (1992). *A history of the mind: Evolution of the birth of consciousness.* New York: Simon & Schuster.

Humphrey, N. (1998). The privatization of sensation. In S. Hameroff, A. Kaszniak, & A. Scott (Eds.), *Toward a science of consciousness: The second Tucson discussions and debates* (pp. 247–257). Cambridge, MA: MIT Press.

Humphreys, P. (1997). Emergence, not supervenience. *Philosophy of Science, 64,* S337–S345.

Hunter, W. (1913). The delayed reaction in animals and children. *Behavior Monographs, 2,* 1–86.

Husserl, E. (1995). *Cartesian meditations.* D. Cairns (Trans.). Dordrecht: Kluwer Academic.

Huttenlocher, J. (1968). Constructing spatial images: A strategy in reasoning. *Psychological Review, 4,* 277–299.

Isaac, G. (1986). Foundation stones: Early artifacts as indicators of activities and abilities. In G. Bailey & P. Callow (Eds.), *Stone age prehistory* (pp. 221–241). Cambridge, UK: Cambridge University Press.

Jackendoff, R. (1987). *Consciousness and the computational mind.* Cambridge, MA: MIT Press.

Jackendoff, R. (1992). *Languages of the mind: Essays on mental representation.* Cambridge, MA: MIT Press.

Jackendoff, R. (1994). *Patterns in the mind: Language and human nature.* New York: Basic Books.

Jackson, F. (1982). Epiphenomenal qualia. *The Philosophical Quarterly, 32,* 127–136.

James, W. (1890). *The principles of psychology.* New York: Henry Holt.

James, W. (1975). *Pragmatism.* Cambridge, MA: Harvard University Press.

Jarrold, C., Carruthers, P., Smith, P., & Boucher, J. (1994). Pretend play: Is it metarepresentational? *Mind and Language, 9,* 445–468.

Jerison, H. (1973). *Evolution of the brain and intelligence.* New York: Academic Press.

Jerison, H. (1991). *Brain size and the evolution of mind.* New York: American Museum of Natural History.

Jerison, H. (1997). Evolution of prefrontal cortex. In N. Krasnegor, G. Lyon, & P. Goldman-Rakic (Eds.), *Development of the prefrontal cortex: Evolution, neurobiology and behavior* (pp. 9–26). Baltimore, MD: Paul H. Brookes.

Joffe, T., & Dunbar, R. (1997). Visual and socio-cognitive information processing in primate brain evolution. *Proceedings of the Royal Society of London, 1386,* 1303–1307.

Johanson, D. (1996). Face-to-face with Lucy's family. *National Geographic Magazine, 189,* 96–117.

Johanson, D., & Edgar, B. (1996). *From Lucy to language*. New York: Simon & Schuster.

Johnson-Laird, P. (1988). *The computer and the mind: An introduction to cognitive science*. Cambridge, MA: Harvard University Press.

Julesz, B. (1983). Textons, rapid local attention shifts and iconic memory. *Behavioral and Brain Sciences, 6*, 25–27.

Julesz, B. (1984). Toward an axiomatic theory of preattentive vision. In G. Edelman, W. Gall, & W. Cowan (Eds.), *Dynamic aspects of neocortical function* (pp. 585–612). New York: Wiley.

Kaas, J. (1987). The organization of the neocortex in mammals: Implications for theories of brain function. *Annual Review of Psychology, 38*, 129–151.

Kaas, J. (1993). Evolution of the multiple areas and modules within neocortex. *Perspectives in Developmental Neurobiology, 1*, 101–107.

Kaas, J. (1995). The evolution of isocortex. *Brain, Behavior, and Evolution, 46*, 187–196.

Kaas, J. (1996). What comparative studies of neocortex tell us about the human brain. *Revista Brasileira de Biologia, 56*, 315–322.

Kandel, E. (1976). *Cellular basis of behavior: An introduction to behavioral neurobiology*. San Francisco: Freeman.

Kandel, E., Schwartz, J., & Jessell, T. (Eds.), (2000). *Principles of neural science*. New York: McGraw-Hill.

Kaneto, H., Morrissey, J., McCracken, R., Reyes, A., & Klahr, S. (1998). Osteopontin expression in the kidney during unilateral ureteral obstruction. *Mineral and Electrolyte Metabolism, 24*, 227–237.

Kaniut, L. (1997). *Some bears kill*. New York: Safari Press.

Kanizsa, G. (1976). Subjective contours. *Scientific American, 234*, 48.

Kanizsa, G. (1979). *Organization in vision: Essays on Gestalt perception*. New York: Praeger.

Kant, I. (1929). *Critique of pure reason*. N. Kemp-Smith (Trans.). New York: Macmillan.

Kant, I. (1987). *Critique of judgment*. W. Pluhar (Trans.). Indianapolis, IN: Hackett.

Kappelman, J. (1996). The evolution of body mass and relative brain size in fossil hominids. *Journal of Human Evolution, 30*, 243–276.

Karmiloff-Smith, A. (1992). *Beyond modularity: A developmental perspective on cognitive science*. Cambridge, MA: MIT Press.

Karten, H. (1998). Evolutionary "progress" or adaptation? Regulation of neuronal numbers has profound down stream effects: Development as a towrope in evolution. *American Journal of Physical Anthropology, 26*, 133.

Karten, H., & Shimazu, T. (1989). The origins of neocortex: Connections and lamination as distinct events in evolution. *Journal of Cognitive Neuroscience, 1,* 291–301.

Keverne, E., Martel, F., & Nevison, C. (1996). Primate brain evolution: Genetic and functional considerations. *Proceedings of the Royal Society of London, 1371,* 689–696.

Kim, J. (1995). Emergent properties. In T. Honderich (Ed.), *The Oxford companion to philosophy* (pp. 220–241). Oxford: Oxford University Press.

Kim, J. (1999). Making sense of emergence. *Philosophical Studies, 95,* 3–36.

Kim, J. (2000). *Mind in a physical world: An essay on the mind–body problem and mental causation.* Cambridge, MA: MIT Press.

Kingdon, J. (2003). *Lowly origins.* Princeton: Princeton University Press.

Kitcher, P. (1989). Explanatory unification and the causal structure of the world. In P. Kitcher & W. Salmon (Eds.), *Scientific explanation* (pp. 33–56). Minneapolis: University of Minnesota Press.

Kitcher, P. (1992). Gene: Current usages. In E. Keller & E. Lloyd (Eds.), *Keywords in evolutionary biology* (pp. 128–136). Cambridge, MA: Harvard University Press.

Kitcher, P. (1993). *The advancement of science: Science without legend, objectivity without illusions.* New York: Oxford University Press.

Koestler, A. (1964). *The act of creation.* New York: Dell.

Kosslyn, S. (1980). *Image and mind.* Cambridge, MA: Harvard University Press.

Kosslyn, S. (1983). *Ghosts in the mind's machine.* New York: Norton.

Kosslyn, S. (1987). Seeing and imagining in the cerebral hemispheres: A computational approach. *Psychological Review, 94,* 148–175.

Kosslyn, S. (1996). *Image and brain: The resolution of the imagery debate.* Cambridge, MA: MIT Press.

Kosslyn, S., et al. (1999a). Identifying objects seen from different viewpoints: A PET investigation. *Brain, 5,* 1055–1071.

Kosslyn, S., et al. (1999b). The role of area 17 in visual imagery: Convergent evidence from PET and rTMS. *Science, 284,* 167–170.

Kosslyn, S., et al. (2001). Neural foundations of imagery. *Nature Reviews Neuroscience, 2,* 635–643.

Kosslyn, S., & Koenig, O. (1995). *Wet mind: The new cognitive neuroscience.* New York: The Free Press.

Kosslyn, S., Thompson, W., Kim, I., & Alpert, N. (1995). Topographical representations in primary visual cortex. *Nature, 378,* 496–498.

Kulin, S., Kishore, R., Helmerson, K., & Locascio, L. (2003). Optical manipulation of liposomes as microcreators. *National Institute of Standards and Technology, 1,* 1–8.

Kulp, C. (Ed.), (1996). *Realism/antirealism and epistemology*. New York: Rowman & Littlefield.

Laland, K., & Brown, G. (2002). *Sense and nonsense: Evolutionary perspectives on human behaviour*. Oxford: Oxford University Press.

Lambert, K. (2001). Free logics. In L. Goble (Ed.), *The Blackwell guide to philosophy of logic* (pp. 258–279). London: Blackwell.

Leakey, M., et al. (2001). New hominin genus from eastern Africa shows diverse middle Pliocene lineages. *Nature, 410*, 433–440.

Lek, S., & Guegan, J. (2000). *Artificial neuronal networks: Application to ecology and evolution*. New York: Telos Press.

Lennox, J. (1993). Darwin was a teleologist. *Biology & Philosophy, 8*, 409–421.

Lerman, G., & Rudolph, L. (1994). *Parallel evolution of parallel processors*. The Hague: Kluwer Academic.

Lewontin, R. (1992). Genotype and phenotype. In E. Keller & E. Lloyd (Eds.), *Keywords in evolutionary biology* (pp. 137–144). Cambridge, MA: Harvard University Press.

Lieberman, D., et al. (1996). Homoplasy and early *Homo*: An analysis of the evolutionary relationships of *H. habilis* sensu stricto and *H. rudolfensis*. *Journal of Human Evolution, 30*, 97–120.

Line, M. (2002). The enigma of the origin of life and its timing. *Microbiology, 148*, 21–27.

Lock, A. (1993). Human language development and object manipulation: Their relation in ontogeny and its possible relevance for phylogenetic questions. In K. Gibson & T. Ingold (Eds.), *Tools, language and cognition in human evolution* (pp. 279–299). Cambridge, MA: Cambridge University Press.

Logothetis, N. (1999). Vision: A window on consciousness. *Scientific American, 281*, 69–75.

Lowe, E. (2000). Causal closure principles and emergentism. *Philosophy, 75*, 571–585.

Lueders, H., et al. (1991). Basal temporal language area. *Brain, 114*, 743–754.

Lumer, E. (2000). Binocular rivalry and human visual awareness. In T. Metzinger (Ed.), *Neural correlates of consciousness* (pp. 231–240). Cambridge, MA: MIT Press.

Lumer, E., Edelman, G., & Tononi, G. (1997). Neural dynamics in a model of the thalamocortical system: The role of neural synchrony tested through perturbations of spike timing. *Cerebral Cortex, 7*, 228–236.

Lumer, E., Friston, K., & Rees, G. (1998). Neural correlates of perceptual rivalry in the human brain. *Science, 280*, 1930–1934.

Lux, S., Marshall, J., Ritzl, A., Zilles, K., & Fink, G. (2003). Neural mechanisms associated with attention to temporal synchrony versus spatial orientation: An fMRI study. *NeuroImage, 20,* S58–S65.

Lycan, W. (1995). *Consciousness.* Cambridge, MA: MIT Press.

Macaluso, E., Frith, C., & Driver, J. (2000). Selective spatial attention in vision and touch: Unimodal and multimodal mechanisms revealed by PET. *The Journal of Neurophysiology, 83,* 3062–3075.

Machamer, P., Darden, L., & Craver, C. (2000). Thinking about mechanisms. *Philosophy of Science, 67,* 1–25.

Mack, R. (1968). *The appeal to immediate experience: Philosophic method in Bradley, Whitehead and Dewey.* New York: Books for Libraries Press.

Mackie, G. (1989). Evolution of cnidarian giant axons. In P. Anderson (Ed.), *Evolution of the first nervous systems* (pp. 395–408). New York: Plenum Press.

Mackintosh, N. (1983). *Conditioning and associative learning.* Oxford: Clarendon Press.

Mackintosh, N. (1995). Categorization by people and by pigeons. *Quarterly Journal of Experimental Psychology, 48B,* 193–214.

MacLean, P. (1967). *A triune concept of the brain and behavior.* Toronto: University of Toronto Press.

MacLean, P. (1991). *The triune brain in evolution.* Dordrecht: Kluwer Academic.

Maconochioe, M., Nonchev, S., Morrison, A., & Krumlauf, R. (1996). Paralogous hox genes: Function and regulation. *Annual Review of Gentics, 30,* 529–556.

Macphail, E. (1996). Cognitive function in mammals: The evolutionary perspective. *Cognitive Brain Research, 3,* 279–290.

Macphail, E. (1998). *The evolution of consciousness.* New York: Oxford University Press.

Mahner, M., & Bunge, M. (2001). Function and functionalism: A synthetic perspective. *Philosophy of Science, 68,* 75–94.

Malenka, R., & Siegelbaum, S. (2001). Synaptic plasticity. In W. Cowan, T. Jessell, & S. Zipursky (Eds.), *Molecular and cellular approaches to neuronal development* (pp. 393–454). New York: Oxford University Press.

Marcel, A. (1983). Consciousness and preconscious perception: Experiments on visual masking and word recognition. *Cognitive Psychology, 15,* 197–237.

Margulis, L., & Dolan, M. (2002). *Early life.* New York: Jones and Bartlett.

Margulis, L., & Sagan, D. (1986). *Microcosmos: Four billion years of microbial evolution.* New York: Summit Books.

Marten, K., & Psarakos, S. (1994). Evidence of self-awareness in the bottlenose dolphin (*Tursiops truncates*). In S. Parker, R. Mitchell, & M. Boccia (Eds.), *Self-awareness in animals and humans* (pp. 361–379). New York: Cambridge University Press.

Martin, R. (1990). *Primate origins and evolution: A phylogenetic reconstruction.* London: Chapman and Hall.

Martin, J., Kogo, N., Fan, T., & Ariel, M. (2003). Morphology of the turtle accessory optical system. *Visual Neuroscience, 20,* 639–649.

Marr, D. (1983). *Vision.* New York: Freeman.

Mattson, B., Sorensen, J., Zimmer, J., & Johansson, B. (1997). Neural grafting to experimental neocortical infarcts improves behavioral outcome and reduces thalamic atrophy in rats housed in enriched but not in standard environments. *Stroke, 28,* 1225–1231.

Maviel, T., Durkin, T., Menzaghi, F., & Bontempi, B. (2004). Sites of neocortical reorganization critical for remote spatial memory. *Science, 305,* 96–99.

Mayer, R. (1995). The search for insight: Grappling with Gestalt psychology's unanswered questions. In R. Sternberg & J. Davidson (Eds.), *The nature of insight* (pp. 3–32). Cambridge, MA: MIT Press.

Mayr, E. (1969). Footnotes on the philosophy of biology. *Philosophy of Science, 36,* 190–200.

Mayr, E. (1976). *Evolution and the diversity of life.* Cambridge, MA: Harvard University Press.

Mayr, E. (1982). *The growth of biological thought.* Cambridge, MA: Harvard University Press.

Mayr, E. (1988). *Toward a new philosophy of biology.* Cambridge, MA: Harvard University Press.

Mayr, E. (1991). *One long argument: Charles Darwin and the genesis of modern evolutionary thought.* Cambridge, MA: Harvard University Press.

Mayr, E. (1993). Proximate and ultimate causation. *Biology & Philosophy, 8,* 95-98.

Mayr, E. (1996). The autonomy of biology: The position of biology among the sciences. *Quarterly Review of Biology, 71,* 98–106.

Mayr, E. (1997). *This is biology: The science of the living world.* Cambridge, MA: Harvard University Press.

Mayr, E. (2001). *What evolution is.* New York: Basic Books.

McFarland, D., & Bosser, T. (1993). *Intelligent behavior in animals and robots.* Cambridge, MA: MIT Press.

McGinn, C. (1982). *The character of mind.* New York: Oxford University Press.

McGrew, W. (2004). *The cultured chimpanzee: Reflections on cultural primatology.* Cambridge, UK: Cambridge University Press.

McHenry, H. (1998). Body proportions in *A. afarensis* and *A. africanus* and the origin of the genus *Homo. Journal of Human Evolution, 35*, 1–22.

McKim, R. (1980). *Experiences in visual thinking.* Monterey, CA: Brooks/Cole.

McLaughlin, B. (1992). Rise and fall of British emergentism. In A. Beckermann, H. Flohr, & J. Kim (Eds.), *Emergence or reduction? Essays on the prospects for nonreductive physicalism* (pp. 30–67). Berlin: Walter De Gruyter.

McLaughlin, B. (1997). Emergence and supervenience. *Intellectica, 2,* 25–43.

McNabb, J., & Ashton, N. (1995). Thoughtful flakers. *Cambridge Archeological Journal, 5,* 289–301.

McTaggart, J. (1921). *The nature of existence.* Cambridge, MA: Cambridge University Press.

Merikle, P., & Daneman, M. (1998). Psychological investigations of unconscious perception. *Journal of Consciousness Studies, 5,* 5–18.

Mesalum, M. (1998). From sensation to cognition. *Brain, 121,* 1013–1052.

Meyer, R. (1989). Systematic thinking fostered by illustrations in scientific text. *Journal of Educational Psychology, 81,* 240–246.

Miles, H., Mitchell, R., & Harper, S. (1996). Simon says: The development of imitation in an enculturated orangutan. *Journal of Comparative Psychology, 105,* 145–160.

Miller, R. (1987). *Fact and method.* Princeton: Princeton University Press.

Millikan, R. (1984). *Language, thought, and other biological categories.* Cambridge, MA: MIT Press.

Millikan, R. (1989). In defense of proper functions. *Philosophy of Science, 56,* 288–302.

Millikan, R. (2002). Biofunctions: Two paradigms. In A. Ariew, R. Cummins, & M. Perlman (Eds.), *Functions: New essays in the philosophy of psychology and biology* (pp. 113–143). Oxford: Oxford University Press.

Milner, A., & Goodale, M. (1995). *The visual brain in action.* Oxford: Oxford University Press.

Mishkin, M., Ungerleider, L., & Macko, K. (1983). Object vision and spatial vision: Two cortical pathways. *Trends in Neurosciences, 6,* 414–417.

Mitchell, R. (1987). A comparative developmental approach to understanding imitation. *Perspectives in Ethology, 7,* 183–215.

Mitchell, R. (1993). Mental models of mirror self-recognition: Two theories. *New Ideas in Psychology, 11,* 295–325.

Mithen, S. (1996). *The prehistory of the mind: The cognitive origins of art, religion and science.* London: Thames and Hudson.

Mithen, S. (1999). Handaxes and ice age carvings: Hard evidence for the evolution of consciousness. In S. Hameroff, A. Kaszniak, & D. Chalmers (Eds.), *Toward a science of consciousness: The third Tucson discussions and debates* (pp. 281–296). Cambridge, MA: MIT Press.

Mithen, S. (2001). Archeological theory and theories of cognitive evolution. In I. Hodder (Ed.), *Archeological theory today* (pp. 98–121). Cambridge, UK: Polity Press.

Moore, B. (1992). Avian movement imitation and a new form of mimicry: Tracing the evolution of a complex form of learning. *Behavior, 122,* 231–263.

Moran, J., & Desimone, R. (1985). Selective attention gates visual processing in the extrastriate cortex. *Science, 229,* 782–784.

Myerson, J., Miezin, F., & Allman, J. (1981). Binocular rivalry in macaque monkeys and humans: A comparative study in perception. *Behavioral Analysis Letter, 1,* 149–159.

Nagel, E. (1961). *The structure of science.* New York: Harcourt, Brace and World.

Neander, K. (1991). Functions as selected effects: The conceptual analyst's defense. *Philosophy of Science, 58,* 168–184.

Neander, K. (1999). Is teleosemantics adaptationist? In V. Hardcastle (Ed.), *Where biology meets psychology* (pp. 3–26). Cambridge, MA: MIT Press.

Nesse, R., & Abelson, J. (1995). Natural selection and fear regulation mechanisms. *Behavioral and Brain Sciences, 18,* 309–310.

Neth, H., & Payne, S. (2003). Thinking by doing? Epistemic actions in the Tower of Hanoi. Online article: http://www.neth.de/Stuff/html/AdditionIPS_CogSci01.html

Nichols, S., & Stich, S. (2000). A cognitive theory of pretence. *Cognition, 74,* 115–147.

Northcutt, R., & Kaas, J. (1995). The emergence and evolution of mammalian neocortex. *Trends in Neuroscience, 18,* 373–379.

Novacek, M. (2002). *Time traveler: In search of dinosaurs and ancient mammals from Montana to Mongolia.* New York: Farrar, Straus and Giroux.

Nüsslein-Volhard, C., & Wieschaus, E. (1980). Mutations affecting segment number and polarity in *Drosophila. Nature, 287,* 795–801.

O'Connor, T. (1994). Emergent properties. *American Philosophical Quarterly, 31,* 91–104.

Olton, D., & Samuelson, R. (1976). Remembrance of places passed: Spatial memory in rats. *Journal of Experimental Psychology: Animal Behavior Processes, 2,* 97–116.

Ostrom, J. (1979). Bird flight: How did it begin? *American Scientist 67,* 46–56.

Oswalt, W. (1976). *An anthropological analysis of food-getting technology.* New York: Wiley.

Otto, S., Christiansen, F., & Feldman, M. (1995). Genetic and cultural inheritance of continuous traits. *Morrison Institute for Population and Resource Studies*, paper 64. Stanford: Stanford University Press.

Oxbury, J., Oxbury, S., & Humphrey, N. (1969). Varieties of colour anomia. *Brain, 92*, 847–860.

Palmer, J., & Palmer, A. (2002). *Evolutionary psychology: The ultimate origins of human behavior.* Needham Heights, MA: Allyn and Bacon.

Parasuraman, R. (Ed.), (1998). *The attentive brain.* Cambridge, MA: MIT Press.

Parker, S. (1996). Apprenticeship in tool-mediated extractive foraging: The origins of imitation, teaching and self-awareness in great apes. *Journal of Comparative Psychology, 106*, 18–34.

Passingham, R. (1993). *The frontal lobes and voluntary action.* Oxford: Oxford University Press.

Patterson, K., & Wilson, B. (1987). A ROSE is a ROSE or a NOSE: A deficit in initial letter identification. *Cognitive Neuropsychology, 7*, 447–477.

Pearce, J. (1997). *Animal learning and cognition.* Hove, UK: Psychology Press.

Peirce, C. (1960). Of science and natural classes. In Peirce Edition Project (Eds.), *The essential Peirce* (pp. 115–132). Bloomington, IN: Indiana University Press.

Peirce, C. (1966). The fixation of belief. In P. Weiner (Ed.), *Charles S. Peirce: Selected writings* (pp. 91–112). New York: Dover.

Pelegrin, J. (1993). A framework for analyzing stone tool manufacture and a tentative application to some early stone industries. In A. Berthelet & J. Chavaillon (Eds.), *The use of tools by human and non-human primates* (pp. 302–314). Oxford: Clarendon Press.

Pelligrino, G., Fadiga, L., Fogassi, L., Gallese, V., & Rizzolatti, G. (1996). Understanding motor events: A neurophysiological study. *Experimental Brain Research, 91*, 176–180.

Pennisi, E. (2004). The birth of the nucleus. *Science, 305*, 766–768.

Peregrin, J. (Ed.), (1996). *The nature of truth (if any).* Proceedings of the International Colloquium, Prague.

Perlman, M. (2004). The modern philosophical resurrection of teleology. *The Monist, 87*, 3–51.

Peterhans, E., & von der Heydt, R. (1991). Subjective contours—Bridging the gap between psychophysics and physiology. *Trends in Neuroscience, 14*, 12.

Petrides, M., Cadoret, G., & Mackey, S. (2005). Orofacial somatomotor responses in the macaque monkey homologue of Broca's area. *Nature, 435*, 1235–1238.

Pinker, S. (1984). Visual cognition: An introduction. *Cognition*, *18*, 54–55.

Pinker, S. (1994). *The language instinct*. New York: Morrow.

Pinker, S. (1997). *How the mind works*. New York: Norton.

Pinker, S. (2002). *The blank slate: The modern denial of human nature*. New York: Penguin Books.

Plantinga, A. (2000). *Warranted Christian belief*. New York: Oxford University Press.

Plotkin, H. (1997). *Evolution in mind: An introduction to evolutionary psychology*. Cambridge, MA: Harvard University Press.

Poggio, T., & Hurlbert, A. (1994). Observations on cortical mechanisms for object recognition and learning. In C. Koch & J. Davis (Eds.), *Large-scale neuronal theories of the brain* (pp. 185–199). Cambridge, MA: MIT Press.

Posner, M., & Dahaene, S. (1994). Attention networks. *Trends in Neuroscience*, *17*, 75–79.

Posner, M., & Petersen, S. (1990). The attention system of the human brain. *Annual Review of Neuroscience*, *13*, 25–42.

Potts, R. (1996). *Humanity's descent: The consequences of ecological instability*. New York: Avon Books.

Preuss, T., Qi, H., & Kaas, J. (1999). Modification of layer IVA of primary visual cortex in ape and human evolution. *American Journal of Physical Anthropology*, *28*, 225.

Primas, H. (1998). Emergence in the exact sciences. *Acta Polytechnica Scandanavica*, *91*, 83–98.

Prince, G. (1970). *The practice of creativity: A manual for dynamic group problem solving*. New York: Harper & Row.

Putnam, H. (1960). Minds and machines. In S. Hook (Ed.), *Dimensions of mind* (pp. 27–37). New York: Collier Books.

Putnam, H. (1975). *Mathematics, matter and method*. Cambridge, UK: Cambridge University Press.

Putnam, H. (1981). *Reason, truth and history*. Cambridge, UK: Cambridge University Press.

Putnam, H. (1987). *The many faces of pragmatism*. LaSalle, IL: Open Court.

Putnam, H. (1988). *Representation and reality*. Cambridge, MA: MIT Press.

Putnam, H. (1995). *Pragmatism*. Oxford: Blackwell.

Pylyshyn, Z. (1980). Computation and cognition: Issues in the foundation of cognitive science. *Behavioral and Brain Sciences*, *3/1*, 111–134.

Pylyshyn, Z. (2003). Return of the mental image: Are there really pictures in the brain? *Trends in Cognitive Sciences*, *7*, 113–118.

Rakic, P., & Kornack, D. (2001). Neocortical expansion and elaboration during primate evolution: A view from neuroembryology. In D. Falk & K. Gibson (Eds.), *Evolutionary anatomy of the cerebral cortex* (pp. 30–56). Cambridge UK: Cambridge University Press.

Receveur, H., & Vossen, J. (1998). Changing rearing environments and problem solving flexibility in rats. *Behavioral Processes, 43*, 193–210.

Rees, G., & Lavine, N. (2001). What can functional imaging reveal about the role of attention in visual awareness? *Neuropsychologia, 39*, 1343–1353.

Rees, G., Kreiman, G., & Koch, C. (2002). Neural correlates of consciousness in humans. *Nature Reviews Neuroscience, 3*, 261–270.

Reichardt, L., & Fariñas, I. (1997). Neurotrophic factors and their receptors: Roles in neuronal development and function. In W. Cowan (Ed.), *Synapses* (pp. 220–263). Baltimore: The Johns Hopkins University Press.

Reiner, A. (1993). Neurotransmitter organization and connections of turtle cortex: Implications for the evolution of mammalian isocortex. *Comparative Biochemical Physiology, 104A*, 735–748.

Reiner, A., Perkel, D., Mello, C., & Jarvis, E. (2004). Songbirds and the revised avian brain nomenclature. *Annals of the New York Academy of Sciences, 1016*, 77–108.

Relethford, J. (1994). *The human species: An introduction to evolutionary anthropology.* Mountain View, CA: Mayfield.

Rescher, N. (1997). *Objectivity: The obligations of impersonal reason.* Notre Dame: University of Notre Dame Press.

Rescher, N. (2005). *Realism and pragmatic epistemology.* Pittsburgh: University of Pittsburgh Press.

Rescorla, R. (1988). Behavioral studies of Pavlovian conditioning. *Annual Review of Neuroscience, 11*, 329–352.

Richert, R., & Lillard, A. (2002). Children's understanding of the knowledge of prerequisites of drawing and pretending. *Developmental Psychology, 38*, 1004–1015.

Rilling, J., & Insel, T. (1998). Evolution of the cerebellum in primates: Differences in relative volume among monkeys, apes and humans. *Brain, Behavior and Evolution, 52*, 308–314.

Ritz, R., & Sejnowski, T. (1997). Synchronous oscillatory activity in sensory systems: New vistas on mechanisms. *Current Opinion in Neurobiology, 7*, 536–546.

Roberts, A., Robbins, T., & Weiskrantz, L. (1998). *The prefrontal cortex: Executive and cognitive functions.* Oxford: Oxford University Press.

Roberts, R. (1989). *Serendipity: Accidental discoveries in science.* New York: Wiley.

Rock, I. (1984). *Perception.* New York: Freeman.

Rodriguez, E., George, N., Lachaux, J., Martinerie, J., Renault, B., & Varela, F. (1999). Perception's shadow: Long-distance synchronization of human brain activity. *Nature*, *397*, 430–433.

Roelfsema, P., Engel, A., König, P., & Singer, W. (1996). The role of neuronal synchronization in response selection: A biologically plausible theory of structured representation in the visual cortex. *Journal of Cognitive Neuroscience*, *8*, 603–625.

Roosta, S. (1999). *Parallel processing and parallel algorithms: Theory and computation.* New York: Springer.

Rorty, R. (1982). *Consequences of pragmatism.* Minneapolis: University of Minnesota Press.

Rorty, R. (1987). Science as solidarity. In J. Nelson, A. Magill, & D. McCloskey (Eds.), *Rhetoric of the human sciences: Language and arguments in scholarship and public affairs* (pp. 38–52). Madison: University of Wisconsin Press, Madison.

Rorty, R. (1991). *Objectivity, realism and truth.* Cambridge, MA: Cambridge University Press.

Rorty, R. (1993). Feminism, ideology, and deconstructionism: A pragmatist view. *Hypatia*, *8*, 96–103.

Rorty, R. (1998). *Truth and progress: Philosophical papers.* Cambridge, MA: Cambridge University Press.

Rose, S., Kamin, L., & Lewontin, R. (1984). *Not in our genes: Biology, ideology and human nature.* Toronto: Penguin Group.

Rosen, G. (1994). What is Constructive Empiricism? *Philosophical Studies*, *74*, 143–178.

Rosen, R. (1968). Recent developments in the theory of control and regulation of cellular processes. *International Review of Cytology*, *23*, 25–88.

Rosenberg, J. (2002). How not to misunderstand Peirce—A pragmatist account of truth. In R. Schantz (Ed.), *What is truth?* (pp. 283–295). Berlin: Walter de Gruyter.

Roskies, A. (1999). The binding problem is a class of problems. *Neuron*, *24*, 7–9.

Roth, G. (2000). The evolution and ontogeny of consciousness. In T. Metzinger (Ed.), *Neural correlates of consciousness* (pp. 77–98). Cambridge, MA: MIT Press.

Rueckl, J., Cave, K., & Kosslyn, S. (1989). Why are "what" and "where" processed by separate cortical systems? A computational investigation. *Journal of Cognitive Science*, *1*, 171–186.

Rueger, A. (2000). Physical emergence, diachronic and synchronic. *Synthese*, *124*, 297–322.

Ruhlen, M. (1994). *The origin of language: Tracing the origin of the mother tongue.* New York: Wiley.

Rumelhart, D., & McClelland, J. (1985). PDP models and general issues in cognitive science. In D. Rumelhart & J. McClelland (Eds.), *Parallel distributed processing: Explorations in the microstructure of cognition: Vol. 1. Foundations* (pp. 110–146). Cambridge, MA: MIT Press.

Ruse, M. (1971). Functional statements in biology. *Philosophy of Science, 38,* 87–95.

Ruse, M. (1973). *The philosophy of biology.* London: Hutchinson.

Ruse, M. (1982). *Darwinism defended.* Reading: Addison-Wesley.

Ruse, M. (1989). *The Darwinian paradigm: Essays on its history, philosophy, and religious implications.* New York: Routledge.

Ruse, M. (1996). *Monad to man: The concept of progress in evolutionary biology.* Cambridge, MA: Harvard University Press.

Ruse, M. (2000). *The evolution wars.* Santa Barbara: ABC-CLIO.

Ruse, M. (2003). *Darwin and design: Does evolution have a purpose?* Cambridge, MA: Harvard University Press.

Rushworth, M., Daus, T., & Sipila, P. (2001). Attention systems and the organization of the human parietal cortex. *Journal of Neuroscience, 21,* 5262–5271.

Russon, A., & Galdikas, B. (1993). Imitation in free-ranging rehabilitant orangutans. *Journal of Comparative Psychology, 107,* 147–161.

Russon, A., & Galdikas, B. (1995). Constraints on great apes' imitation: Model and action selectivity in rehabilitant orangutan (*Pan pygmaeus*) imitation. *Journal of Comparative Psychology, 109,* 5–17.

Sacco, W., Copes, W., Sloyer, C., & Stark, R. (1988). *Information theory: Saving bits.* Dedham, MA: Janson.

Salthe, S., & Matsuno, K. (1995). Self-organization in hierarchical systems. *Journal of Social and Evolutionary Systems, 18,* 327–338.

Samuels, R. (1998). Evolutionary psychology and the massive modularity hypothesis. *British Journal of the Philosophy of Science, 49,* 575–602.

Sanes, D., Reh, T., & Harris, W. (2000). *Development of the nervous system.* New York: Academic Press.

Savage-Rumbaugh, E., & Boysen, S. (1978). Linguistically-meditated tool use and exchange by chimpanzees (*Pan troglodytes*). *Brain and Behavioral Science, 4,* 539–553.

Scher, S., & Rauscher, F. (2003). Nature read in truth or flaw: Locating alternatives in evolutionary psychology. In S. Scher & F. Rauscher (Eds.), *Evolutionary psychology: Alternative approaches* (pp. 1–30). Boston: Kluwer Academic.

Schneider, T. (1986). Information content of binding sites on nucleotide sequences. *Journal of Molecular Biology, 188,* 415–431.

Schopf, J. (Ed.), (2002). *Life's origin: The beginnings of biological evolution*. Berkeley: University of California Press.

Schwartz, E. (Ed.), (1990). *Computational neuroscience*. Cambridge, MA: MIT Press.

Schwartz, J., & Begley, S. (2002). *The mind and brain: Neuroplasticity and the power of mental force*. New York: HarperCollins.

Schwartz, P. (2002). The continuing usefulness account of proper function. In A. Ariew, R. Cummins, & M. Perlman (Eds.), *Functions: New essays in the philosophy of psychology and biology* (pp. 244–260). Oxford: Oxford University Press.

Scott, S., et al. (1997). Impaired auditory recognition of fear and anger following bilateral amygdala lesions. *Nature, 385*, 254–257.

Searle, J. (1990a). Is the brain a digital computer? *Proceedings and Addresses of the American Philosophical Association, 64*, 21–37.

Searle, J. (1990b). Collective intentions and actions. In P. Cohen, M. Pollack, & J. Morgan (Eds.), *Intentions in communication* (pp. 401–414). Cambridge, MA: MIT Press.

Searle, J. (1992). *The rediscovery of the mind*. Cambridge, MA: MIT Press.

Sekuler, R., & Blake, R. (2002). *Perception*. New York: McGraw-Hill.

Sellars, W. (1963). *Science, perception and reality*. New York: Humanities Press.

Sereno, M., et al. (1995). Borders of multiple visual areas in humans revealed by functional magnetic resonance imaging. *Science, 268*, 889–893.

Shallice, T. (1988). *From neuropsychology to mental structure*. Cambridge, UK: Cambridge University Press.

Shallice, T. (1997). Modularity and consciousness. In N. Block et al. (Eds.), *The nature of consciousness* (pp. 277–297). Cambridge, MA: MIT Press.

Shannon, C. (1948). A mathematical theory of communication. *Bell System Technical Journal, 27*, 379–423, 623–656.

Shatz, C. (1992). The developing brain. *Scientific American, 267*, 60–67.

Shatz, C., & Stryker, M. (1978). Ocular dominance in layer IV of the cat's visual cortex and the effects of monocular deprivation. *Journal of Physiology, 281*, 267–283.

Shephard, R., & Cooper, L. (1992). *Mental images and their transformations*. Cambridge, MA: MIT Press.

Shephard, R., & Metzler, N. (1971). Mental rotation of three-dimensional objects. *Science, 171*, 701–703.

Sherry, D., & Schacter, D. (1987). The evolution of multiple memory systems. *Psychological Review, 94*, 439–454.

Sherwood, J., et al. (2003). Evolution of specialized pyramidal neurons in primate visual and motor cortex. *Brain, Behavior and Evolution, 61*, 28–44.

Shettleworth, S. (2000). Modularity and the evolution of cognition. In C. Heyes & L. Huber (Eds.), *The evolution of cognition* (pp. 43–60). Cambridge, MA: MIT Press.

Sigala, N., & Logothetis, N. (2002). Visual categorization shapes feature selectivity in the primate temporal cortex. *Nature, 415,* 318–320.

Silberstein, M. (2002). Reduction, emergence and explanation. In M. Silberstein & P. Machamer (Eds.), *The Blackwell guide to the philosophy of science* (pp. 80–107). Malden, MA: Blackwell.

Silberstein, M., & McGreever, J. (1999). The search for ontological emergence. *The Philosophical Quarterly, 49,* 182–200.

Simon, H. (1975). The functional equivalence of problem-solving skills. *Cognitive Psychology, 7,* 268–288.

Singer, W. (1995). Development and plasticity of cortical processing architectures. *Science, 270,* 758–764.

Singer, W. (1999). Neuronal synchrony: A versatile code for the definition of relations? *Neuron, 24,* 49–65.

Singer, W. (2000). Phenomenal awareness and consciousness from a neurobiological perspective. In T. Metzinger (Ed.), *Neural correlates of consciousness* (pp. 121–138). Cambridge, MA: MIT Press.

Singer, W., & Gray, C. (1995). Visual feature integration and the temporal correlation hypothesis. *Annual Review of Neuroscience, 18,* 555–586.

Sinha, P., Balas, B., Ostrovsky, Y., & Russell, R. (2006). *Face recognition: Advanced modeling and methods.* New York: Academic Press.

Sklar, L. (1999). The reduction (?) of thermodynamics to statistical mechanics. *Philosophical Studies, 95,* 187–199.

Smart, J. (1963). *Philosophy and scientific realism.* London: Routledge.

Smith, E., & Jonides, J. (1997). Working memory: A view from neuroimaging. *Cognitive Psychology, 33,* 5–42.

Smith, E., Jonides, J., & Koeppe, R. (1996). Dissociating verbal and spatial memory using PET. *Cerebral Cortex, 6,* 11–20.

Smith, J. (1987). When learning guides evolution. *Nature, 329,* 761–762.

Smith, S. (1995). Fixation, incubation, and insight in memory and creative thinking. In S. Smith, T. Ward, & R. Finke (Eds.), *The creative cognition approach* (pp. 135–156). Cambridge, MA: MIT Press.

Smolensky, P. (1988). On the proper treatment of connectionism. *Behavioural and Brain Sciences, 11,* 1–23.

Sober, E. (1990). Putting the function back into functionalism. In W. Lycan (Ed.), *Mind and cognition* (pp. 97–106). Cambridge, MA: Blackwell.

Sober, E. (1993). *Philosophy of biology.* Boulder, CO: Westview Press.

Spelke, E. (1991). Physical knowledge in infancy: Reflections on Piaget's theory. In S. Carey & S. Gelman (Eds.), *Epigenesis of mind: Studies in biology and culture* (pp. 131–169). Hillsdale, NJ: Lawrence Erlbaum Associates.

Sperber, D. (1994). The modularity of thought and the epidemiology of representations. In L. Hirschfeld & S. Gelman (Eds.), *Mapping the mind: Domain specificity in cognition and culture* (pp. 39–67). Cambridge: Cambridge University Press.

Sperry, R. (1980). Mind–brain interaction: Mentalism, yes; dualism, no. *Neurosciences, 5,* 195–206.

Squire, L., & Kandel, E. (1999). *Memory: From mind to molecules.* New York: Freeman.

Staddon, J. (1987). Optimality theory and behavior. In J. Dupre (Ed.), *The latest of the best: Essays on evolution and optimality* (pp. 34–63). Cambridge, MA: MIT Press.

Stamp Dawkins, M. (1993). *Through our eyes only? The search for animal consciousness.* Oxford: Oxford University Press.

Stanford, C. (2000). *Significant others: The ape–human continuum and the quest for human nature.* New York: Basic Books.

Steinmetz, P., Roy, A., Fitzgerald, P., Hsiao, S., Johnson, K., & Niebur, E. (2000). Attention modulates synchronized neuronal firing in primate somatosensory cortex. *Nature, 404,* 187–190.

Sterelny, K. (2001). *The evolution of agency and other essays.* Cambridge, UK: Cambridge University Press.

Sterelny, K., & Griffiths, P. (1999). *Sex and death: An introduction to philosophy of biology.* Chicago: University of Chicago Press.

Sternberg, R. (1988). *The triatic mind: A new theory of human intelligence.* New York: Viking Press.

Sternberg, R. (1996). *Cognitive psychology.* Fort Worth, TX: Harcourt Brace College.

Sternberg, R. (2000). *Practical intelligence in everyday life.* Cambridge, UK: Cambridge University Press.

Sternberg, R. (Ed.), (1984). *Mechanisms of cognitive development.* New York: Freeman.

Sternberg, R. (Ed.), (1998). *The nature of cognition.* Cambridge, MA: MIT Press.

Sternberg, R. (Ed.), (1999). *Handbook of creativity.* Cambridge, UK: Cambridge University Press.

Sternberg, R. (2001). *Complex cognition: The psychology of human thought.* New York: Oxford University Press.

Sternberg, R., & Frensch, P. (Eds.), (1991). *Complex problem solving: Principles and mechanisms*. Mahwah, NJ: Lawrence Erlbaum Associates.

Sternberg, R., & Kaufman, J. (Eds.), (2002). *The evolution of intelligence*. Mahwah, NJ: Lawrence Erlbaum Associates.

Stevens, C., & Wesseling, J. (1999). Identification of a novel process limiting the rate of synaptic vesicle cycling at hippocampal synapses. *Neuron, 24*, 1017–1028.

Stich, S., & Warfield, T. (Eds.), (2003). *The Blackwell guide to philosophy of mind*. London: Blackwell.

Strickberger, M. (1985). *Genetics*. New York: Macmillan.

Strickberger, M. (2000). *Evolution*. Sudbury, MA: Jones and Bartlett.

Striedter, G. (1998). Stepping in the same river twice: Homologues as recurring attractors in epigenetic landscapes. *Brain, Behavior and Evolution, 52*, 218–231.

Stringer, C. (2002). Modern human origins: Progress and prospects. *Philosophical Transactions of the Royal Society of London, 357B*, 563–579.

Stringer, C., & Andrews, P. (2005). *The complete world of human evolution*. London: Thames & Hudson.

Stout, R. (1996). *Things that happen because they should: A teleological approach to action*. Oxford: Oxford University Press.

Swanson, C. (1973). *The natural history of man*. Englewood Cliffs: Prentice-Hall.

Swisher, C. (1994). Dating hominid sites in Indonesia. *Science, 266*, 1727.

Tabery, J. (2004). Synthesizing activities and interactions in the concept of a mechanism. *Philosophy of Science, 71*, 1–15.

Tallerman, M. (Ed.), (2005). *Language origins: Perspectives on evolution*. New York: Oxford University Press.

Tanaka, K. (1993). Neuronal mechanisms of object recognition. *Science, 262*, 685–688.

Tattersall, I. (2001). How we came to be human. *Scientific American, 285*, 57–63.

Tattersall, I. (2002). *The monkey in the mirror: Essays on the science of what makes us human*. Oxford: Oxford University Press.

Terzis, G. (2001). How crosstalk creates vision-related eureka moments. *Philosophical Psychology, 14*, 393–421.

Terzis, G., & Arp, R. (Eds.), (2008). *Information and living systems: Essays in philosophy of biology*. Cambridge, MA: MIT Press.

Thearling, K., & Ray, T. (1997). Evolving parallel computation. *Complex Systems, 10*, 1–8.

Tiles, J. (1988). *Dewey*. New York: Routledge.

Tomasello, M. (1990). Cultural transmission in the tool use and communicatory signaling of chimpanzees. In S. Parker & K. Gibson (Eds.), *"Language" and intelligence in monkeys and apes* (pp. 274–311). Cambridge, UK: Cambridge University Press.

Tomasello, M., et al. (1987). Observational learning of tool use by young chimpanzees. *Human Evolution, 2*, 175–185.

Tomasello, M., et al. (1993). Imitative learning of actions on objects by children, chimpanzees, and enculturated chimpanzees. *Child Development, 64*, 1688–1705.

Tononi, G., & Edelman, G. (1998). Consciousness and integration of information in the brain. *Advances in Neurology, 77*, 245–279.

Tononi, G., Srinivasan, R., Russell, D., & Edelman, G. (1998). Investigating neural correlates of conscious perception by frequently-tagged neuromagnetic responses. *Proceedings of the National Academy of Sciences, 95*, 3198–3203.

Tovee, M. (1998). Face processing: Getting by with a little help from its friends. *Current Biology, 8*, R317–R320.

Tovee, M., & Cohen-Tovee, E. (1993). The neural substrates of face processing models. *Cognitive Neuropsychology, 10*, 505–528.

Treisman, A. (1977). Selective attention stimulus integration. In S. Dornie (Ed.), *Attention and performance VI* (pp. 333–361). Hillsdale, NJ: Lawrence Erlbaum Associates.

Treisman, A. (1988). Features and objects: The fourteenth Bartlett memorial lecture. *The Quarterly Journal of Experimental Biology, 40A*, 206–237.

Trivers, R. (1985). *Social evolution.* Menlo Park, CA: Benjamin Cummings.

Trout, J. (1998). *Measuring the intentional world: Realism, naturalism and quantitative methods in the behavioral sciences.* New York: Oxford University Press.

Turing, A. (1950). Computing machinery and intelligence. *Mind, 59*, 433–460.

Tye, M. (1991). *The imagery debate.* Cambridge, MA: MIT Press.

Tyler, C., et al. (1998). Anatomical comparison of the macaque and marsupial visual cortex: Common features that may reflect retention of essential cortical elements. *Journal of Comparative Neurology, 400*, 449–468.

Ungerleider, L., & Haxby, J. (1994). "What" and "where" in the human brain. *Current Opinions in Neurobiology, 4*, 157–165.

Ungerleider, L., & Mishkin, M. (1982). Two cortical visual systems. In D. Ingle (Ed.), *Analysis of visual behavior* (pp. 213–217). Cambridge, MA: MIT Press.

Usher, M., & Donnelly, N. (1998). Visual synchrony affects binding and segmentation in perception. *Nature, 394*, 179–182.

Uylings, H., & van Eden, C. (1990). Qualitative and quantitative comparison of the prefrontal cortex in rats and in primates, including humans. In H. Uylings (Ed.), *The prefrontal cortex: Its structure, function and pathology* (pp. 31–62). New York: Oxford University Press.

Vaadia, E., Aertsen, A., & Nelken, I. (1995). Dynamics of neuronal interactions in monkey cortex in relation to behavioral events. *Nature, 373,* 515–518.

van Essen, D. (1985). Functional organization of primate visual cortex. In A. Peters & E. Jones (Eds.), *Cerebral cortex* (pp. 279–299). New York: Plenum Press.

van Essen, D. (1997). A tension-based theory of morphogenesis and compact wiring in the central nervous system. *Nature, 385,* 313–318.

van Essen, D., et al. (1998). A common network of functional areas for attention and eye movements. *Neuron, 21,* 761–773.

van Essen, D., Anderson, C., & Felleman, D. (1992). Information processing in the primate visual system: An integrated systems perspective. *Science, 255,* 419–423.

van Essen, D., Anderson, C., & Olshausen, B. (1994). Dynamic routing strategies in sensory, motor, and cognitive processing. In C. Koch & J. Davis (Eds.), *Large-scale neuronal theories of the brain* (pp. 271–300). Cambridge, MA: MIT Press.

van Essen, D., & Gallant, J. (1994). Neural mechanisms of form and motion processing in the primate visual system. *Neuron, 13,* 1–10.

van Essen, D., & Maunsell, J. (1983). Hierarchical organization and functional streams in the visual cortex. *Trends in Neurosciences, 6,* 370–375.

Van Gulick, R. (2001). Reduction, emergence and other recent options on the mind/body problem: A philosophic overview. *Journal of Consciousness Studies, 8,* 1–34.

van Praag, H., Kempermann, G., & Gage, F. (2000). Neural consequences of environmental enrichment. *Nature Reviews Neuroscience, 1,* 191–198.

Vaughan, R. (1997). *The Hardy–Littlewood method.* Cambridge: Cambridge University Press.

Velmans, M. (1992). Is consciousness integrated? *Behavioral and Brain Sciences, 15,* 229–230.

Vlastos, G. (1981). *Platonic studies.* Princeton: Princeton University Press.

Voet, D., Voet, J., & Pratt, C. (2002). *Fundamentals of biochemistry.* New York: Wiley.

von der Malsburg, C. (1981). Binding in models of perception and brain function. *Current Opinion in Neurobiology, 5,* 520–526.

von Neumann, J. (1958). *The computer and the brain.* New Haven, CT: Yale University Press.

Walters, C. (1998). Causal regularities in the biological world of contingent distributions. *Biology & Philosophy, 13,* 5–36.

Watson, J., & Arp, R. (2008). Checks and balances: The welcomed tension between philosophy and science. *The Quarterly Review of Biology*, in press.

Weaver, W., & Shannon, C. (1949). *The mathematical theory of communication*. Urbana: University of Illinois Press.

Weir, A., Chappell, J., & Kacelnik, A. (2002). Shaping of hooks in New Caledonian crows. *Science, 297*, 981.

Weisberg, R. (1995). Case studies of creative thinking: Reproduction versus restructuring in the real world. In S. Smith, T. Ward, & R. Finke (Eds.), *The creative cognition approach* (pp. 53–72). Cambridge, MA: MIT Press.

Weiskrantz, L. (1986). *Blindsight: A case study and its implications*. Oxford: Oxford University Press.

Weiskrantz, L. (Ed.), (1988). *Thought without language*. Oxford: Oxford University Press.

Weiskrantz, L. (1997). *Consciousness lost and found*. Oxford: Oxford University Press.

Wertheimer, M. (1912/1961). Experimental studies on the seeing of motion. In T. Shipley (Ed.), *Classics in psychology* (pp. 1032–1088). New York: Philosophical Library.

Wertheimer, M. (1923/1958). Principles of perceptual organization. In D. Beardslee & M. Wertheimer (Eds.), *Readings in perception* (pp. 115–135). Princeton: Van Nostrand.

Wheeler, M., & Atkinson, A. (2001). Domains, brains and evolution. In D. Walsh (Ed.), *Naturalism, evolution and mind* (pp. 239–266). Cambridge, UK: Cambridge University Press.

White, T. (2003). Early hominids: Diversity or distortion? *Nature, 299*, 1994–1997.

Whiten, A., & Custance, D. (1996). Studies of imitation in chimpanzees and children. In C. Heyes & B. Galef (Eds.), *Social learning in animals: The roots of culture* (pp. 291–318). San Diego: Academic Press.

Whiten, A., & Ham, R. (1992). On the nature and evolution of imitation in the animal kingdom. In P. Slater (Ed.), *Advances in the study of behavior: Vol. 21* (pp. 239–283). New York: Academic Press.

Whiten, A., et al. (1996). Imitative learning of artificial fruit processing in children (*Homo sapiens*) and chimpanzees (*Pan troglodytes*). *Journal of Comparative Psychology, 110*, 3–14.

Whiten, A., et al. (1999). Cultures in chimpanzees. *Nature, 399*, 682–685.

Will, F. (1996). *Pragmatism and realism*. New York: Rowman & Littlefiled.

Williams, R. (1988). Toward a theory of reinforcement-learning connectionist systems. *Technical Reprt NU-CCS-88-3*, Northeastern University.

Wilson, D. (2003). Human evolutionary psychology: Pardon our dust. *Evolution, 56,* 2334–2338.

Wilson, F., et al. (1993). Dissociation of object and spatial processing domains in primate prefrontal cortex. *Science, 260,* 1955–1958.

Wimsatt, W. (1994). The ontology of complex systems: Levels, perspectives and causal thickets. *Canadian Journal of Philosophy, 20,* 207–274.

Wimsatt, W. (1997). Aggregativity: Reductive heuristics for finding emergence. *The Philosophy of Science Association, 96,* 372–384.

Wippel, J. (1984). *Metaphysical themes in Thomas Aquinas.* Washington, DC: The Catholic University of America Press.

Wise, S. (1996). Evolutionary and comparative neurobiology of the supplementary sensorimotor cortex. *Advances in Neurobiology, 70,* 71–83.

Wittgenstein, L. (1953). *Philosophical investigations.* New York: Macmillan.

Wolpoff, M. (1999). *Paleoanthropology.* Boston: McGraw-Hill.

Wood, B. (1994). The problems of our origins. *Journal of Human Evolution, 27,* 323–330.

Wright, A. (1989). Memory processing by pigeons, monkeys, and people. *Psychology of Learning and Motivation, 24,* 25–70.

Wright, A. (1997). Memory of auditory lists by rhesus monkeys (*Macaca mulatta*). *Journal of Experimental Psychology: Animal Behavior Processes, 23,* 441–449.

Wright, C. (1993). *Realism, meaning and truth.* London: Blackwell.

Wright, L. (1973). Functions. *Philosophical Review, 82,* 139–168.

Wright, L. (1976). *Teleological explanations: An etiological analysis of goals and functions.* Berkeley: University of California Press.

Wurtz, R., Goldberg, M., & Robinson, D. (1982). Brain mechanisms of visual attention. *Scientific American, 246,* 100–107.

Wynn, T. (1979). The intelligence of later Acheulian hominids. *Man, 14,* 371–391.

Wynn, T. (1981). The intelligence of Oldowan hominids. *Journal of Human Evolution, 10,* 529–541.

Wynn, T. (1991). Tools, grammar and the archeology of cognition. *Cambridge Archeological Journal, 1,* 191–206.

Wynn, T. (1993). Layers of thinking in tool behavior. In K. Gibson & T. Ingold (Eds.), *Tools, language and cognition in human evolution* (pp. 389–406). Cambridge: Cambridge University Press.

Wynn, T., & McGrew, W. (1989). An ape's view of the Oldowan man. *Man, 24,* 383–398.

Yao, X., & Liu, Y. (1997). A new evolutionary system for evolving artificial neural networks. *IEEE Transactions on Neural Networks, 8,* 694–713.

Yao, X., & Liu, Y. (1998). Towards designing artificial networks by evolution. *Applied Mathematics and Computation, 91,* 83–90.

Yando, R., Seitz, V., & Ziqler, E. (1978). *Imitation: A developmental perspective.* Mahwah, NJ: Lawrence Erlbaum Associates.

Young, J. (1995). *Global anti-realism.* Aldershot: Avebury Press.

Zeki, S. (1993). *A vision of the brain.* New York: Blackwell.

Zeki, S., Watson, J., Weck, C., Friston, K., Kennard, C., & Frackowiak, R. (1991). A direct demonstration of functional specialization in human visual cortex. *Journal of Neuroscience, 11,* 641–649.

Zentall, T., et al. (1990). Memory strategies in pigeons' performance of a radial-arm-maze analog task. *Journal of Experimental Psychology: Animal Behavior Processes, 16,* 358–371.

Zhang, L., Tao, H., Holt, C., Harris, W., & Poo, M. (1998). A critical window for cooperating competition among developing retinotectal synapses. *Nature, 395,* 37–44.

Zigmond, M., Bloom, F., Landis, S., Roberts, J., Squire, L., & Wooley, R. (Eds.), (1999). *Fundamental neuroscience.* San Diego: Academic Press.

Zornetzer, S., Davis, J., & Lau, C. (Eds.), (1990). *An introduction to neural and electronic networks.* New York: Academic Press.

Zylstra, U. (1992). Living things as hierarchically organized structures. *Synthese, 91,* 111–133.

Index

Adaptation, 35, 54, 138
Adaptive radiation, 25
Animal cognition, 78, 84,
    150–153
  birds and, 78, 150–151
  cats and, 78
  chimpanzees and, 78, 120, 122
  monkeys and, 78
  octopi and, 151–152
  orangutans and, 120, 151
  rats and, 150
Antirealism, 38–39
Argument from the sciences,
    42–45
Argument from miracles, 47, 49
As-if realism, 4, 36, 38–47
Associations, mental, 8–9, 120, 150–
    153. *See also* Animal cognition;
    Bissociation
Attention, 81, 68–69

Binding problems, 71, 163
Bissociation, 8–9, 150–153
Brain
  evolution and (*see* Evolution)
  visual system and, 60–66

Causation
  bottom-up, 14–15, 33–34, 162
  top-down, 14–15, 33–34, 162
Cell functions, 32–33

Cognition. *See* Animal cognition;
    Associations, mental; Bissociation;
    Vision
Cognitive fluidity, 147–150
Component, 12
Computer processing, 70, 141
Consciousness. *See* Scenario
    visualization
Constraint, 21
Constructivism, 39
Cosmides, Leda, and Tooby, John,
    135–139
Critical period, 86

Data selectivity
  in organisms generally, 17–21
  in the visual system, 67–69
Drosophila, 26
Dummett-style assertibility conditions,
    46

Emergentism, 29–31, 136
  nomological emergence and,
    30–35
  representational emergence and,
    36–46
Environment, 23, 84
Environmental-organismic information
    exchange
  in organisms generally, 23–26
  in the visual system, 84–88

Eureka moments, 153
Evolution, 91–95
  brain and, 99–102
  Darwin and, 92
  environments and, 94–95, 123–125,
    140–141
  genetic variability and, 91–95
  hominins and, 7–8, 103–105, 140–141
  javelin and, 118–123
  mutations and, 92–93
  natural selection and, 91–95
  nervous systems and, 95–99
  principle of economy and, 98, 142
  scenario visualization and (see
    Scenario visualization)
  sieve illustration and, 94
  visual system and, 105–109
Evolutionary psychology, 8, 135–146
  broad evolutionary psychology,
    135–148
  narrow evolutionary psychology,
    135–148
Exaptation, 52

Face-selective cells, 63
Fallibilism, 46
Functions, 5, 36–38, 47–55
  Cummins' organizational view of,
    49–55
  Griffiths/Godfrey-Smith's modern
    history view of, 49–55

General intelligence, 138, 147
Gestalt psychology, 87
Geological time, 102
Good trick, 124–125

Hierarchical organization, 4, 11–12, 15
  of living systems generally, 11–17
  of visual systems (see Vision)
Homeostasis
  generalized, 4, 13–14, 31–35
  particularized, 4, 13–14, 31–35

Homeostatic organization view, 4,
    31–36
Hominin evolution (see Evolution)
Homunculus problem, 163–165
Humphrey's distinction between "in
  here" and "out there," 96, 98

Imagination, 155
Information, 17–18
Informational integration
  in organisms generally, 21–23
  in the visual system, 69–74
Integration. See Selectivity and
  integration
Internal-hierarchical data exchange
  of living systems generally,
    12, 15–17
  of the visual system, 57–67

Javelin, 118–125
Just-so stories, 119

Kantianism, 41, 155–156
Knowledge, 38

Long-term potentiation. See Memory

MacLean's model of evolution, 99–101
Mayr, Ernst, 11–12
Memory, 79–81
Mind-body problems, 77
Mithen, Steven, 9, 147–150
Modularity, 9
  evolutionary psychology and,
    135–139
  visual system and, 71–72

Nervous system
  central, 98–100, 109
  peripheral, 98–100
Neurulation, 85
Neuronal synchrony, 82–84
Neurotrophic theory, 86

Organisms, 11–27

Parallel processing, 72, 141
Phenotypic traits, 25
Philosophy of science
  epistemological issues in, 36–46
  metaphysical issues in, 29–35
Pictorialist approach, 128
Pleistocene epoch and its importance,
  139–146
Pragmatism, 38–42
Preaptation, 52
Problem solving
  creative (nonroutine), 2, 9, 126–128,
    133–135, 146 (*see also* Bissociation)
  routine, 2, 9, 133–135

Realism. *See* As-if realism
Reductionism, 29–31, 136

Scenario visualization
  consciousness and, 2–3, 7–9, 113–118,
    149, 153–158, 162–163
  goal-directness and, 117–118
  illustrations of, 115, 159, 161
  neurobiological evidence and, 7–8,
    129–131
  psychological evidence and, 7–8,
    125–129
  psychological-neurobiological-
    biological continuum and, 10,
    162–166
  selectivity, integration and, 7–8, 113–
    115, 153–158, 163
  steps involved in, 113–114
  tool-making and, 6–7, 109–125,
    158–161
  trial-and-error learning and, 124–125
Selectivity and integration, 3–4, 8–10
  in organisms generally, 17–21
  in scenario visualization (*see* Scenario
    visualization)
  in the visual system, 67–74

Sensory systems, 59–60
Skepticism, 38
Swiss Army Knife model of the mind,
  144
Synfire chain, 82
System, 12–15

Thought-experiments, as helpful to a
  point, 53–54
Tool-making, 109–113. *See also*
  Scenario visualization
Tool-making industries, 110–113
Truth, 39–41, 43

Veil of perceptions, 47
Vision
  cognitive awareness and, 6, 75–78,
    83–84, 89
  conscious awareness and, 6, 75–78, 84
  disorders and, 75–76
  evolution of, 6, 91
  eye evolution and, 105–106
  hierarchical organization of, 57–67
  illustrations of areas in, 64–65
  levels of processing in, 6, 75–78
  neuronal wiring of, 60–67, 129–132
  what system in, 60, 64–67
  where system in, 60, 64–67
Visual integration, 6, 71–72, 83, 89
Visual modularity, 6, 71–72, 83, 89